ISAEUS

THE ORATORY OF CLASSICAL GREECE

Translated with Notes ◆ *Michael Gagarin, Series Editor*

VOLUME 11

ISAEUS

Translated with introduction and notes by

Michael Edwards

 UNIVERSITY OF TEXAS PRESS, AUSTIN

Requests for permission to reproduce material from
this work should be sent to:
  Permissions
  University of Texas Press
  P.O. Box 7819
  Austin, TX 78713-7819
  www.utexas.edu/utpress/about/bpermission.html

♾ The paper used in this book meets the minimum
requirements of ANSI/NISO Z39.48-1992 (R1997)
(Permanence of Paper).

Library of Congress Cataloging-in-Publication Data

Isaeus, ca. 420–ca. 350 B.C.
    Isaeus / translated with introduction and notes by
Michael Edwards.
        p.   cm. — The oratory of classical Greece ; v. 11)
    Includes bibliographical references and index.
    ISBN-13: 978-0-292-71645-2 (cloth : alk. paper)
    ISBN-10: 0-292-71645-1 (alk. paper)
    ISBN-13: 978-0-292-71646-9 (pbk. : alk. paper)
    ISBN-10: 0-292-71646-X (alk. paper)
    1. Inheritance and succession (Greek law)—
Sources.   2. Inheritance and succession—Greece—
Athens—Sources.   3. Forensic orations—Greece—
Athens.   4. Isaeus, ca. 420–ca. 350 B.C.—
Translations into English.   5. Speeches, addresses,
etc., Greek—Translations into English.
I. Edwards, Michael, 1958–   II. Title.
    KL4196.I83   2007
    346.3805'2—dc22
                                        2006102746

For
Sylvia, a very dear friend

CONTENTS

SERIES EDITOR'S PREFACE

This is the eleventh volume in a series of translations of *The Oratory of Classical Greece*. The aim of the series is to make available primarily for those who do not read Greek up-to-date, accurate, and readable translations with introductions and explanatory notes of all the surviving works and major fragments of the Attic orators of the classical period (ca. 420–320 BC): Aeschines, Andocides, Antiphon, Demosthenes, Dinarchus, Hyperides, Isaeus, Isocrates, Lycurgus, and Lysias. This volume includes all the surviving speeches and major fragments of Isaeus, most of them from inheritance cases. These are an important source for our knowledge of Athenian inheritance law, and they also give us a valuable picture of the sometimes complex relations among members of extended families in classical Greece.

This volume, like the others in the series, has benefited greatly from the careful attention of many at the University of Texas Press. These include Director Joanna Hitchcock, Humanities Editor Jim Burr, manuscript editor Lynne Chapman, and copy editor Nancy Moore. As always, they have been a pleasure to work with.

—M. G.

TRANSLATOR'S PREFACE

Many people have helped me in the preparation of this book over the long period that I have been working on it, both by their encouragement and in offering helpful suggestions, and I hope they will forgive me if I do not even attempt to mention them all by name here. John Lawless read the typescript for the University of Texas Press and made a number of pertinent observations, and Jim Burr and the staff of the Press have been most supportive. I must, however, record my gratitude above all to Michael Gagarin, whose meticulous reading of my first submission and many suggestions for improvement have made the final version so much better and more readable than it would otherwise have been.

—M. E.

SERIES INTRODUCTION
Greek Oratory

༺༄༺༄༺༄༺༄༺༄༺༄༺༄༺༄༺༄༺༄༺༄༺༄༺༄༺༄༺༄༺༄༺༄༺༄༺༄༺

By Michael Gagarin

ORATORY IN CLASSICAL ATHENS

From as early as Homer (and undoubtedly much earlier) the Greeks
placed a high value on effective speaking. Even Achilles, whose great-
ness was primarily established on the battlefield, was brought up
to be "a speaker of words and a doer of deeds" (*Iliad* 9.443); and
Athenian leaders of the sixth and fifth centuries,[1] such as Solon, The-
mistocles, and Pericles, were all accomplished orators. Most Greek
literary genres—notably epic, tragedy, and history—underscore the
importance of oratory by their inclusion of set speeches. The formal pleadings of the envoys to Achilles in the *Iliad,* the messenger
speeches in tragedy reporting events like the battle of Salamis in
Aeschylus' *Persians* or the gruesome death of Pentheus in Euripides'
Bacchae, and the powerful political oratory of Pericles' funeral oration in Thucydides are but a few of the most notable examples of the
Greeks' never-ending fascination with formal public speaking, which
was to reach its height in the public oratory of the fourth century.

In early times, oratory was not a specialized subject of study but
was learned by practice and example. The formal study of rhetoric as
an "art" (*technē*) began, we are told, in the middle of the fifth century
in Sicily with the work of Corax and his pupil Tisias.[2] These two are

---

[1] All dates in this volume are BC unless the contrary is either indicated or
obvious.

[2] See Kennedy 1963: 26–51. Cole 1991 has challenged this traditional picture,
arguing that the term "rhetoric" was coined by Plato to designate and deni-
grate an activity he strongly opposed. Cole's own reconstruction is not without

scarcely more than names to us, but another famous Sicilian, Gorgias of Leontini (ca. 490–390), developed a new style of argument and is reported to have dazzled the Athenians with a speech delivered when he visited Athens in 427. Gorgias initiated the practice, which continued into the early fourth century, of composing speeches for mythical or imaginary occasions. The surviving examples reveal a lively intellectual climate in the late fifth and early fourth centuries, in which oratory served to display new ideas, new forms of expression, and new methods of argument.[3] This tradition of "intellectual" oratory was continued by the fourth-century educator Isocrates and played a large role in later Greek and Roman education.

In addition to this intellectual oratory, at about the same time the practice also began of writing speeches for real occasions in public life, which we may designate "practical" oratory. For centuries Athenians had been delivering speeches in public settings (primarily the courts and the Assembly), but these had always been composed and delivered impromptu, without being written down and thus without being preserved. The practice of writing speeches began in the courts and then expanded to include the Assembly and other settings. Athens was one of the leading cities of Greece in the fifth and fourth centuries, and its political and legal systems depended on direct participation by a large number of citizens; all important decisions were made by these large bodies, and the primary means of influencing these decisions was oratory.[4] Thus, it is not surprising that oratory flourished in Athens,[5] but it may not be immediately obvious why it should be written down.

---

problems, but he does well to remind us how thoroughly the traditional view of rhetoric depends on one of its most ardent opponents.

[3]Of these only Antiphon's *Tetralogies* are included in this series. Gorgias' *Helen* and *Palamedes*, Alcidamas' *Odysseus*, and Antisthenes' *Ajax* and *Odysseus* are translated in Gagarin and Woodruff 1995.

[4]Yunis 1996 has a good treatment of political oratory from Pericles to Demosthenes.

[5]All our evidence for practical oratory comes from Athens, with the exception of Isocrates 19, written for a trial in Aegina. Many speeches were undoubtedly delivered in courts and political forums in other Greek cities, but it may be that such speeches were written down only in Athens.

The pivotal figure in this development was Antiphon, one of the fifth-century intellectuals who are often grouped together under the name "Sophists."[6] Like some of the other sophists he contributed to the intellectual oratory of the period, but he also had a strong practical interest in law. At the same time, Antiphon had an aversion to public speaking and did not directly involve himself in legal or political affairs (Thucydides 8.68). However, he began giving general advice to other citizens who were engaged in litigation and were thus expected to address the court themselves. As this practice grew, Antiphon went further, and around 430 he began writing out whole speeches for others to memorize and deliver. Thus began the practice of "logography," which continued through the next century and beyond.[7] Logography particularly appealed to men like Lysias, who were metics, or non-citizen residents of Athens. Since they were not Athenian citizens, they were barred from direct participation in public life, but they could contribute by writing speeches for others.

Antiphon was also the first (to our knowledge) to write down a speech he would himself deliver, writing the speech for his own defense at his trial for treason in 411. His motive was probably to publicize and preserve his views, and others continued this practice of writing down speeches they would themselves deliver in the courts and (more rarely) the Assembly.[8] Finally, one other type of practical oratory was the special tribute delivered on certain important public occasions, the best known of which is the funeral oration. It is convenient to designate these three types of oratory by the terms

---

[6]The term "sophist" was loosely used through the fifth and fourth centuries to designate various intellectuals and orators, but under the influence of Plato, who attacked certain figures under this name, the term is now used of a specific group of thinkers; see Kerferd 1981.

[7]For Antiphon as the first to write speeches, see Photius, *Bibliotheca* 486a7–11 and [Plut.], *Moralia* 832c–d. The latest extant speech can be dated to 320, but we know that at least one orator, Dinarchus, continued the practice after that date.

[8]Unlike forensic speeches, speeches for delivery in the Assembly were usually not composed beforehand in writing, since the speaker could not know exactly when or in what context he would be speaking; see further Trevett 1996.

Aristotle later uses: forensic (for the courts), deliberative (for the Assembly), and epideictic (for display).[9]

THE ORATORS

In the century from about 420 to 320, dozens—perhaps even hundreds—of now unknown orators and logographers must have composed speeches that are now lost, but only ten of these men were selected for preservation and study by ancient scholars, and only works collected under the names of these ten have been preserved. Some of these works are undoubtedly spurious, though in most cases they are fourth-century works by a different author rather than later "forgeries." Indeed, modern scholars suspect that as many as seven of the speeches attributed to Demosthenes may have been written by Apollodorus, son of Pasion, who is sometimes called "the eleventh orator."[10] Including these speeches among the works of Demosthenes may have been an honest mistake, or perhaps a bookseller felt he could sell more copies of these speeches if they were attributed to a more famous orator.

In alphabetical order the Ten Orators are as follows:[11]

- AESCHINES (ca. 395–ca. 322) rose from obscure origins to become an important Athenian political figure, first an ally, then a bitter enemy of Demosthenes. His three speeches all concern major public issues. The best known of these (Aes. 3) was delivered at the trial in 330, when Demosthenes responded with *On the Crown* (Dem. 18). Aeschines lost the case and was forced to leave Athens and live the rest of his life in exile.

---

[9] *Rhetoric* 1.3. Intellectual orations, like Gorgias' *Helen,* do not easily fit into Aristotle's classification. For a fuller (but still brief) introduction to Attic oratory and the orators, see Edwards 1994.

[10] See Trevett 1992.

[11] The Loeb volumes of Minor Attic Orators also include the prominent Athenian political figure Demades (ca. 385–319), who was not one of the Ten; but the only speech that has come down to us under his name is a later forgery. It is possible that Demades and other fourth-century politicians who had a high reputation for public speaking did not put any speeches in writing, especially if they rarely spoke in the courts (see above, n. 8).

* ANDOCIDES (ca. 440–ca. 390) is best known for his role in the scandal of 415, when just before the departure of the fateful Athenian expedition to Sicily during the Peloponnesian War (431–404), a band of young men mutilated statues of Hermes, and at the same time information was revealed about the secret rites of Demeter. Andocides was exiled but later returned. Two of the four speeches in his name give us a contemporary view of the scandal: one pleads for his return, the other argues against a second period of exile.

* ANTIPHON (ca. 480–411), as already noted, wrote forensic speeches for others and only once spoke himself. In 411 he participated in an oligarchic coup by a group of 400, and when the democrats regained power he was tried for treason and executed. His six surviving speeches include three for delivery in court and the three Tetralogies—imaginary intellectual exercises for display or teaching that consist of four speeches each, two on each side. All six of Antiphon's speeches concern homicide, probably because these stood at the beginning of the collection of his works. Fragments of some thirty other speeches cover many different topics.

* DEMOSTHENES (384–322) is generally considered the best of the Attic orators. Although his nationalistic message is less highly regarded today, his powerful mastery of and ability to combine many different rhetorical styles continues to impress readers. Demosthenes was still a child when his wealthy father died. The trustees of the estate apparently misappropriated much of it, and when he came of age, he sued them in a series of cases (27–31), regaining some of his fortune and making a name as a powerful speaker. He then wrote speeches for others in a variety of cases, public and private, and for his own use in court (where many cases involved major public issues), and in the Assembly, where he opposed the growing power of Philip of Macedon. The triumph of Philip and his son Alexander the Great eventually put an end to Demosthenes' career. Some sixty speeches have come down under his name, about a third of them of questionable authenticity.

* DINARCHUS (ca. 360–ca. 290) was born in Corinth but spent much of his life in Athens as a metic (a noncitizen resident). His public fame came primarily from writing speeches for the prosecutions

surrounding the Harpalus affair in 324, when several prominent figures (including Demosthenes) were accused of bribery. After 322 he had a profitable career as a logographer.

* HYPERIDES (389/8–322) was a political leader and logographer of so many different talents that he was called the pentathlete of orators. He was a leader of the Athenian resistance to Philip and Alexander and (like Demosthenes) was condemned to death after Athens' final surrender. One speech and substantial fragments of five others have been recovered from papyrus remains; otherwise, only fragments survive.

* ISAEUS (ca. 415–ca. 340) wrote speeches on a wide range of topics, but the eleven complete speeches that survive, dating from ca. 390 to ca. 344, all concern inheritance. As with Antiphon, the survival of these particular speeches may have been the result of the later ordering of his speeches by subject; we have part of a twelfth speech and fragments and titles of some forty other works. Isaeus is said to have been a pupil of Isocrates and the teacher of Demosthenes.

* ISOCRATES (436–338) considered himself a philosopher and educator, not an orator or rhetorician. He came from a wealthy Athenian family but lost most of his property in the Peloponnesian War, and in 403 he took up logography. About 390 he abandoned this practice and turned to writing and teaching, setting forth his educational, philosophical, and political views in essays that took the form of speeches but were not meant for oral delivery. He favored accommodation with the growing power of Philip of Macedon and panhellenic unity. His school was based on a broad concept of rhetoric and applied philosophy; it attracted pupils from the entire Greek world (including Isaeus, Lycurgus, and Hyperides) and became the main rival of Plato's Academy. Isocrates greatly influenced education and rhetoric in the Hellenistic, Roman, and modern periods until the eighteenth century.

* LYCURGUS (ca. 390–ca. 324) was a leading public official who restored the financial condition of Athens after 338 and played a large role in the city for the next dozen years. He brought charges of corruption or treason against many other officials, usually with success. Only one speech survives.

* LYSIAS (ca. 445–ca. 380) was a metic—an official resident of Athens but not a citizen. Much of his property was seized by the Thirty during their short-lived oligarchic coup in 404–403. Perhaps as a result he turned to logography. More than thirty speeches survive in whole or in part, though the authenticity of some is doubted. We also have fragments or know the titles of more than a hundred others. The speeches cover a wide range of cases, and he may have delivered one himself (Lys. 12), on the death of his brother at the hands of the Thirty. Lysias is particularly known for his vivid narratives, his *ēthopoiïa*, or "creation of character," and his prose style, which became a model of clarity and vividness.

THE WORKS OF THE ORATORS

As soon as speeches began to be written down, they could be preserved. We know little about the conditions of book "publication" (i.e., making copies for distribution) in the fourth century, but there was an active market for books in Athens, and some of the speeches may have achieved wide circulation.[12] An orator (or his family) may have preserved his own speeches, perhaps to advertise his ability or demonstrate his success, or booksellers may have collected and copied them in order to make money.

We do not know how closely the preserved text of these speeches corresponded to the version actually delivered in court or in the Assembly. Speakers undoubtedly extemporized or varied from their text on occasion, but there is no good evidence that deliberative speeches were substantially revised for publication.[13] In forensic oratory a logographer's reputation would derive first and foremost from his success with jurors. If a forensic speech was victorious, there would be no reason to alter it for publication, and if it lost, alteration would probably not deceive potential clients. Thus, the published texts of forensic speeches were probably quite faithful to the texts

---

[12]Dover's discussion (1968) of the preservation and transmission of the works of Lysias (and perhaps others under his name) is useful not just for Lysias but for the other orators too. His theory of shared authorship between logographer and litigant, however, is unconvincing (see Usher 1976).

[13]See further Trevett 1996: 437–439.

that were provided to clients, and we have little reason to suspect substantial alteration in the century or so before they were collected by scholars in Alexandria (see below).

In addition to the speaker's text, most forensic speeches have breaks for the inclusion of documents. The logographer inserted a notation in his text—such as *nomos* ("law") or *martyria* ("testimony")—and the speaker would pause while the clerk read out the text of a law or the testimony of witnesses. Many speeches survive with only a notation that a *nomos* or *martyria* was read at that point, but in some cases the text of the document is included. It used to be thought that these documents were all creations of later scholars, but many (though not all) are now accepted as genuine.[14]

With the foundation of the famous library in Alexandria early in the third century, scholars began to collect and catalogue texts of the orators, along with many other classical authors. Only the best orators were preserved in the library, many of them represented by over 100 speeches each (some undoubtedly spurious). Only some of these works survived in manuscript form to the modern era; more recently a few others have been discovered on ancient sheets of papyrus, so that today the corpus of Attic Oratory consists of about 150 speeches, together with a few letters and other works. The subject matter ranges from important public issues and serious crimes to business affairs, lovers' quarrels, inheritance disputes, and other personal or family matters.

In the centuries after these works were collected, ancient scholars gathered biographical facts about their authors, produced grammatical and lexicographic notes, and used some of the speeches as evidence for Athenian political history. But the ancient scholars who were most interested in the orators were those who studied prose style, the most notable of these being Dionysius of Halicarnassus (first century BC), who wrote treatises on several of the orators,[15] and Hermogenes of Tarsus (second century AD), who wrote several literary studies, including *On Types of Style*.[16] But relative to epic or tragedy, oratory was little studied; and even scholars of rhetoric whose

---

[14]See MacDowell 1990: 43–47; Todd 1993: 44–45.

[15]Dionysius' literary studies are collected and translated in Usher 1974–1985.

[16]Wooten 1987. Stylistic considerations probably also influenced the selection of the "canon" of ten orators; see Worthington 1994.

interests were broader than style, like Cicero and Quintilian, paid little attention to the orators, except for the acknowledged master, Demosthenes.

Most modern scholars until the second half of the twentieth century continued to treat the orators primarily as prose stylists.[17] The reevaluation of Athenian democracy by George Grote and others in the nineteenth century stimulated renewed interest in Greek oratory among historians; and increasing interest in Athenian law during that century led a few legal scholars to read the orators. But in comparison with the interest shown in the other literary genres—epic, lyric, tragedy, comedy, and even history—Attic oratory had been relatively neglected until the last third of the twentieth century. More recently, however, scholars have discovered the value of the orators for the broader study of Athenian culture and society. Since Dover's ground-breaking works on popular morality and homosexuality,[18] interest in the orators has been increasing rapidly, and they are now seen as primary representatives of Athenian moral and social values, and as evidence for social and economic conditions, political and social ideology, and in general those aspects of Athenian culture that in the past were commonly ignored by historians of ancient Greece but are of increasing interest and importance today, including women and the family, slavery, and the economy.

GOVERNMENT AND LAW IN CLASSICAL ATHENS

The hallmark of the Athenian political and legal systems was its amateurism. Most public officials, including those who supervised the courts, were selected by lot and held office for a limited period,

---

[17]For example, the most popular and influential book ever written on the orators, Jebb's *The Attic Orators* (1875) was presented as an "attempt to aid in giving Attic Oratory its due place in the history of Attic Prose" (I.xiii). This modern focus on prose style can plausibly be connected to the large role played by prose composition (the translation of English prose into Greek, usually in imitation of specific authors or styles) in the Classics curriculum, especially in Britain.

[18]Dover (1974, 1978). Dover recently commented (1994: 157), "When I began to mine the riches of Attic forensic oratory I was astonished to discover that the mine had never been exploited."

typically a year. Thus a great many citizens held public office at some point in their lives, but almost none served for an extended period of time or developed the experience or expertise that would make them professionals. All significant policy decisions were debated and voted on in the Assembly, where the quorum was 6,000 citizens, and all significant legal cases were judged by bodies of 200 to 500 jurors or more. Public prominence was not achieved by election (or selection) to public office but depended rather on a man's ability to sway the majority of citizens in the Assembly or jurors in court to vote in favor of a proposed course of action or for one of the litigants in a trial. Success was never permanent, and a victory on one policy issue or a verdict in one case could be quickly reversed in another.[19] In such a system the value of public oratory is obvious, and in the fourth century oratory became the most important cultural institution in Athens, replacing drama as the forum where major ideological concerns were displayed and debated.

Several recent books give good detailed accounts of Athenian government and law,[20] and so a brief sketch can suffice here. The main policy-making body was the Assembly, open to all adult male citizens; a small payment for attendance enabled at least some of the poor to attend along with the leisured rich. In addition, a Council of 500 citizens, selected each year by lot with no one allowed to serve more than two years, prepared material for and made recommendations to the Assembly; a rotating subgroup of this Council served as an executive committee, the Prytaneis. Finally, numerous officials, most of them selected by lot for one-year terms, supervised different areas

----

[19]In the Assembly this could be accomplished by a reconsideration of the question, as in the famous Mytilenean debate (Thuc. 3.36–50); in court a verdict was final, but its practical effects could be thwarted or reversed by later litigation on a related issue.

[20]For government, see Sinclair 1988, Hansen 1991; for law, MacDowell 1978, Todd 1993, and Boegehold 1995 (Bonner 1927 is still helpful). Much of our information about the legal and political systems comes from a work attributed to Aristotle but perhaps written by a pupil of his, *The Athenian Constitution* (*Ath. Pol.*—conveniently translated with notes by Rhodes 1984). The discovery of this work on a papyrus in Egypt in 1890 caused a major resurgence of interest in Athenian government.

of administration and finance. The most important of these were the nine Archons (lit. "rulers"): the eponymous Archon after whom the year was named, the Basileus ("king"),[21] the Polemarch, and the six Thesmothetae. Councilors and almost all these officials underwent a preliminary examination (*dokimasia*) before taking office, and officials submitted to a final accounting (*euthynai*) upon leaving; at these times any citizen who wished could challenge a person's fitness for his new position or his performance in his recent position.

There was no general taxation of Athenian citizens. Sources of public funding included the annual tax levied on metics, various fees and import duties, and (in the fifth century) tribute from allied cities; but the source that figures most prominently in the orators is the Athenian system of liturgies (*leitourgiai*), by which in a regular rotation the rich provided funding for certain special public needs. The main liturgies were the *chorēgia*, in which a sponsor (*chorēgos*) supervised and paid for the training and performance of a chorus which sang and danced at a public festival,[22] and the trierarchy, in which a sponsor (trierarch) paid to equip and usually commanded a trireme, or warship, for a year. Some of these liturgies required substantial expenditures, but even so, some men spent far more than required in order to promote themselves and their public careers, and litigants often tried to impress the jurors by referring to liturgies they had undertaken (see, e.g., Lys. 21.1–n5). A further twist on this system was that if a man thought he had been assigned a liturgy that should have gone to someone else who was richer than he, he could propose an exchange of property (*antidosis*), giving the other man a choice of either taking over the liturgy or exchanging property with him. Finally, the rich were also subject to special taxes (*eisphorai*) levied as a percentage of their property in times of need.

The Athenian legal system remained similarly resistant to professionalization. Trials and the procedures leading up to them were supervised by officials, primarily the nine Archons, but their role was purely administrative, and they were in no way equivalent to mod-

---

[21]Modern scholars often use the term *archōn basileus* or "king archon," but Athenian sources (e.g., *Ath. Pol.* 57) simply call him the *basileus*.

[22]These included the productions of tragedy and comedy, for which the main expense was for the chorus.

ern judges. All significant questions about what we would call points of law were presented to the jurors, who considered them together with all other issues when they delivered their verdict at the end of the trial.[23] Trials were "contests" (*agōnes*) between two litigants, each of whom presented his own case to the jurors in a speech, plaintiff first, then defendant; in some cases each party then spoke again, probably in rebuttal. Since a litigant had only one or two speeches in which to present his entire case, and no issue was decided separately by a judge, all the necessary factual information and every important argument on substance or procedure, fact or law, had to be presented together. A single speech might thus combine narrative, argument, emotional appeal, and various digressions, all with the goal of obtaining a favorable verdict. Even more than today, a litigant's primary task was to control the issue—to determine which issues the jurors would consider most important and which questions they would have in their minds as they cast their votes. We only rarely have both speeches from a trial,[24] and we usually have little or no external evidence for the facts of a case or the verdict. We must thus infer both the facts and the opponent's strategy from the speech we have, and any assessment of the overall effectiveness of a speech and of the logographer's strategy is to some extent speculative.

Before a trial there were usually several preliminary hearings for presenting evidence; arbitration, public and private, was available and sometimes required. These hearings and arbitration sessions allowed each side to become familiar with the other side's case, so that discussions of "what my opponent will say" could be included in one's speech. Normally a litigant presented his own case, but he was often assisted by family or friends. If he wished (and could afford it), he

---

[23]Certain religious "interpreters" (*exēgētai*) were occasionally asked to give their opinion on a legal matter that had a religious dimension (such as the prosecution of a homicide), but although these opinions could be reported in court (e.g., Dem. 47.68–73), they had no official legal standing. The most significant administrative decision we hear of is the refusal of the Basileus to accept the case in Antiphon 6 (see 6.37–46).

[24]The exceptions are Demosthenes 19 and Aeschines 2, Aeschines 3 and Demosthenes 18, and Lysias 6 (one of several prosecution speeches) and Andocides 1; all were written for major public cases.

could enlist the services of a logographer, who presumably gave strategic advice in addition to writing a speech. The speeches were timed to ensure an equal hearing for both sides,[25] and all trials were completed within a day. Two hundred or more jurors decided each case in the popular courts, which met in the Agora.[26] Homicide cases and certain other religious trials (e.g., Lys. 7) were heard by the Council of the Areopagus or an associated group of fifty-one Ephetae. The Areopagus was composed of all former Archons—perhaps 150–200 members at most times. It met on a hill called the Areopagus ("rock of Ares") near the Acropolis.

Jurors for the regular courts were selected by lot from those citizens who registered each year and who appeared for duty that day; as with the Assembly, a small payment allowed the poor to serve. After the speakers had finished, the jurors voted immediately without any formal discussion. The side with the majority won; a tie vote decided the case for the defendant. In some cases where the penalty was not fixed, after a conviction the jurors voted again on the penalty, choosing between penalties proposed by each side. Even when we know the verdict, we cannot know which of the speaker's arguments contributed most to his success or failure. However, a logographer could probably learn from jurors which points had or had not been successful, so that arguments that are found repeatedly in speeches probably were known to be effective in most cases.

The first written laws in Athens were enacted by Draco (ca. 620) and Solon (ca. 590), and new laws were regularly added. At the end of the fifth century the existing laws were reorganized, and a new procedure for enacting laws was instituted; thereafter a group of Law-Givers (*nomothetai*) had to certify that a proposed law did not conflict with any existing laws. There was no attempt, however, to organize legislation systematically, and although Plato, Aristotle, and other philosophers wrote various works on law and law-giving, these were either theoretical or descriptive and had no apparent influence on legislation. Written statutes generally used ordinary language rather than precise legal definitions in designating offenses, and ques-

---

[25]Timing was done by means of a water-clock, which in most cases was stopped during the reading of documents.

[26]See Boegehold 1995.

tions concerning precisely what constituted a specific offense or what was the correct interpretation of a written statute were decided (together with other issues) by the jurors in each case. A litigant might, of course, assert a certain definition or interpretation as "something you all know" or "what the lawgiver intended," but such remarks are evidently tendentious and cannot be taken as authoritative.

The result of these procedural and substantive features was that the verdict depended largely on each litigant's speech (or speeches). As one speaker puts it (Ant. 6.18), "When there are no witnesses, you (jurors) are forced to reach a verdict about the case on the basis of the prosecutor's and defendant's words alone; you must be suspicious and examine their accounts in detail, and your vote will necessarily be cast on the basis of likelihood rather than clear knowledge." Even the testimony of witnesses (usually on both sides) is rarely decisive. On the other hand, most speakers make a considerable effort to establish facts and provide legitimate arguments in conformity with established law. Plato's view of rhetoric as a clever technique for persuading an ignorant crowd that the false is true is not borne out by the speeches, and the legal system does not appear to have produced many arbitrary or clearly unjust results.

The main form of legal procedure was a *dikē* ("suit") in which the injured party (or his relatives in a case of homicide) brought suit against the offender. Suits for injuries to slaves would be brought by the slave's master, and injuries to women would be prosecuted by a male relative. Strictly speaking, a *dikē* was a private matter between individuals, though like all cases, *dikai* often had public dimensions. The other major form of procedure was a *graphē* ("writing" or "indictment") in which "anyone who wished" (i.e., any citizen) could bring a prosecution for wrongdoing. *Graphai* were instituted by Solon, probably in order to allow prosecution of offenses where the victim was unable or unlikely to bring suit himself, such as selling a dependent into slavery; but the number of areas covered by *graphai* increased to cover many types of public offenses as well as some apparently private crimes, such as *hybris*.

The system of prosecution by "anyone who wished" also extended to several other more specialized forms of prosecution, like *eisangelia* ("impeachment"), used in cases of treason. Another specialized prosecution was *apagōgē* ("summary arrest"), in which someone could arrest a common criminal (*kakourgos*, lit. "evil-doer"), or have him arrested, on the spot. The reliance on private initiative meant that Athenians never developed a system of public prosecution; rather, they presumed that everyone would keep an eye on the behavior of his political enemies and bring suit as soon as he suspected a crime, both to harm his opponents and to advance his own career. In this way all public officials would be watched by someone. There was no disgrace in admitting that a prosecution was motivated by private enmity.

By the end of the fifth century the system of prosecution by "anyone who wished" was apparently being abused by so-called sykophants (*sykophantai*), who allegedly brought or threatened to bring false suits against rich men, either to gain part of the fine that would be levied or to induce an out-of-court settlement in which the accused would pay to have the matter dropped. We cannot gauge the true extent of this problem, since speakers usually provide little evidence to support their claims that their opponents are sykophants, but the Athenians did make sykophancy a crime. They also specified that in many public procedures a plaintiff who either dropped the case or failed to obtain one-fifth of the votes would have to pay a heavy fine of 1,000 drachmas. Despite this, it appears that litigation was common in Athens and was seen by some as excessive.

Over the course of time, the Athenian legal and political systems have more often been judged negatively than positively. Philosophers and political theorists have generally followed the lead of Plato (427– 347), who lived and worked in Athens his entire life while severely criticizing its system of government as well as many other aspects of its culture. For Plato, democracy amounted to the tyranny of the masses over the educated elite and was destined to collapse from its own instability. The legal system was capricious and depended entirely on the rhetorical ability of litigants with no regard for truth or justice. These criticisms have often been echoed by modern scholars, who particularly complain that law was much too closely interwoven with politics and did not have the autonomous status it achieved in Roman law and continues to have, at least in theory, in modern legal systems.

Plato's judgments are valid if one accepts the underlying presuppositions, that the aim of law is absolute truth and abstract justice and that achieving the highest good of the state requires thorough and systematic organization. Most Athenians do not seem to have subscribed to either the criticisms or the presuppositions, and most scholars now accept the long-ignored fact that despite major external disruptions in the form of wars and two short-lived coups brought about by one of these wars, the Athenian legal and political systems remained remarkably stable for almost two hundred years (508–320). Moreover, like all other Greek cities at the time, whatever their form of government, Athenian democracy was brought to an end not by internal forces but by the external power of Philip of Macedon and his son Alexander. The legal system never became autonomous, and the rich sometimes complained that they were victims of unscrupulous litigants, but there is no indication that the people wanted to yield control of the legal process to a professional class, as Plato recommended. For most Athenians—Plato being an exception in this and many other matters—one purpose of the legal system was to give everyone the opportunity to have his case heard by other citizens and have it heard quickly and cheaply; and in this it clearly succeeded.

Indeed, the Athenian legal system also served the interests of the rich, even the very rich, as well as the common people, in that it provided a forum for the competition that since Homer had been an important part of aristocratic life. In this competition, the rich used the courts as battlegrounds, though their main weapon was the rhetoric of popular ideology, which hailed the rule of law and promoted the ideal of moderation and restraint.[27] But those who aspired to political leadership and the honor and status that accompanied it repeatedly entered the legal arena, bringing suit against their political enemies whenever possible and defending themselves against suits brought by others whenever necessary. The ultimate judges of these public competitions were the common people, who seem to have relished the dramatic clash of individuals and ideologies. In this respect fourth-century oratory was the cultural heir of fifth-century drama and was similarly appreciated by the citizens. Despite the disapproval of intellectuals like Plato, most Athenians legitimately considered their legal system a hallmark of their democracy and a vital presence in their culture.

---

[27]Ober 1989 is fundamental; see also Cohen 1995.

THE TRANSLATION OF GREEK ORATORY

The purpose of this series is to provide students and scholars in all fields with accurate, readable translations of all surviving classical Attic oratory, including speeches whose authenticity is disputed, as well as the substantial surviving fragments. In keeping with the originals, the language is for the most part nontechnical. Names of persons and places are given in the (generally more familiar) Latinized forms, and names of officials or legal procedures have been translated into English equivalents where possible. Notes are intended to provide the necessary historical and cultural background; scholarly controversies are generally not discussed. The notes and introductions refer to scholarly treatments in addition to those listed below, which the reader may consult for further information.

Cross-references to other speeches follow the standard numbering system, which is now well established except in the case of Hyperides (for whom the numbering of the Oxford Classical Text is used).[28] References are by work and section (e.g., Dem. 24.73); spurious works are not specially marked; when no author is named (e.g., 24.73), the reference is to the same author as the annotated passage.

ABBREVIATIONS

Aes.	=	Aeschines
And.	=	Andocides
Ant.	=	Antiphon
Arist.	=	Aristotle
Aristoph.	=	Aristophanes
Ath. Pol.	=	The Athenian Constitution
Dem.	=	Demosthenes
Din.	=	Dinarchus
Herod.	=	Herodotus
Hyp.	=	Hyperides
Is.	=	Isaeus
Isoc.	=	Isocrates

---

[28]For a listing of all the orators and their works, with classifications (forensic, deliberative, epideictic) and rough dates, see Edwards 1994: 74–79.

Lyc.	=	Lycurgus
Lys.	=	Lysias
Plut.	=	Plutarch
Thuc.	=	Thucydides
Xen.	=	Xenophon

NOTE ON CURRENCY

The main unit of Athenian currency was the drachma; this was divided into obols, and larger amounts were designated minas and talents.

1 drachma	=	6 obols
1 mina	=	100 drachmas
1 talent	=	60 minas (6,000 drachmas)

It is impossible to give an accurate equivalence in terms of modern currency, but it may be helpful to remember that the daily wage of some skilled workers was a drachma in the mid-fifth century and 2–2½ drachmas in the later fourth century. Thus it may not be too misleading to think of a drachma as worth about $50 or £33 and a talent as about $300,000 or £200,000 in 1997 currency.

BIBLIOGRAPHY OF WORKS CITED

Boegehold, Alan L., 1995: *The Lawcourts at Athens: Sites, Buildings, Equipment, Procedure, and Testimonia.* Princeton.

Bonner, Robert J., 1927: *Lawyers and Litigants in Ancient Athens.* Chicago.

Carey, Christopher, 1997: *Trials from Classical Athens.* London.

Cohen, David, 1995: *Law, Violence and Community in Classical Athens.* Cambridge.

Cole, Thomas, 1991: *The Origins of Rhetoric in Ancient Greece.* Baltimore.

Dover, Kenneth J., 1968: *Lysias and the Corpus Lysiacum.* Berkeley.

———, 1974: *Greek Popular Morality in the Time of Plato and Aristotle.* Oxford.

———, 1978: *Greek Homosexuality.* London.

———, 1994: *Marginal Comment.* London.

Edwards, Michael, 1994: *The Attic Orators*. London.

Gagarin, Michael, and Paul Woodruff, 1995: *Early Greek Political Thought from Homer to the Sophists*. Cambridge.

Hansen, Mogens Herman, 1991: *The Athenian Democracy in the Age of Demosthenes*. Oxford.

Jebb, Richard, 1875: *The Attic Orators*. 2 vols. London.

Kennedy, George A., 1963: *The Art of Persuasion in Greece*. Princeton.

Kerferd, G. B., 1981: *The Sophistic Movement*. Cambridge.

MacDowell, Douglas M., 1978: *The Law in Classical Athens*. London.

———, ed. 1990: *Demosthenes, Against Meidias*. Oxford.

Ober, Josiah, 1989: *Mass and Elite in Democratic Athens*. Princeton.

Rhodes, P. J., trans., 1984: *Aristotle, The Athenian Constitution*. Penguin Books.

Sinclair, R. K., 1988: *Democracy and Participation in Athens*. Cambridge.

Todd, Stephen, 1993: *The Shape of Athenian Law*. Oxford.

Trevett, Jeremy, 1992: *Apollodoros the Son of Pasion*. Oxford.

———, 1996: "Did Demosthenes Publish His Deliberative Speeches?" *Hermes* 124: 425–441.

Usher, Stephen, 1976: "Lysias and His Clients," *Greek, Roman and Byzantine Studies* 17: 31–40.

———, trans., 1974–1985: *Dionysius of Halicarnassus, Critical Essays*. 2 vols. Loeb Classical Library. Cambridge, MA.

———, 1999: *Greek Oratory: Tradition and Originality*. Oxford.

Wooten, Cecil W., trans., 1987: *Hermogenes' On Types of Style*. Chapel Hill, NC.

Worthington, Ian, 1994: "The Canon of the Ten Attic Orators," in *Persuasion: Greek Rhetoric in Action,* ed. Ian Worthington. London: 244–263.

Yunis, Harvey, 1996: *Taming Democracy: Models of Political Rhetoric in Classical Athens*. Ithaca, NY.

ISAEUS

INTRODUCTION

LIFE

One of the very few facts we know about Isaeus is that he was a professional speechwriter (*logographos*). The man behind the speeches, however, is almost entirely obscure. His name does not appear in the historical record until the critical essay written about him in the late first century BCE by Dionysius of Halicarnassus, and Dionysius himself already had little or no reliable information about his subject.[1] His birthplace was either Athens (according to Hermippus) or Chalcis (according to Demetrius of Magnesia),[2] but if he did not play a prominent role in Athenian politics, this does not necessarily indicate that he was, like the earlier orator Lysias, a resident alien (metic) at Athens.

Isaeus' logographic activity, on the evidence of the dating of the speeches that survive, began in the very early 380s and continued until the later 340s, and so a birth date of ca. 415–410 is feasible.[3] This date would fit with one of the two facts recorded about Isaeus by Hermippus (Dionysius of Halicarnassus, *Isaeus* 1): first, that he studied under Isocrates, who began teaching in Athens in ca. 390. If that is the case, it is interesting that if Speech 5 is correctly dated to

---

[1]E.g., "He was in his prime after the Peloponnesian War, as I deduce from his speeches, and survived until the rule of Philip" (*Isaeus* 1). Cf. the very brief biography in [Plut.], *Lives of the Ten Orators* (839e–f).

[2]Cf. Harpocration, s.v. *Isaios*. Hermippus was third century, Demetrius, first century BCE.

[3]Speech 5 may be the earliest surviving speech, from 389; Speech 12 dates to 344/3.

389, Isaeus either seems to have been a student for only a short time or was already writing speeches while learning the trade. Hermippus' second fact was that Isaeus taught Demosthenes, a tradition that recurs in the pseudo-Plutarchan *Lives* of the two orators (839f, 844b–c), in the expanded form that Isaeus lived in Demosthenes' house and composed for him the early speeches prosecuting his guardians. It was his teaching of Demosthenes that chiefly won Isaeus fame, according to the opening sentence of Dionysius' essay, and one of Demosthenes' rivals, Pytheas, accused him of "digesting the whole of Isaeus and his rhetorical technique" (Dionysius of Halicarnassus, *Isaeus* 4).

WORKS

The pseudo-Plutarchan *Life* records that Isaeus "left behind sixty-four speeches, of which fifty were genuine, and his own rhetorical manuals" (839f). Eleven speeches survive, as well as an extended fragment quoted by Dionysius (*Isaeus* 17), which is regularly printed as Speech 12; in addition, we have from various sources (including Dionysius and the later lexicographers) the names, with fragments in some cases, of over forty lost speeches, some of which probably overlap, plus a number of other fragments and single words of unknown origin. We therefore have a good idea of the range of Isaeus' activity, but it is clear from the surviving speeches and many of the fragments that he concentrated mainly on composing forensic speeches for suits concerned with matters of inheritance. There is some variety in the types of suit involved, including the actual inheritance claims (*diadikasiai*), subsequent prosecutions for false testimony (*dikai pseudomartyriōn*), the prosecution of a surety (*dikē engyēs*), and prosecution for maltreatment of an orphan (*eisangelia kakōseōs orphanou*). Nevertheless, the common subject matter makes Isaeus the Attic orator closest to being a legal expert. Unfortunately, the complex nature of this material has also prompted negative evaluations of his ability, from Dionysius' contrasting of Isaeus' cleverness (*deinotēs*) with Lysias' charm (*charis*) to Dobson's evaluation of his "efficiency which is admirable, but dull."[4] We shall return to this topic presently

---

[4]Dionysius of Halicarnassus, *Isaeus* 3; J. F. Dobson, *The Greek Orators* (London, 1919), 105.

and merely note here the crucial importance of Isaeus' speeches as sources in a central area of Athenian law.

STYLE AND METHOD

Dionysius, as we saw, begins his essay on Isaeus with the statement that his fame was due mainly to his being the teacher of Demosthenes. Dionysius views Isaeus as a link between the older forensic style of Lysias and the mature forensic style of Demosthenes, the unquestioned master of Attic oratory.[5] The critic, however, firmly classifies Isaeus with Lysias and Isocrates as being among the best orators of the earlier generation, not in the later group of Demosthenes, Hyperides, and Aeschines (Dionysius of Halicarnassus, *On the Ancient Orators* 4); and in his stylistic analysis he compares Isaeus primarily with Lysias. Lysias is a clear winner in the comparison: although in many respects (such as clarity, vividness, and conciseness) their language is very similar, that of Lysias is plainer and has a greater moral flavor, his composition is more natural, his figures are simpler, and he has plenty of grace and charm; whereas Isaeus' language has more technical skill and attention to detail, is more elaborate, and contains a variety of figures (Dionysius of Halicarnassus, *Isaeus* 3). Isaeus displays the same cleverness in his writing that is the source of Demosthenes' rhetorical power, yet the cleverness and rhetorical skill make Dionysius suspect of both orators' speeches, which he opposes to the more natural, straightforward works of Lysias and Isocrates (*Isaeus* 4, cf. 16). In the structure and argument of his speeches, Dionysius observes, Lysias is more simple than Isaeus, whose arguments are developed at great length, backed by emotional appeal and blackening of the opponent's character (*Isaeus* 3). In these and other features, such as his extensive use of rhetorical questions (*Isaeus* 12–13) and the arrangement of his material (*Isaeus* 14–15), Isaeus is the forerunner of Demosthenes, though lacking his supreme talent.

Dionysius' observations are characteristically acute, but we should beware of accepting them and thereby underestimating Isaeus' abil-

---

[5]See Usher 1974: 170–171.

ity as a logographer. Confronted by the intricacies of family histories
and the obscurities of inheritance laws, Isaeus is ready to dispense
with the standard order of forensic speeches of proem, narrative,
proofs, and epilogue. He breaks up his narratives into several sections, each with arguments attached, and pays close attention to the
beginnings and endings of his speeches. Speech 11 opens forcefully
with a discussion of the laws, while Speech 8 closes equally forcefully
with a deposition proving the opponent's adultery. Indeed, while
Isaeus lacks Lysias' supreme ability of characterization (*ēthopoiia*),
he is not at all deficient in using the character of his client or opponent as a means of proof.[6] If, then, Isaeus won a reputation for
deception and "being clever at devising speeches for the worse cause"
(Dionysius of Halicarnassus, *Isaeus* 4), it must redound to his credit
that he did everything he could to help his client's case (id. 3). He
was, without doubt, the man to turn to for help in family disputes.

ISAEUS' MODERN REPUTATION

Modern criticism of Isaeus has been shaped not so much by
Dionysius as by a scholar who took his suspicions to their extremes:
William Wyse. Todd (1990)[7] offers a succinct examination of the
decline in importance of the orators in the classical curriculum of
the late nineteenth century, as scholars became increasingly suspicious of their veracity (and hence their honor). The most notable
product of the new thinking was Wyse's monumentally learned
commentary, which doubts Isaeus' words at every turn and indeed
has virtually nothing positive to say about him. Wyse's commentary
and his skepticism have dominated Isaean scholarship ever since,
although in more recent times a reaction has begun against the latter.[8] In my Introductions and Notes to the speeches I attempt to
give a more balanced view, and if legal historians are destined to be
frustrated by what many will continue to regard as Isaean chicanery,

---

[6]See, e.g., Kennedy 1963: 144.

[7]S. C. Todd, "The Use and Abuse of the Attic Orators," *G&R* 37 (1990),
159–178, at 161–162.

[8]See, e.g., Thompson 1976; Usher 1999: 128 n. 6.

it is hoped that the brilliant rhetoric in which Isaeus entangles his readers will come to be recognized in its own right.

THE FAMILY, PROPERTY, AND ATHENIAN INHERITANCE LAW

At the core of Athenian society lay the family unit, the *oikos* ("house" or "household"). The *oikos* comprised both people and possessions: members of the family (its head, his wife and children, unmarried or widowed female relatives, and other dependents), slaves and sometimes concubines and illegitimate children, the house itself (usually called the *oikia*), and the land and other property. Additionally, and very importantly, the *oikos* was the center of a family's religious observance, with its hearth and ceremonies and, above all, the ancestral graves. Hence the preservation of the individual *oikos* was a matter of vital concern to both the family and the state.

The head of the household was called its *kyrios* ("legal representative"), and he controlled the property and cult and was responsible for the well-being of the women and children. Throughout their lives Athenian women remained in the guardianship of a *kyrios,* who normally was their father when they were single and their husband when they married. They had a very limited procedural capacity and could not, for example, appear in court as witnesses: they relied on their *kyrios* to initiate legal proceedings on their behalf (e.g., 3.2–3). Nor could Athenian women own significant amounts of property, beyond personal clothing and jewelry; and it seems unlikely (though this is a much-debated topic) that women in Athens could own land. Similarly, a father was the *kyrios* of his son until the latter reached his eighteenth year. At that point the son would become legally independent, but usually he would still live in the *oikos* of his father, who might, on entering old age, then hand over to him the *kyrieia* ("control") of the *oikos*.

The worst eventuality that could befall an Athenian *oikos* was that it become extinct. The primary method of preserving the *oikos* was through marriage and the procreation of legitimate male children. There were two forms of marriage in Athens (cf. 6.14): by far, the more common was the process of betrothal (*engyē*) and giving away (*ekdosis*) of the woman by her *kyrios*. The other way was by the awarding (*epidikasia*) of an heiress to a man after judicial process, to which we shall return presently. In marriage by *engyē* the prospective husband came to an agreement with the *kyrios* of the woman, who at least in theory would have no say in the matter and need not even be present at the betrothal. The formal granting of the woman by the *kyrios* was the essential part of the marriage. The actual handing over of the bride and transference of the *kyrieia* to her new husband would usually follow soon after, regularly with a wedding (*gamos;* for an example, see Hyp. 1.3–7), but might take place several years later if the bride-to-be was still a young girl (as in the case of Demosthenes' sister, who was promised to Demophon by her father on his deathbed when she was only five; cf. Dem. 27.4, 28.15). There was a wide range of relatives to whom a woman might be married, including a half-brother by the same father, a brother by adoption, and an uncle or cousin; she could not, however, legally be betrothed to a direct ascendant (father, grandfather) or descendant (son, grandson), brother, or half-brother by the same mother. The other main restriction in our period, originating in Pericles' citizenship law of 451/0, was that both parties should be Athenians, born of an Athenian father and mother.

It was regular practice (though not a legal requirement) for the bride's *kyrios* to offer her for marriage with a dowry (*proix*).[9] The prosecutor of Nicodemus raises suspicion against his sister's alleged marriage to Pyrrhus by playing on the lack of a dowry (3.8–9, 28–29, 78). The dowry regularly took the form of money but might also include land and other property. It acted as a form of protection for the wife, since if the marriage ended in divorce, or if either partner died and there were no children, it had to be returned to the donor. The husband did not own the dowry but was expected to use it as capital for generating income to support his wife and children.

Divorce was a straightforward matter for the husband, who could simply send his wife away. This *apopempsis* was a legal requirement if he caught his wife in adultery. Similarly, the wife's natal *kyrios* could simply take her away from her husband (*aphairesis*), either at all times or possibly until she had borne a child. At least in theory, the wife

---

[9] See 3.28n.

could initiate divorce by leaving her husband (*apoleipsis*), though she had to inform the Archon (3.78; cf. Dem. 30.17, 26); in the only example we have, Alcibiades simply carried his wife Hipparete back home (And. 4.14; Plut., *Alcibiades* 8.6). Hipparete was understandably upset by her husband bringing home his mistresses (*hetairai*), but his behavior reflects that husbands (unlike wives) were not legally required to be sexually faithful to their partners. Indeed, a man might take a concubine (*pallakē*), regularly a slave (as in Ant. 1) or, if kept "with a view to free children" (Dem. 23.53), a free noncitizen, such as Pericles' consort Aspasia (the possibility of citizen women living as *pallakai* is attested by 3.39). The free children of these unions were called *nothoi* ("bastards"), and their rights in the family and city as a whole were restricted by their illegitimate status.

The child of a married citizen couple would, if accepted by the father, be formally acknowledged and named at a family religious ceremony ten days after the birth (the *dekatē*); otherwise, the child might be exposed. This acknowledgement of paternity by the father in front of witnesses was highly important for establishing the legitimacy and citizenship of the child, which in turn had consequences for the succession. Inheritance at Athens was based on various key principles. Foremost among these was that direct descendants of the deceased took precedence over collateral relatives (i.e., those who shared a common ancestor with him). Inheritance was male-oriented, though not agnatic (i.e., through the male line): sons inherited to the exclusion of daughters, but inheritance could pass through the female line, as was the case with heiresses (see below). Further, it was partible (i.e., male children shared equally, as opposed to a rule of primogeniture); and it had a principle of representation *per stirpes* ("by lines of descent") not *per capita* ("by heads"). Thus, for example, if a man had two sons, one of whom predeceased his father but had two sons of his own, they would inherit half the estate of their grandfather, and their uncle would inherit the other half.

A legitimate son (or grandson or a son adopted during his adoptive father's lifetime) automatically inherited all the deceased's property and took over from him control of the *oikos* if he was its *kyrios*. He did not need to go through any legal process but simply took possession of the estate by *embateusis* ("entry"), and if anybody made a rival claim, he could block it by testimony (*diamartyria*) that he was the legitimate son (or grandson or adopted son).[10] If he was a minor when his father died, the son became an orphan (*orphanos*), whether or not his mother was still alive, and came under the general protection of the Eponymous Archon (Aesch. 1.158; Dem. 43.75). This official, who gave his name to the Athenian civil year, would ensure that a guardian or guardians were appointed, if the deceased had not already made arrangements; Demosthenes had three such guardians. The boy would usually live with and under the *kyrieia* of the guardian until he came of age, and in this period, the guardian was expected to maintain and increase his estate. In a society in which so many men lost their lives in war, the state was particularly concerned to ensure the welfare of its future citizens; maltreatment (*kakōsis*) of an orphan could lead to prosecution of the guardian by *eisangelia* (as in Speech 11), in which the usual penalties suffered by a prosecutor who failed to obtain one-fifth of the votes in a public suit (a heavy fine and loss of the right to bring similar cases in future) did not apply.

In all other circumstances, recourse to a judicial decision was necessary. If a claim was uncontested, it was termed an *epidikasia;* if there were rival claimants, it was a *diadikasia.* If somebody testified (by *diamartyria*) that the inheritance was "not awardable" because there was in existence a legitimate son or a son adopted during the deceased's lifetime (see below), this prevented further claims, unless the testimony was itself challenged by a prosecution for false witness (*pseudomartyria*). There were three alternative scenarios to the regular succession of a son (or direct male descendant): the deceased left no son but a daughter or daughters (or granddaughter or great-granddaughter); he adopted a son (or more rarely a daughter, as when Hagnias adopted his niece, 11.8); or the estate was claimed by the nearest collateral relative.

When the deceased left only a daughter (or other female descendant), she was called an *epiklēros* (pl. *epiklēroi*). This word is regularly translated as "heiress," but an heiress in Athens did not own the property; rather, it was vested in her until her son became an adult. The heiress would therefore need to be married to the nearest relative of her father (often her uncle) or, if he declined, the next nearest (and so on; see below for the order of precedence). To ensure offspring, the

---

[10]See the Introduction to Speech 2.

husband was required by law to have intercourse with his wife three times a month (Plut. *Solon* 20.2–5). He likewise did not own the estate, but he did have control of it until their son grew up, and so the estate of a wealthy heiress was an attractive proposition. Therefore, if the heiress was already married but childless, her nearest relative could claim her by *epidikasia* before the Archon and require her to divorce her husband (cf. 3.64, 10.19); similarly, a man might divorce his wife to claim an heiress. On the other hand, when the heiress belonged to the lowest property class, and there might not be a ready claimant, the Archon could compel the nearest relative to marry her or to give her in marriage with a dowry he had to provide (unless he was also from that class). Andocides makes capital out of his own and his cousin Leagrus' willingness to marry two impoverished heiresses (And. 1.117–119).

A father who had no male children might make arrangements to adopt a son during his lifetime. The adoptee would usually be a relative and an adult who had at least one brother (so that his own *oikos* was not in danger of becoming extinct; cf. 2.10, 21). By the adoption, the adoptee would lose membership of his natal family (cf. 10.4) and legally become the son of the adopter. If the father had a daughter, his adopted son would usually marry her. The advantage of such an adoption *inter vivos* ("between living people") was that the adoptee became the undisputed heir and could take possession of the estate by *embateusis*. Since, however, an adoption *inter vivos* could not be annulled, problems might arise if the adopter later had a son of his own, in which case the son and adopted son had to divide the estate (6.63). Consequently, adoption *inter vivos* would typically be carried out by an older man, with the danger that he might die before the process was completed (the circumstances in Speech 7), or that the adoption might be challenged on the ground of his being under the influence of a woman (see Speech 2).

An alternative method was testamentary adoption. Since there were clear rules of succession in Athens, the scope for making a will was limited, and its main purpose was to ensure an heir in the absence of a son or daughter or adopted son. The attraction of this method of adoption was that the adopter, often a younger man who might, for example, be facing the dangers of military service, could make provisional arrangements (cf. 6.7) or later amend the will; the downside was that the adoptee did not have the right of *embateusis* but had to make a claim by *epidikasia,* which might then be contested (as in Speech 1). A third method of adoption was posthumous adoption (11.49), which was used, for example, in the case of the son of an *epiklēros* who was posthumously adopted as the son of his maternal grandfather (Dem. 43.11–15).

Finally, the group of kin who had inheritance rights as collateral relatives in the absence of a daughter or adopted son was legally defined and known as the *ankhisteia,* though where the precise limits of this group lay is the subject of the Hagnias inheritance dispute (Speech 11). Ascendants of the deceased probably had no rights, nor did his widow. The relatives who did have rights were organized by order of precedence into eight categories, beginning with four on the father's side of the deceased: brothers and half-brothers by the same father and their descendants (probably without limit); sisters and half-sisters by the same father and their descendants; paternal uncles, their children, and grandchildren; and paternal aunts, their children, and grandchildren. The next four categories were on the mother's side: half-brothers by the same mother and their descendants; half-sisters by the same mother and their descendants; maternal uncles, their children, and grandchildren; and maternal aunts, their children, and grandchildren. More distant relatives on the father's side could claim if there were no *ankhisteis.*

THE TEXT

The translation is based on the Greek text of Forster's 1927 Loeb edition. I have, however, followed my published readings at 4.7, 5.9, and 26 (see notes). The manuscripts of Isaeus contain Arguments (*Hypotheseis*) to the speeches, which were composed in later antiquity and therefore have no independent authority. These are translated in the Appendix.

FURTHER READING

Andrewes, A., 1961: "Philochoros on Phratries," *JHS* 81, 1–15.
Avramovic, S., 1990: "Plaidoyer for Isaeus, or. IX," in G. Nenci and G. Thür (eds.), *Symposion 1988: Vorträge zur griechischen und hellenistischen Rechtsgeschichte.* Köln-Wien: 41–55.

Cox, C. A., 1998: *Household Interests: Property, Marriage Strategies, and Family Dynamics in Ancient Athens.* Princeton.

Davies, J. K., 1971: *Athenian Propertied Families 600–300 B.C.* Oxford.

Develin, R., 1989: *Athenian Officials 684–321 B.C.* Cambridge.

Edwards, M. J., 2002: "Two Awkward Women in Isaeus (Is. 5.9, 26)," *CQ* 52, 592–597.

Forster, E. S., 1927: *Isaeus.* Loeb Classical Library. Cambridge, MA.

Harrison, A. R. W., 1968: *The Law of Athens: The Family and Property.* Oxford.

Humphreys, S. C., 1983: "The Date of Hagnias' Death," *CP* 78, 219–225.

MacDowell, D. M., 1982: "Love versus the Law: An Essay on Menander's *Aspis,*" *G&R* 29, 42–52.

Parker, R., 1996: *Greek Religion: A History.* Oxford.

Rubinstein, L., 1993: *Adoption in IV. Century Athens.* Copenhagen.

————, 2000: *Litigation and Cooperation: Supporting Speakers in the Courts of Classical Athens.* Historia Einzelschriften 147. Stuttgart.

Thompson, W. E., 1970: "Isaeus VI: The Historical Circumstances," *CR* 20, 1–4.

————, 1976: De Hagniae Hereditate: *An Athenian Inheritance Case.* Leiden.

Wevers, R. F., 1969: *Isaeus: Chronology, Prosopography, and Social History.* The Hague.

Wyse, W., 1904: *The Speeches of Isaeus.* Cambridge.

The most recent studies of Isaeus have been in Italian:

Avramovic, S., 1997: *Iseo e il diritto attico.* Napoli.

Cobetto Ghiggia, P., 2002: *Contro Leocare (sulla successione di Diceogene).* Pisa.

Ferrucci, S., 1998: *L' Atene di Iseo. L'organizzazione del privato nella prima metà del IV sec. a. C.* Pisa.

————, 2005: *Iseo. La successione di Kiron.* Pisa.

See also the works by Kennedy, MacDowell, Todd, and Usher listed in the Series Introduction.

1. ON THE ESTATE OF CLEONYMUS

〰〰

Cleonymus,[1] son of Polyarchus, died childless, leaving his estate in a will to some relatives whose precise number and relationship to him cannot be determined.[2] The validity of the will was challenged in a rival inheritance claim (*diadikasia*) made by Cleonymus' nephews, one of whom delivered the present speech. It is a possible, but by no means necessary, inference from remarks made by the speaker that the opponents were twice as many in number, since he claims their friends and relatives thought the two parties deserved an equal share in the estate (1.2, 35; cf. 28) and that the nephews deserved a one-third share (1.16). One of the legatees was called Pherenicus (1.31, 45), another was probably Poseidippus (1.22–23; cf. 14–15), and a third was Diocles (1.14, 23). Poseidippus and Diocles may have been the brothers referred to in 1.45, but the Greek does not make it clear how many brothers there were or even if they were the brothers of Pherenicus, though this is perhaps the natural interpretation. What is clear is that the other names mentioned in the speech, Cephisander (1.16, 28) and Simon (1.31–32), were not among the heirs.

As for their relationship to Cleonymus, the heirs must have been further removed than the nephews, who challenge the validity of the will on the ground of closer affinity to Cleonymus (1.20; cf. 17, 36). Details of the nephews are equally obscure. The speaker is unnamed,

---

[1] In the stemmata, M denotes an unnamed male, F denotes an unnamed females, X denotes unnamed parents, and = denotes marriage.

[2] We might have expected him to adopt one of them, but there is no mention of this, and the will may not have been concerned with testamentary adoption. See Rubinstein 1993: 118.

Stemma

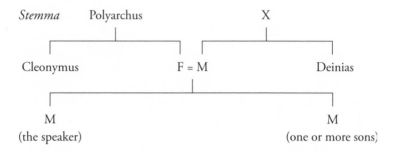

and the number of brothers he has is not stated. They were probably the sons of Cleonymus' sister, since it was their uncle Deinias rather than Cleonymus who became their guardian on the death of their father, and Deinias and Cleonymus clearly were not brothers (cf. 1.9, "their previous friendship"). It is likely, therefore, that Deinias was their paternal uncle, though it is possible that Deinias was nominated guardian of his sister's children in their father's will because the father, like Deinias, was at odds with his brother Cleonymus. This in turn would have been a reason for the speaker not to mention his father's circumstances, since it was a further motive for Cleonymus not to leave his estate to his nephews.

On the face of it, Isaeus' client does not have a strong case. In the absence of direct or adopted descendants of Cleonymus, his will should have been decisive: it had evidently been drawn up a number of years before Cleonymus' death and had been deposited with the City Magistrates (*astynomoi*), and so there was no question of arguing that Cleonymus was of unsound mind or under other duress when he wrote it or that the will was a forgery. Cleonymus' behavior on his death bed (1.14), however, opened up an avenue of attack. The heirs claimed that in sending for the magistrate, Cleonymus wished merely to make corrections to the will (1.18), and indeed there had been plenty of opportunity for him previously to change it in favor of his nephews. It may also be inferred that the heirs either were living with Cleonymus at the time of his death or were in close contact with him: otherwise, why did he not send one of his nephews to the magistrate if he intended to alter the will in their favor?

The speaker seizes the opportunity to put a different interpretation on this action, that Cleonymus wished to revoke the will, which therefore did not represent his last wishes. To support this he adduces two arguments. The first is that the nephews were the next of kin. The speaker's evasiveness on the exact relationship of the heirs to Cleonymus (cf. 1.36) serves to emphasize his claim to the succession through closer affinity, and there is no doubt that many of the jurors would have sympathized with him—the bias of Athenian juries in favor of kinship over wills was notorious (cf. Arist., *Problems* 29.3), and the speaker plays on this in particular at 1.41–43 (cf. 1.17).[3] His second argument is the subjective claim, reiterated throughout the speech, that Cleonymus was closer in affection to his nephews than the heirs: he brought the nephews up and looked after their affairs, and the quarrel that led to the will being made in the heirs' favor was not with them but with Deinias. Moreover, the speaker alleges that Cleonymus had fallen out with some of the heirs just before his death, though in fact he cleverly generalizes from a dispute between Cleonymus and Pherenicus (1.30–34). This pervasive theme of Cleonymus' greater affection for his nephews than his heirs, when added to the kinship argument, will doubtless have had a significant effect on the minds of the jurors.

Furthermore, Isaeus makes the most of the case rhetorically. In the proem (1.1–8) he sets out the main points of his clients' case and goes on the attack right from the start, assuming in the very first section of the speech what he is trying to prove,[4] that Cleonymus bequeathed his property to his nephews. He begins the characterization of the nephews as innocent victims and repeatedly emphasizes the shamelessness of their opponents in seeking to deprive them of their inheritance (1.2, 5, 8; cf. 26). The opposing attitudes of the parties are further highlighted by the commonplace argument (*topos*) that litigation between kin was undesirable (1.6).

In the narrative (1.9–16) the speaker carefully contrasts Cleonymus' enmity against Deinias with his kind treatment of his nephews, from which he argues Cleonymus' real intentions could be inferred. He immediately bolsters this with the story of Cleonymus' attempt at the last to change his will. In the proofs section, which forms the core of

---

[3]He also claims in passing, and with little conviction, that the wishes of his grandfather Polyarchus were that, if anything happened to Cleonymus, he was to leave the property to his nephews (1.4).

[4]The figure *petitio principii;* cf. 3.1, 8.1.

the speech (1.17–47), the speaker begins by summarizing the theme of his main refutatory argument: kinship is the most important factor in inheritance cases (1.17). Arguments from probability (*eikos*) demonstrate that a sane Cleonymus must have wanted to change the will in the nephews' favor (1.18–21); the opponents' behavior, if they really believed Cleonymus was going to alter it in their favor, was absurd (1.22–23); and his intended alteration of the will must mean that he was dissatisfied with it (1.24–26). An attack on the opponents' shamelessness follows (1.26–29), which lays the foundation for the charge that Cleonymus had quarreled with them (1.30–35).

On the assumption now that Cleonymus was on bad terms with the heirs and wanted to annul the will,[5] the speaker argues that the nephews' closer ties of kinship and friendship should be decisive (1.36–38); then it is argued that obligations to care for next of kin should in turn mean that the closest relatives are entitled to inherit (1.39–40). The speaker next returns to the argument that jurors should decide on the basis of kinship, not on the basis of a will (1.41–43). The proofs section culminates in an argument from reciprocity, that Cleonymus would, if still alive, have been entitled to inherit the nephews' estate because they were childless but not that of the other relatives, whose children would have inherited; hence in the reverse situation, the nephews, not the other relatives, should inherit Cleonymus' estate (1.44–47). In the brief epilogue (1.48–51) the speaker pleads once again that his opponents' arguments, if true, merely demonstrate that Cleonymus was insane, whereas his own contentions show that Cleonymus wanted to revoke the will. He thereby attempts to place the jurors in a dilemma that he first raised in 1.21,[6] and the speech comes to an end with a pathetic paradox.[7]

---

[5] I.e., that in effect Cleonymus died intestate.

[6] If Cleonymus did not wish to annul the will, he was insane, and it should therefore be declared void by the jurors; if he did, the speaker must win his case.

[7] The opponents had admitted the nephews were entitled to a share of the estate, but a verdict in their favor would entitle them to all of it, thus giving them more than they themselves felt was due to them and depriving the nephews even of what their opponents had conceded. For the term, see Usher 1999: 367.

We do not know if the jurors were persuaded by Isaeus' forceful rhetoric, and there are no indications in the speech of the date of the trial. Wevers orders Isaeus' speeches by statistical analysis of the rhythms at the end of sentences (*clausulae*) and suggests ca. 355 for this speech (Wevers 1969: 21).[8]

I

[1] The change in my circumstances occasioned by Cleonymus' death, gentlemen, has been great indeed. In life he left his property to us; in death he has caused us to risk losing it. In those days he brought us up with such modesty that we never even went into a lawcourt as listeners; today we have come to fight for everything we possess, since they are claiming not just Cleonymus' property but our patrimony as well and are alleging besides that we owe his estate money. [2] Their own friends and relatives think we should have an equal share with them even of the undisputed property Cleonymus left, but our opponents have become so shameless that they are seeking to deprive us of our patrimony as well, not through ignorance of what is just, gentlemen, but because they have observed our extreme destitution. [3] Consider the basis of the claims each side is making as we come before you. Our opponents are relying on a will he made in anger at one of our relatives, not because he had any complaint against us, and which he annulled before his death by sending Poseidippus to the magistrate. [4] But we were his next of kin and were closer to him than anybody, while the laws have granted us the right of succession on the ground of kinship and so did Cleonymus himself because of the friendship existing between us. Moreover, Polyarchus, Cleonymus' father and our grandfather, prescribed that if Cleonymus died childless, he was to leave his property to us. [5] Despite such strong claims on our side, our opponents, who are our relatives and have nothing just to say, are not ashamed to bring us to trial on matters it would be shameful even for nonrelatives to dispute. [6] But I don't believe, gentlemen, that we feel the same way towards one another. For I think that the greatest of my present

---

[8]For a generally positive review of Wever's method, see D. M. MacDowell, "Dating by Rhythms," *CR* 85 (1971), 24–26.

troubles is not that I am unjustly in danger but that I am fighting a case against relatives, against whom it is not good even to defend oneself. As they are relatives I would think it no less a misfortune to injure them in defending myself than to have been injured by them in the first place. [7] Our opponents do not share this opinion but have attacked us. They have called on their friends to help, procured orators,[9] and done everything in their power as if, gentlemen, they intended to punish enemies rather than harm kinsmen and relatives. [8] You'll understand their shamelessness and greed even better when you have heard everything. I'll begin my account at the point where I think you will most readily understand what our dispute is about.

[9] Deinias, our father's brother, became our guardian, as he was our uncle and we were orphans.[10] Now, he happened to have a dispute with Cleonymus, gentlemen. Which of the two was to blame for the quarrel it is perhaps not my business to decide, except that I might justly blame them both for turning their previous friendship so casually into mutual hostility for no real reason after an exchange of words. [10] Anyway, at that point because of this anger Cleonymus made this will, not because he had any complaint against us, as he later said, but because he saw we were the wards of Deinias and he was afraid in case he should die himself while we were still minors, and that Deinias would gain control of his property if it were ours— he thought it terrible to leave his bitterest enemy as guardian of his relatives and in charge of his property, and to have a man he was in dispute with while alive perform the customary rites over him until we grew up.[11] [11] It was with these thoughts in mind that, rightly or not, he made this will. Deinias then immediately asked him if he had some complaint against us or our father, and he replied in the

---

[9] I.e., politicians to speak on their behalf, probably as "co-pleaders" (*synēgoroi*). Further on supporting speakers, see Speech 2, n. 2.

[10] In Athens, an "orphan" had no father but might still have a mother; see the Introduction to this volume.

[11] Performance of rites by the guardian is not attested elsewhere. The guardian's primary role was to manage the property, and on reaching his majority, the ward might accuse him of mismanagement and corruption, as happened most famously in the case of Demosthenes' guardians.

presence of every citizen[12] that he had nothing bad to complain of, thereby giving evidence that he made this will out of anger against Deinias and not from good judgment. For if he had been of sound mind, gentlemen, how could he have wanted to harm us, when we had done no harm to him? [12] What he did afterwards furnishes the strongest proof of our contention that he had no wish to harm us even by this action. When Deinias died and we were having a bad time of things, he didn't allow us to want for anything but took us into his own house and brought us up, saved our property from creditors who were plotting to take it away, and took care of our affairs as if they were his own. [13] Now, we should judge his intentions from these actions rather than from the will, and use as evidence not what he did in anger, which naturally leads all of us astray, but what he did later, which made his intentions clear. For towards the end he showed still more how he felt about us. [14] When he was already weak from the illness that killed him, he wanted to revoke this will and instructed Poseidippus to fetch the magistrate, but he not only failed to do so but even dismissed one of the magistrates who came to the door. Cleonymus was angry at him and again gave instructions, to Diocles this time, to summon the magistrates for the next day, even though he was in no fit state due to his illness. But although there was still plenty of hope for his recovery, he died suddenly that night.

[15] I will now present witnesses, first, that he made the will not because he had a complaint against us but because of his fight with Deinias; then that after Deinias died he took care of all our affairs, received us into his own house, and brought us up; and furthermore that he sent Poseidippus for the City Magistrate (*astynomos*),[13]

---

[12]Implying that Cleonymus and Deinias quarreled in the Assembly or (allowing for rhetorical exaggeration) at some other public gathering. The speaker may be trying to gloss over the lack of witnesses to support this part of his story.

[13]The official in question is now specified; earlier references have been more vaguely to "magistrates" (1.3, 14; cf. 18, 21, 22, 25). There were ten *astynomoi*: five in the city and five in Piraeus, whose duties included the hire of entertainers and keeping the streets clean and safe (cf. [Arist.], *Ath. Pol.* 50.2). They had no specific connection with the administration of testamentary law.

but this man not only failed to summon him but even dismissed him when he came to the door. [16] To prove I'm telling the truth, please call the witnesses.

[WITNESSES]

Next, please also call witnesses that our opponents' friends, including Cephisander, thought we should share the property and have a third of all Cleonymus' possessions.

[WITNESSES]

[17] I think then, gentlemen, that when anyone laying claim to an estate can prove, as we can, that they are nearer the deceased both in kinship and in friendship, it is superfluous to advance other arguments. But since our opponents, with neither of these grounds, have the audacity to claim what doesn't belong to them and are fabricating false arguments, I would like to respond briefly to these points too. [18] They rely on the will and say that Cleonymus sent for the magistrate not because he wanted to revoke it but to revise it and confirm his bequest to them. But consider whether it is more likely that when he became friendly towards us Cleonymus wanted to revoke the will he had made in anger or that he was seeking even more firmly to deprive us of his property. [19] Other men repent afterwards of wrongs done to their relatives in anger; but our opponents argue instead that, when he was on most intimate terms with us, he wanted to confirm the will he made in anger. If we admitted this and you yourselves believed it, understand that our opponents are accusing him of sheer insanity. [20] For what could be greater madness than that during his dispute with Deinias he should harm us and make a will by which he didn't punish him but wronged his closest relatives, but now, when he was close to us and valued us above all, he wanted, as our opponents claim, to leave only his nephews without a share of his property? Who in his right mind, gentlemen, would manage his property in this way? [21] So by these arguments they have made a decision on their case easy for you. If he sent for the magistrate because he wanted to revoke the will, as we contend, they have no possible argument; but if he was so insane that he never had the least consideration for us, his closest kin and most intimate friends, you would surely be justified in declaring such a will invalid.

[22] Next, remember that they allege that Cleonymus called for the magistrate to confirm their bequest, yet when ordered they didn't dare to bring him in, but even sent away the magistrate who came to the door. Faced with a choice either to have their bequest confirmed or to offend Cleonymus by not doing as he asked, they chose his enmity in preference to this bequest. How could anything be less credible than this? [23] Those who stood to gain so much by doing this avoided rendering the service as if they were going to be penalized for it, while Cleonymus showed such zeal for their advantage that he was angry with Poseidippus for his negligence and the next day asked the same thing again of Diocles!

[24] Gentlemen, if as they say Cleonymus bequeathed the property to them in the will as presently written, I can't help wondering what revision he thought would make it more valid; for everybody else, gentlemen, this is the ultimate form of bequest. [25] Furthermore, if he wanted to add something to it, why didn't he leave this written down in another document when he couldn't get the original document from the magistrates? Gentlemen, he could not revoke any document other than the one deposited with the magistrate, but he could write anything he liked in another one and leave no chance of dispute between us. [26] So if we concede that Cleonymus wanted to revise the will, it is doubtless obvious to all of you that he didn't think it was right. Here again consider their shamelessness: they claim this will is valid, when they admit the testator himself did not think it was right, and then try to persuade you to reach a verdict contrary to the laws, justice, and the intentions of the deceased. [27] And the most shameless of all their statements is when they have the audacity to say that Cleonymus didn't want us to have any of his property. Who else could he have wanted to have it, gentlemen, if not those relatives to whom he gave the most help out of his property when alive? [28] The most amazing thing of all would be if even though Cephisander, their relative, thought it fair for each of us to have a share of the property, Cleonymus, our closest relative—the one who took us into his own house, brought us up, and took care of our affairs as if they were his own—was the only one who did not want us to share in his property. [29] Could any of you believe that our opponents are kinder and fairer towards us than our closest relatives? Or that he, who was obliged to treat us

well and would be shamed if he neglected us, should leave us none of his property, but these men, who have no obligation and for whom neglect brings no shame, should share what they say doesn't belong to us? All this, gentlemen, is utterly incredible.[14]

[30] Now, if Cleonymus still felt the same about both sides at his death as he felt when he made this will, some of you might reasonably believe my opponents' version; but as it is, you will find the exact opposite is true. At the time he made the will he was in dispute with our guardian Deinias, was not yet close to us, and was on friendly terms with all these people; but at the time of his death he was quarreling with some of these people and was closer to us than to anybody else. [31] There is no point in talking about the reasons for his dispute with my opponents, but I'll give you some strong proofs of it and shall also produce witnesses. First, when he was sacrificing to Dionysus he asked all his relatives and many other citizens to come, but he did not invite Pherenicus.[15] Then, shortly before his death, while traveling to Panormus[16] with Simon, he met Pherenicus and could not bring himself to speak to him. [32] Further, when Simon inquired about the dispute, he told him all about their mutual hostility and threatened that one day he'd show Pherenicus exactly how he felt about him. And to prove I'm telling the truth, call witnesses.

[WITNESSES]

---

[14]The speaker's argument here is based on the assumption that the changes Cleonymus wanted to make to his will must have been in favor of his nephews. Cephisander, a kinsman of the opponents, realized this and therefore proposed the compromise that the estate be shared, to prevent them losing all of it. This allows the speaker to argue that if, as the opponents claimed, Cleonymus was antipathetic towards his nephews, the compromise offer would indicate that their opponents were better disposed towards them than their uncle, which was patently absurd—so he cannot have been antipathetic. As Wyse observes (1904: 207–208), the opponents will have argued that the changes to the will did not involve the nephews; rather, their proposed compromise showed them as being conciliatory towards the nephews, who for their part were rapacious.

[15]For Pherenicus and Simon, see the Introduction.

[16]A harbor town between Sunion and Thoricus in southeast Attica.

[33] Do you think, gentlemen, that a man who was so disposed towards each side acted towards us, with whom he was on the closest terms, in a way that did not leave us so much as an argument but considered how to confirm that they would receive his whole property, even though he was quarreling with some of them? And that despite this hostility, he thought more of them and tried rather to harm us, despite the growth of such intimacy and friendship? [34] As I see it, if they wanted to attack the will or the deceased, I don't know what else they could have said to you. They represent the will as being neither right nor approved of by the testator and accuse him of sheer madness when they claim he thought more of those who were quarreling with him than those who were friends, left his property to those with whom he was not even on speaking terms when alive, and didn't think the ones he was closest to should have even the smallest share. [35] So could any of you vote for the validity of this will, which the testator rejected as being not right, which our opponents are in fact annulling in their willingness for us to have an equal share of the property, and which in addition we can prove to you is contrary to the law, to justice, and to the wishes of the deceased?

[36] But I think you can most clearly learn the justice of our case from our opponents. If they were asked on what grounds they think they should be Cleonymus' heirs, they might reply that they are in some way related to him and for some time he was friendly towards them. Wouldn't they thus be speaking in our favor rather than theirs? [37] For if the right of succession depends on the degree of kinship, we are more closely related; if on existing friendship, everyone knows that he was on closer terms with us. So you must learn the justice of the case not from us but from them. [38] It would be very strange indeed if you voted in other cases for those who prove themselves to be either nearer in kinship to the deceased or on friendlier terms with him but in our case should decide that we, who all admit are both of these, should alone have no share in his property.

[39] If Polyarchus, Cleonymus' father and our grandfather, were alive and lacked life's necessities, or Cleonymus had died leaving daughters in need, we would have been obliged by our kinship to look after our grandfather in his old age and either to marry Cleonymus' daughters ourselves or to provide dowries and marry them

to others.[17] Kinship, the laws, and the shame we would feel before you would have obliged us to do this or else encounter the severest penalties and extreme disgrace. [40] But since property has been left, will you think it just for others to inherit it rather than us? You will not vote justly, then, or in your own interests or in accordance with the laws if you force the next of kin to share in misfortunes but give everyone a greater right than them to the money that has been left.

[41] You should vote, gentlemen, as you do, on grounds of kinship and the true facts of the case in favor of those whose claims are based on kinship rather than a will. You all know the connection of kinship, and it's impossible to lie about this to you, but many before now have produced false wills, some of them complete forgeries, some made by people who were misguided. [42] In this case you all know the kinship and relationship on which we base our claim, but none of you knows that the will is valid on which our opponents rely in falsely accusing us.[18] Moreover, you will find that our kinship is admitted even by our opponents, yet the will is contested by us, since they prevented its annulment when he wanted this. [43] So, gentlemen, it's far more fitting for you to vote according to the kinship admitted by both sides than according to the will that was not drawn up rightly. Also remember that Cleonymus annulled it when of sound mind but made it when angry and misguided, and so it would be really extraordinary if you allowed his anger to prevail over his wishes.

[44] I think you consider it your right to inherit, and to feel aggrieved if you don't, from those who stand to inherit from you. Supposing, then, that Cleonymus were still alive, and our family or our opponents' family had been left without heirs, consider from which of us he would inherit. For it's only fair that those from whom he had the right to inherit should have his property. [45] Now if Pher-

---

[17]On the obligations of relatives towards unmarried girls, cf. And. 1.117–120; Dem. 43.54

[18]The Greek verb here is *sykophanteō,* "to act the sykophant" (see the Series Introduction, p. xxvii). Since this case was a *diadikasia,* the speaker's opponents were not his prosecutors, against whom the term was regularly used. See further Speech 3, n. 49.

enicus or one of the brothers[19] had died, their children and not Cleonymus were going to become entitled to the property left behind. If, however, we had met such a fate, Cleonymus was going to become heir to everything, because we had no children or other relatives, but he was our next of kin and the one with the closest personal ties to us. [46] For these reasons, the laws have granted him the right of succession, and we would not have thought anyone else should have this bequest. Surely, we would not have put our property in his hands during our lifetime,[20] thus making his wishes stronger than our own as regards our possessions, and then when we died have wanted there to be heirs other than our closest kin. [47] Therefore, gentlemen, you'll find us bound to him both in bequest and inheritance, but you'll find my opponents acting shamelessly and talking about intimacy and kinship, because they expect to gain something. But in making a bequest they would have put many relatives and friends before him as being closer.

[48] To sum up what I've said—and you should all pay close attention. As long as my opponents are using these arguments to show and try to persuade you that Cleonymus made this will and never afterwards regretted it, but still wanted us to receive none of his property and to confirm his bequest to them—[49] but while emphasizing all these points they are not showing either that they are closer kin of Cleonymus or that they were on closer terms with him than we were—understand that they are accusing him but are not showing you that their case is just. [50] So if you believe what they say, you should still not make them his heirs but pronounce Cleonymus insane; while if you believe us, you should consider that he was well advised in wanting to annul the will and that we are not behaving as sykophants[21] but are claiming this estate justly. [51] Finally, gentlemen, you should realize that it's impossible for you to decide

---

[19]See the Introduction.

[20]As Wyse notes (1904: 228), the nephews did not put their property in Cleonymus' hands, because when he took them on after Deinias' death, they were minors with no say in the matter.

[21]See 42n. The word is used more appropriately here, since the speaker is the one making the claim against the will and would therefore be more open to the charge of sykophancy than his opponents.

the case on the basis of their arguments. It would be really extraordinary if you vote that our opponents should have the whole estate when they recognize our right to receive a part of it, and think they should receive more than they considered themselves entitled to, but don't think that we deserve even what our opponents concede to us.

2. ON THE ESTATE OF MENECLES

In Athenian law, a direct male heir had the right of automatic succession to an estate without the verdict of a court.[1] If anybody made a rival claim (*diadikasia*) to the Archon, the direct heir could block it by the process of declaration (*diamartyria*), in which he presented a witness (*martys*) that the estate was not actionable because there were legitimate sons of the deceased. The rival claimant was then entitled to prosecute the *martys* for false witness by a *dikē pseudomartyriōn*. If he lost this case, the direct heir inherited; if he won, the heir was forced to abandon his claim to the estate, though the claimant still had to establish his right to it in court and might himself be challenged by other claimants.

The present speech was delivered in just such a trial for false witness. When Menecles' first wife died, he married the daughter of his friend Eponymus of Acharnae. The second marriage, like the first, was childless, and so after a time, Menecles divorced his wife, who was then given in marriage by her two brothers to Elius of Sphettus. Menecles in due course adopted one of Eponymus' sons to continue his line; but when he died twenty-three years after the adoption, Menecles' brother challenged the validity of the adoption and claimed the estate for himself as next of kin. The son entered a *diamartyria*, putting forward as a witness to the adoption his father-in-law Philonides. Menecles' brother then prosecuted Philonides for

---

[1]Direct heirs consisted of any male descendant in the male line, usually a son or a son's son, both by birth and by adoption, when the adoption was carried out during the lifetime of the adopter (*inter vivos*).

Stemma

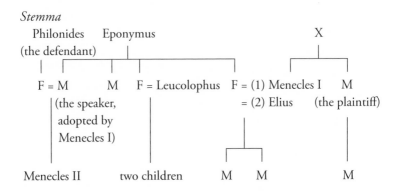

false witness, and the son delivered this speech on his behalf as an advocate (*synēgoros*).[2] The result of the trial is unknown.

As far as we can tell from the speech, the prosecution's case was based on the provision in a law of Solon that adoptions were invalid if the adopter was insane or senile or "under the influence of a woman."[3] It is the third of these that the speaker concentrates on, trying to prove that Menecles was not under the spell of his second wife, the speaker's younger sister, who had remarried before the adoption took place and given birth to two sons (2.19). It is probable, as the speaker claims, that the prosecutor devoted a large part of his speech to the woman's relationship with Menecles, both when she was married to him and subsequently, and he will have given a very different version of it from the idyllic one presented in 2.4–9. It seems from 2.5 that the prosecutor insisted she had no dowry and will possibly have argued from this and from the brevity of their time together (2.7) that the couple were never properly married; he will certainly have attacked the morals of the speaker and of his brother and sister.[4] It is also clear from 2.28 that he strongly objected to the

---

[2]The speech may be termed a *synēgoria;* other terms for supporting speeches (in Isaeus Speeches 2 and 4) are *epilogos* ("afterword") and *deuterologia* ("second speech"). Further on *synēgoroi,* see Todd 1993: 94–95 (who also classifies Speeches 5 and 6 under this heading); Rubinstein 2000: 28–29, 38–39 (who classifies Speeches 2, 4, 6, and 12 as *synēgoriai,* but not 5).

[3]Cf. 2.1, 4.14, 6.9; [Arist.], *Ath. Pol.* 35.2; Dem. 46.14.

[4]Harrison (1968: 49 n. 1) contends that the prosecution did not argue about the validity of the marriage but stressed the mercenary attitude of the brother.

adoption during Menecles' lifetime, though he will presumably have had to explain why he did not try to prevent the son's registration in Menecles' deme and phratry (2.14–15).

In reply, the speaker produces evidence that Menecles' wife brought a dowry with her (2.5) and stresses that she had remarried long before his adoption.[5] Since by that time she had two children, it would have been in her interest, if she was so minded, to persuade Menecles to adopt one of her sons rather than her brother. But the speaker's main contention, which is underscored by fine use of pathos, is that the ageing and lonely Menecles naturally wanted to adopt a son, and since his brother had only one son himself (2.10, 21),[6] he equally naturally turned to the family of his old friend Eponymus. He is then at pains to demonstrate that the adoption was both permitted by law in Menecles' circumstances and carried out in the proper manner (2.13–17) and that subsequently he enjoyed a normal relationship with his adoptive father, who arranged a marriage for him (2.18), while he acted as a son should (e.g., 2.43) and on his father's death performed the requisite funeral rites (2.36–37).

The speaker also explores an alleged motive for the prosecutor's behavior, that it stemmed from a quarrel between Menecles and his brother over their land (2.27–37). Menecles was a guardian of the orphaned children of a certain Nicias and used part of their inheritance to pay back his ex-wife's dowry, putting up the family property as security. When one of the orphans came of age, Menecles tried to sell the property to raise the money he owed him, but his brother objected and forced him to reserve a part of it for himself. After Menecles had sold his portion, he brought an action against his brother for restraint of sale, which was referred to arbitrators. These found in favor of the brother (the speaker unsurprisingly accuses the arbitrators of being friends of the brother), and oaths of reconciliation were sworn. The outcome of all this, according to the speaker, was that Menecles' brother now had possession of land worth ten minas, whereas Menecles and in turn his adopted son had

---

[5]He does not state precisely how long or that Menecles no longer saw his ex-wife, but his later adoption of her brother implies that he remained on good terms with Eponymus' family.

[6]The use of the plural "children" in 2.23 implies that the brother also had one or more daughters.

only a small house and what little remained from the proceeds of the sale after the orphan was recompensed (2.35).[7] This in turn leads to the emotive argument that the prosecution (the brother and his son) were breaking their oath, by which they had tacitly recognized the adopted son's position, whereas the speaker was undertaking the case not for money (since there was none) but as a matter of honor (2.38–43).

None of this proves that the speaker's sister did not have influence over Menecles after their separation, and it cannot indeed have been easy for either party to persuade the jurors to accept their version of events that took place such a long time before. But the notable characterization, especially at the end of the speech, of the dutiful son resisting a vindictive uncle gave the speaker every chance of doing so.

The speech begins with a brief proem (2.1–2), in which conventional material abounds.[8] A long narrative follows (2.3–12), detailing the family backgrounds of Menecles and the speaker and culminating in the latter's adoption. There is a good deal of characterization here, especially of Menecles as the old family friend who nobly ended his marriage because of his concern that his wife should have children and then became concerned about his own lack of children, which he determined to remedy through adoption. The wife was perfectly respectable, only reluctantly separating from her husband; so too her brothers, who agreed to help Menecles in his difficulty. Given, however, that the prosecution were claiming the undue influence of the wife in the adoption, there is also a businesslike and rational tone to the narrative: three marriages and an adoption are arranged with the minimum of fuss, and there is no mention of Menecles and his wife being in love.[9]

---

[7] If this was true, we might wonder why the brother took the risk of going to law over such a small estate—the speaker naturally accuses him of jealousy and shamelessness (2.27).

[8] Note the hypothetical inversion "I thought. . . . But since. . . ."; the *topos* of compulsion on the speaker; and a strong plea for the jurors' goodwill.

[9] Interestingly, the only time the word appears is at the start of 2.8, in what is manifestly a later gloss, or marginal explanation, that has found its way into the text.

In the first proofs section (2.13–27), the speaker starts by demonstrating that Menecles was legally entitled to adopt a son and that he adopted the speaker with all the necessary formalities (2.13–17); the brief description of the speaker's marriage to the daughter of Philonides (2.18) is a first indication of the normal relationship between the two men after the adoption and paves the way for arguments against the contention that Menecles had acted under his ex-wife's influence (2.19–20). The speaker next demands of his opponent by the use of *hypophora*[10] who else Menecles could have adopted (2.21–22) and accuses him of blaming Menecles for adopting anybody at all, though this is what he would have done himself in the same circumstances (2.23–26). Having thereby shown his opponent to be spiteful, the speaker ends this section of proofs with a transitional passage in which he indicates that he will now examine the reason for this attitude (2.27). This he does by narrating the quarrel between Menecles and his brother over the sale of their property, which ended in legal action, arbitration, and the swearing of oaths of reconciliation (2.28–34).

In the second section of proofs that follows (2.35–43), the speaker contrasts the vindictiveness of Menecles' brother with his own filial loyalty (2.35–37); he then returns to the question of his sister's influence on Menecles and his state of mind, and can now put forward the clever argument that his opponent was himself a witness in his favor, since the oaths they swore indicated that at the time Menecles' brother accepted the legitimacy of the adoption (2.38–40). He ends the proofs by emphasizing his obligation to his adoptive father in a pathetic paradox (2.41–43).[11] In the epilogue (2.44–47) the speaker recapitulates his arguments, again contrasting his own sense of duty with the opponent's vindictiveness and, in regular fashion, makes final appeals to the jurors for acquittal.

This speech, along with 7, *On the Estate of Apollodorus*, is one of the latest in the extant Isaean corpus and can be dated from the reference in 2.6 to the speaker's service in Thrace under Iphicrates. Iphicrates went there with a force of mercenaries in ca. 383 to support the

---

[10]A series of questions answered by the speaker himself.

[11]It was a disgrace if he acted as Menecles' son during his lifetime, when he had money, but abandoned him now that he was dead.

prince Cotys, whose sister he had married.[12] Allowing for this service and the birth of his elder sister's two children (2.6), for "some time" before the adoption took place (2.10), and then for a further twenty-three years before Menecles died, we come down to the mid 350s, perhaps ca. 354/3.

2

[1] I thought, gentlemen, that if anybody was ever adopted by someone according to the laws, then I was that man, and nobody could ever dare say that Menecles adopted me when out of his mind or under the influence of a woman.[13] But since my uncle, acting misguidedly as I contend, is trying in every way he can to establish that his brother died childless, showing no respect for his family gods or for any of you, I am compelled to help the father who adopted me, and myself. [2] I will therefore show you from the start that the adoption took place rightfully and according to the law and that the estate of Menecles is not adjudicable, since I am his son, but the witness made a true declaration.[14] I beg and entreat and supplicate you all to receive my speech with goodwill.

[3] Gentlemen, my father Eponymus of Acharnae was a friend and confidant of Menecles and was close to him. He had four children, two sons and two daughters. After our father died, we married our elder sister to Leucolophus when she was the right age, with a dowry of twenty minas.[15] [4] Four or five years after this, our younger sister was almost of marriageable age, and Menecles' first wife died. So when he had performed the customary funeral rites, he asked for the hand of our sister, reminding us of the friendship between him and our father and of his friendly feelings towards us. [5] Knowing

---

[12]See Davies 1971: 249–250. It is possible that the speaker is referring to Iphicrates' expedition to the Hellespont and local regions in ca. 389/8 (cf. Xen., *Hellenica* 4.8.34), but most commentators have rejected this.

[13]Two of the grounds for annulling an adoption; see the Introduction.

[14]By a *diamartyria*, on which see the Introduction. Philonides' testimony is referred to again at 2.17.

[15]A not inconsiderable sum (2,000 dr.). On the giving of a dowry, see 3.28 and n. 19.

that our father would not have given her to anybody else with greater pleasure, we gave her to him, not without a dowry as my opponent says at every opportunity but with a dowry of the same amount we gave our elder sister; and in this way, instead of being his friends, we became his relatives. And first I wish to produce the following deposition that Menecles received a dowry of twenty minas with my sister.

[DEPOSITION] [16]

[6] So we gave our sisters in marriage, gentlemen, and then ourselves joined the army, as we were of military age. We served abroad with Iphicrates in Thrace,[17] where we proved our worth and saved some money before sailing back to Athens. Here we found our elder sister with two children but the younger one, Menecles' wife, childless. [7] Two or three months later, while lavishing praise on our sister, he spoke to us and said that he was worried about his age and childlessness. He said she ought not to be rewarded for her virtue by growing old with him and remaining childless; it was enough, he said, that he was himself unfortunate.[18] [8] He therefore begged us to do him the favor of marrying her to someone else with his blessing. We told him to persuade her of this and said we would do whatever she agreed. [9] At first she would not even listen to his proposal, but after a while she reluctantly agreed. So we married her to Elius of Sphettus, and Menecles, who had obtained part of the estate of Nicias' children by lease,[19] handed over her dowry to him, and gave

---

[16]After ca. 380, witnesses no longer gave evidence orally in court; rather, their statements were read out by the clerk and they confirmed these as correct. Hence, a deposition (*martyria*) was in effect the same as a witness (*martys*).

[17]As mercenaries. For the date, see the Introduction.

[18]This sentence is followed in the manuscripts by a manifestly later addition (see above, n. 9): "And it's clear from these words that he loved her when he rejected her; for nobody makes supplications for one he hates."

[19]I.e., in acting as guardian of Nicias' children, Menecles had ready money from their inheritance with which to repay his wife's dowry. It was common practice for a guardian to invest the estate's cash in real estate. Accordingly, Menecles took some of the estate's cash, using part of his own land as security. If (as was often the case) the original dowry was in the form of real property, he probably would have used this property as the security.

her the clothes she'd brought with her to his house and the jewelry she had.[20] [10] Some time after this, Menecles began to consider how not to remain childless but instead to have someone to look after him in his old age, bury him when he died, and afterwards perform the customary rites for him. He saw that my opponent had only one son, so he thought it would be wrong to ask him to give him this son for adoption and deprive him of male children. [11] He could therefore find no other relative closer than us.[21] So he spoke to us and said he thought it a good thing, since fate had decreed he should have no children by our sister, that he should adopt a son from the family out of which he would have wanted to have children naturally. "So I wish," he said, "to adopt one of you, whichever one it suits." [12] When he heard this, my brother approved his proposal and said that because of his age and present state of loneliness he needed someone who would take care of him and be in Athens. "I," he said, "happen to be living abroad, as you know, but my brother here" (meaning me) "will take care of your affairs and mine, if you want to adopt him." Menecles said he liked his suggestion and in this way adopted me.

[13] I wish now to show you that the adoption was carried out legally. Please read for me the law that says that a man is entitled to dispose of his own property in whatever way he likes, as long as he has no legitimate male children. The lawgiver, gentlemen, enacted this law because he saw that for those without children, the only refuge in their loneliness and the only comfort in life lay in being able to adopt whomever they wished. [14] Since, then, the law allowed him to adopt because he was childless, he adopted me, not by writing it in a will, gentlemen, when he was about to die or was ill, as some other citizens do, but when he was well, of sound mind, and fully aware of what he was doing, he adopted me and introduced me in the presence of my opponents to the members of his phratry, and he registered me among his demesmen and the members of his reli-

---

[20]The bride's trousseau and jewelry might be part of the dowry (as in 8.8) but (as here) might be separate from it, in which case the husband was under no legal obligation to return them on divorce, though they were treated like the woman's own possessions and normally went with her. So this act demonstrated Menecles' love for his wife.

[21]I.e., the speaker and his brother.

gious association.[22] [15] At the time, my opponents did not object to his actions at all on the ground of his not being of sound mind, although it would have been much better if they had tried to persuade him to see their point of view when he was alive rather than to insult him when he is dead and leave his house without heirs. After the adoption he lived on not for one or two years but for twenty-three, and in all that long time he never regretted what he'd done because everybody agreed that he had been well advised in doing it. [16] And to prove I'm telling the truth, I'll produce for you as witnesses to the adoption the members of his phratry and of his religious association and his demesmen, and to prove that he was entitled to adopt, the clerk will read you the law itself, in accordance with which the adoption was made. Please read these depositions and the law.

[DEPOSITIONS. LAW]

[17] The law itself shows that Menecles was allowed to adopt any son he liked for himself, and his phratry members, his demesmen, and the members of his religious association have testified that he did adopt one. So we have manifestly proved, gentlemen, that the witness testified truthfully,[23] and my opponents cannot dispute the actual fact of the adoption.

[18] When he'd done this, Menecles began to look for a wife for me and said I ought to marry, so I married the daughter of Philonides. Menecles was concerned for me as is reasonable for a father to be for his son, and I and my wife together took care of him and respected

---

[22]The phratry ("brotherhood") was a type of kinship group, which had officials and meetings and passed phratry decrees but had very limited juristic significance (cf. 3.76). Most citizens belonged to a phratry, and while it appears that membership of a phratry was not compulsory, as was membership in a deme, it provided further evidence of a man's citizenship. Attica and Athens itself were divided into 139 demes (villages or town districts), and a man's citizenship depended on his registration in his father's deme at the age of eighteen (cf. [Arist.], *Ath. Pol.* 42.1). The religious associations referred to here (cf. Lost Speech XXXV) consisted of members (*orgeōnes*) who were devoted to the rites of a particular god or hero. Further on these, see Andrewes 1961, esp. 8–9; Parker 1996: 109–111.

[23]I.e., Philonides in the earlier *diamartyria;* see the Introduction.

him in the same way as if he were my natural father; and so he praised us to all his demesmen.

[19] That Menecles was not out of his mind or under the influence of a woman when he adopted me but was of sound mind you can easily conclude from this. First, there's my sister. My opponent has devoted most of his speech to arguing that it was under her influence that he adopted me. But she had remarried long before the adoption took place, so if he adopted his son under her influence, he would have adopted one of her children, since she has two. [20] But, gentlemen, he was not under her influence when he adopted me as his son. His main motivation was his loneliness, second were the causes I've mentioned and his fondness for my father, and third was because he had no other relative from whose family he could have adopted a son. These were the reasons why he adopted me at the time, and so he was clearly not insane or under the influence of a woman, unless of course my opponent wants to apply these names to his loneliness and childlessness.

[21] I would be pleased to hear from my opponent, who claims to be of sound mind, which of his relatives Menecles should have adopted? My opponent's son? But he wouldn't have given him to Menecles and left himself childless—he's not so greedy for money as that. The son of his sister or of his male or female cousin? But he did not have any of these relatives whatsoever. [22] He was forced, therefore, to adopt somebody else or grow old childless, as my opponent now thinks he should have done. And I think you would all agree that when he did adopt, he could not have adopted anybody closer to him than I. Let my opponent show you someone closer. But he couldn't possibly, because Menecles had no other relative but these.

[23] But it is clear that my opponent is not blaming Menecles for failing to adopt his own son but for adopting in the first place rather than dying childless. That's his criticism, and he's being invidious and unjust—he has his own children, yet he openly blames Menecles for the misfortune of being childless. [24] All other men, Greeks and barbarians, think this law about adoption is a good one, and because of this they all use it. But my uncle here isn't ashamed now to deprive his own brother of this right of adoption, which nobody has ever begrudged even those who are not relatives at all. [25] I

think if anybody asked my opponent what he would have done if he had found himself in the same situation as Menecles, even he would not say anything other than that he would have adopted somebody who would take care of him while he lived and bury him when he died; and clearly the adoption would have taken place under the very same law as mine. So he himself would have adopted if he had been childless; but he says Menecles, who did exactly the same thing, was insane and adopted me under the influence of a woman. [26] Isn't it clear that he's saying wicked things? I think it's much more my opponent who is insane in what he's now saying and doing. What he's arguing is clearly contrary to the laws and justice and what he himself would have done, and he is not ashamed of making the law on adoption valid for himself but seeking to make this same law invalid for his brother.

[27] Next, gentlemen, you deserve to hear the ground for the dispute that causes my opponent to seek to make his own brother childless. If he disagrees with me about my name and disdains the thought of my being Menecles' son, isn't he quite simply jealous? If it's a question of money, let him show you what land or apartment block or house Menecles left that I now have. If he left none of these, but my opponent took from him while he was still alive what he had left after he paid back the money to the orphan,[24] isn't that clear proof of his shamelessness? I'll show you how it is. [28] When Menecles had to pay back the money to the orphan but didn't have the resources to do so, and interest had been accumulating for a long time, he tried to sell the land. My opponent seized the opportunity and, wanting to take out his anger on him because he had adopted me, tried to prevent the land from being sold, so that it would continue to be held as a pledge and Menecles would be obliged to relinquish it to the orphan. He therefore claimed a part of the land from Menecles, although he'd never previously made any claim, and tried to prevent the buyers from buying it. [29] Menecles was upset, of course, and was forced to reserve the part that my opponent contested. The rest he sold to Philippus of Pithos for seventy minas, and with this he paid off the orphan, giving him one talent and seven minas from the

---

[24]For the orphan, cf. 2.9.

price of the land;[25] and he brought a suit for restraint of sale against my opponent. After much discussion and hostility, so that nobody could ever say I was money-loving and was making them enemies although they were brothers, we thought we should entrust the matter to my opponent's brother-in-law and our friends for arbitration. [30] They told us that if we were entrusting it to them to decide the justice of the case, they would refuse to arbitrate, for they had no desire to offend either side. But if we allowed them to decide what was in everyone's best interest, they said they would arbitrate. And so we entrusted the dispute to them on these terms, in order to resolve it, as we thought. [31] They swore an oath at the altar of Aphrodite at Cephale[26] that they would decide in the interests of all, and then they decided that we should relinquish what my opponent claimed and make him a gift of it. They said there was no other solution to the matter unless these men got a share of his property. [32] For the future they decided we should treat each other well in our words and deeds, and they obliged both sides to swear at the altar that we would indeed do this. So we swore that we would treat each other well in the future, as far as we could in our words and deeds. [33] And that the oath was sworn and these men have what was awarded to them by my opponent's friends, and this is how they are now treating us well, by wanting to make the deceased childless and insolently throw me out of his family, I'll produce as witnesses the very men who made the decision, if they are willing to mount the stand (for they are my opponent's friends),[27] and if not, those who were present. [34] Please read these depositions; and you, stop the water.[28]

[DEPOSITIONS]

Please take those depositions that the land was sold for seventy minas and the orphan received sixty-seven minas from the proceeds.

[DEPOSITIONS]

---

[25]I.e., 67 minae.

[26]A deme about 12 miles north of Sunion in southern Attica.

[27]A person who was summoned to be a witness could swear an oath of denial (exōmosia) that he had any knowledge of the facts.

[28]The speeches of each side were timed by a waterclock (klepsydra), which was turned off during the giving of evidence.

[35] So then, gentlemen, it's my uncle here who has inherited Menecles' property in fact and not nominally, as I have, and he has a far larger share than I. I received the three hundred drachmas that were left over from the price of the land, plus a small house that is not worth three minas. But my opponent has land worth more than ten minas and now besides has come to court with the purpose of leaving Menecles' house without heirs. [36] Yet I, Menecles' adopted son, took care of him while he was alive, I and my wife, the daughter of Philonides here, and named my little boy after him, so that his house would not lose the name; and I buried him when he died in a manner befitting both of us, and I set up a fine grave monument for him and performed the ninth-day offerings and all the other rites at the tomb in the finest way possible, so that all my demesmen praised me. [37] But my opponent, his relative who criticizes him for adopting a son, deprived him of his remaining land when he was alive and, now that he is dead, wants to leave him without children and without a name. That's the kind of man he is. And to prove that I buried him and performed the ceremonies on the third and ninth days and all the other rites at the tomb, the clerk will read you the depositions of those who know the facts.

[DEPOSITIONS]

[38] Next, gentlemen, to prove that Menecles was neither out of his mind nor under the influence of a woman when he adopted me, I want to produce as witnesses my opponents themselves, who testify that I am telling the truth not in word but in deed, by their own conduct.[29] For both of them[30] clearly carried out the reconciliation with me, not with Menecles, and swore oaths to me as I did to them. [39] Yet if the adoption had not been carried out legally and I had not been recognized as the heir to Menecles' property by my opponents themselves, why did they need to swear to me or receive oaths from me? Surely they didn't. Therefore since they did this, it is clear that they themselves testify that I was legally adopted and am the rightful heir to Menecles' property. [40] I think it's clear to you all

---

[29]Note the commonplace argument that the opponents or those connected with them by their conduct were in effect testifying on the speaker's behalf (cf. 3.55, 6.12, 7.18, 8.14; Dem. 41.19).

[30]I.e., Menecles' brother and nephew.

that even my opponents agree that it's not Menecles who was insane but rather my opponent who is now, since despite settling the hostility between us and swearing oaths, he has now come forward again in violation of his agreements and oaths and thinks I should be deprived of these remnants of the estate, small though they are. [41] If I didn't think it was utterly disgraceful and shameful to betray the man whose son I was called and who adopted me, I would quickly have relinquished my right to his property to my opponent—after all, there's nothing left of it, as I think you realize. [42] But as it is, I think it's a terrible disgrace in the sense that if, when Menecles had some property, I allowed myself to be adopted as his son, and from his property, before the land was sold, acted as gymnasiarch[31] for the deme and gained honor as his son, and served with his tribe and deme on all the campaigns that took place at that time; [43] but now that he is dead, if I betray him and go away leaving his family without heirs, wouldn't this be a disgrace and wouldn't I be laughed at and provide those who want to slander me plenty of opportunity to do so? And these are not the only things that are making me contest this case, but what grieves me is if I am thought to be so mean and worthless that I could not be adopted by someone of sound mind, nor even by one of my friends but only by a man who was insane.

[44] I therefore beg and entreat and supplicate you all, gentlemen, to pity me and acquit the witness here. I have shown you first that I was adopted by Menecles as legally as anybody could be and that the adoption was not made verbally or by a will but by action; and I produced as witnesses of this his phratry members, his demesmen, and the members of his religious association. [45] I also showed that he lived on for twenty-three years. Then I further showed you the laws that allow those who are childless to adopt sons. And besides this, I clearly took care of him during his lifetime and buried him when he died. [46] My opponent now wants to deprive me of my father's

---

[31]A liturgy (compulsory public service performed by the wealthy) in which the gymnasiarch organized and paid the costs of festival torch races. The state liturgy was very expensive; service for the deme would have cost much less. The point is that Menecles' property provided the speaker with the means for carrying out this liturgy, from which he gained honor and status. Further on liturgies, see the Series Introduction, p. xxiii.

estate, whether it's large or small, and make the deceased childless and without a name, so that there will be nobody to honor the family cults on his behalf or to make the annual offerings for him, and he will be deprived of the honors due to him. Menecles foresaw this, and being in control of his own property, he adopted a son, to secure all these things. [47] Therefore, gentlemen, don't be persuaded by my opponents and deprive me of my name, the only part of my inheritance that still remains, or make his adoption invalid. Since the matter has come to you and you have the authority to judge it, help us and also him who is in Hades, and by the gods and spirits I beg you, don't allow Menecles to be insulted by my opponents but remember the law and the oath you have sworn[32] and the arguments I have used to support my case, and vote in accordance with the laws for what's just and in accordance with your oath.

---

[32]The dicastic oath sworn by jurors at the start of every year that they would judge according to the law. See further Todd 1993: 54–55.

3. ON THE ESTATE OF PYRRHUS

~~~~~~

This speech was delivered at another trial for false witness.[1] Pyrrhus adopted by will his nephew Endius, a son of his sister (3.1, 56). After Pyrrhus' death, Endius inherited without opposition and held the estate for over twenty years. Since he had no children, however, within two days of his death, rival claimants to Pyrrhus' estate came forward. Xenocles claimed the estate on behalf of his wife, Phile, saying that she was the legitimate daughter of Pyrrhus, and he tried to seize some of the property (3.22); but he was opposed by Endius' younger brother (the unnamed speaker) on behalf of his mother, who denied Phile's legitimacy and entered a counter-claim as Pyrrhus' sister and next of kin. Xenocles therefore entered a declaration (*diamartyria*), with evidence that his wife's mother had been legally married to Pyrrhus, but he was successfully prosecuted by Endius' brother for false witness. Xenocles, however, announced his intention to prosecute the witnesses to Pyrrhus' will (3.56), and the present suit may have been designed to forestall this by prosecuting Xenocles' main witness at the first trial, Nicodemus, who was the brother of Phile's mother. We do not know the outcome of the trial or whether the saga continued in subsequent litigation.

A remarkable feature of the speech is its heavy dependence on arguments from probability (*eikos*). The speaker naturally begins his prosecution by recalling his earlier victory against Xenocles, which indicated that Nicodemus' testimony was also false (3.1–7). He cannot rely on this, however, since Athenian juries were not bound by

---

[1] A more accurate title would in fact be *Against Nicodemus for False Witness*.

Stemma

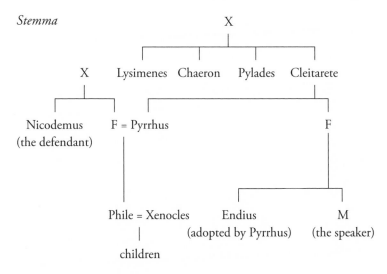

decisions in previous trials, and many of the arguments he adduces in the speech are doubtless repeated from before, as are a number of depositions. After posing a series of indignant questions that are picked up later in the speech (3.8–10; cf. 78–79), he examines the likelihood that Pyrrhus married a woman of the character of Nicodemus' sister (3.11–16). She behaved before, during, and after the supposed marriage like a prostitute, and the speaker reproduces the depositions confirming this from the previous trial. Such behavior in itself does not, of course, preclude the marriage, as the speaker admits (3.17),[2] and so he goes on to examine Nicodemus' version of the betrothal (3.16–27). Nicodemus summoned only one witness, Pyretides, when many would be expected, and Pyretides subsequently denied that the absentee deposition (*ekmartyria*) produced in his name by Xenocles was genuine. Further, the speaker claims that two witnesses to the deposition were completely unreliable. Pyrrhus' three maternal uncles also witnessed the betrothal on his invitation, and the speaker asks whether it was likely that Pyrrhus invited relations to his betrothal to a woman of this kind.

---

[2]Nor was Pyrrhus perfect (3.13).

Another probability argument follows, that it was unlikely that Nicodemus married his sister to Pyrrhus without a dowry, as he stated: since Pyrrhus was wealthy, Nicodemus would have secured from him the settlement on her of a fictitious dowry, which would have prevented Pyrrhus from easily divorcing her (3.28–29). The three uncles again had testified to the betrothal without a dowry, and their credibility is now assailed—they even got Phile's name wrong (3.30–34). Returning to the matter of the dowry, the speaker concludes the first half of the speech by attacking Nicodemus: what would he gain from a marriage that might end at any moment if no dowry had been agreed? He surely would have secured an agreement about a dowry, because if his sister died without children, he could claim the money for himself (3.35–39).

Whatever the strength of these individual arguments, clearly none is conclusive. For instance, the alleged betrothal, which was a private affair, had taken place over twenty years previously, and it is odd that the speaker does not call Pyretides himself as a witness that he disavowed his absentee deposition[3] or present some evidence of the bad character of Dionysius and Aristolochus, the witnesses to it (3.23). Further, a dowry was not a legal requirement for a valid marriage, and if Phile's mother really was the sort of woman she is portrayed as here, Nicodemus might well have been delighted to give her away without one, while the argument concerning the extortion of a fictitious dowry is pure hypothesis.[4] Nor is it a secure argument that the uncles who could not remember the real name of their nephew's daughter had therefore lied, because the change of name may not have been unusual.[5]

In the second half of the speech the speaker reverts to the law and poses a string of hard-hitting questions. In particular he asks why, if Phile really was Pyrrhus' legitimate daughter and heiress, Nicodemus did not oppose the succession of Endius (3.40–44) or prosecute him for giving her in marriage as an illegitimate daughter to Xenocles: Endius, as an adopted son, would normally have married the heiress himself (3.45–54). An answer to the first question may lie in Phile's

---

[3]Or at least explain his current absence.

[4]We have no other evidence for an arrangement of this kind.

[5]See below, 30n.

age at the time of her father's death.[6] Since she was only a child, Pyrrhus may have made provision in his will for the adoption of Endius and his marriage to Phile when she came of age, and so there will have been no reason for Nicodemus to challenge Endius' succession at that point.[7]

The second question is perhaps the speaker's strongest argument, if indeed it was the case that a son adopted by will was required in law to marry the legitimate daughter of his adoptive father or the will became invalid (cf. 3.42, 68–69); this, however, is doubtful.[8] But the speaker does assume rather than prove that Endius thought Phile was illegitimate.[9] The size of the dowry is no firm indication,[10] and it has been suggested that Endius (who was far older than Phile and was to remain unmarried) and Nicodemus came to an arrangement whereby Endius did not fulfill his legal obligation to marry Pyrrhus' daughter but married her to Xenocles while retaining possession of the estate.[11] This would not have affected Phile's position, since Endius was childless and had himself been adopted: he therefore could not dispose of the property, but it would have reverted on his death to the daughter and her children. We should note, however, that such an agreement might well have been represented by the speaker as demonstrating Endius' fine character, in that he did not force himself on the young girl but was looking out for her interests.[12]

Finally, the speaker examines the conduct of Xenocles (3.54–62), Pyrrhus' uncles (3.63–71), and Pyrrhus himself (3.72–76), which

---

[6]Pyrrhus had been dead for over twenty years (3.1, 57), while Phile had been married to Xenocles for over eight years (3.31) and will probably have been fourteen or fifteen at the time of the marriage.

[7]See Wyse 1904: 321. We might have expected the speaker to produce the will, especially if it did not include Phile in its provisions, but it may no longer have existed and Xenocles had denounced the witnesses to it (3.56).

[8]See below, 42n.

[9]He does not, for example, produce any witnesses to her betrothal to Xenocles.

[10]See below, 49n.

[11]See Wyse 1904: 328.

[12]Contrast the behavior of Smicrines in Menander's *Aspis;* see MacDowell 1982.

in his opinion showed that they all thought Phile was illegitimate. For example, he asks why Xenocles too had not previously disputed Endius' claim to the estate, since he denied Endius' adoption and is not claiming for Phile in the name of Endius' sister; and why, instead of going to the Archon for a judgment, he did not simply take possession of the estate with Phile and prosecute anybody who tried to stop them. Again, the possibility of a deal between Endius and Nicodemus might explain Xenocles' earlier inactivity, as due to fear that Endius might exercise his right to claim Phile as his next of kin, even if his adoption was shown to be invalid.

The point that Xenocles was not claiming for Phile as Endius' sister carries no legal weight, since the estate reverted to Pyrrhus' family on Endius' death without issue, hence the claim by Pyrrhus' sister (Endius' mother). The second argument is apparently undermined by the speaker's own statement in 3.22 that Xenocles did try to seize part of the estate, and his failure may have prompted the legal action. The main argument concerning Pyrrhus' uncles, that they would have claimed Phile if she was legitimate, might also be countered by the supposed deal. Finally, Pyrrhus' adoption of Endius is perfectly reasonable if Phile was legitimate, since she was a child and therefore needed to be protected; her age might have precluded her from being introduced to her father's phratry; and the nonperformance of a wedding feast is no proof that Pyrrhus' marriage was invalid.[13] After recapitulating his arguments, the speaker ends with a deposition proving that Pyrrhus never performed the regular celebrations of the marriage in his phratry and deme, which does not, however, prove that the marriage never took place.

The defense will presumably have based their case on the testimony of witnesses (cf. 3.26–27, 30) and an explanation of why Endius was allowed to betroth Phile to Xenocles instead of marrying her himself. Yet there is no reason to suppose that their proofs were any more cogent than the prosecution's, and, in the wake of Xenocles' defeat, Nicodemus will have faced an uphill task to convince the jurors

---

[13]For these and further arguments, see Wyse 1904: 336–338, 347–349, 354–355.

that the marriage was legal, for the cumulative effect of the prosecutor's arguments is enhanced by the effectiveness of Isaeus' rhetoric. The speaker dispenses with a formal proem and opens with a narrative (3.1–7), immediately impressing on the jurors that their colleagues had already decided in his favor once. The questions that follow (3.8–10) culminate in the remark that Phile's mother was available to anybody, and her low character is a key theme of the speech, which is immediately taken up in 3.11–16.[14] This neatly prepares the jurors for the section on the betrothal (3.16–27),[15] where the speaker has to overcome the obstacle that his opponents have witnesses. One of these, Pyretides, is comfortably dealt with, since (it is claimed) he retracted his absentee deposition (3.18). It was a harder task to dispose of the evidence of Pyrrhus' three uncles, and the speaker begins by generalizing about the appropriate choice of witnesses (which enables him to attack the two who allegedly witnessed Pyretides' deposition, damning their characters without adducing any proof; 3.23); then he relies again on the theme of the mother's bad character in the *eikos*-argument that Pyrrhus would not have selected three relatives to witness a shameful marriage of this kind (3.27), and an attack on their credibility is sandwiched between further *eikos*-arguments concerning the dowry (3.28–29, 35–39; see above).

The speaker next turns to the question of Phile's legitimacy, considering in turn the actions of all the men connected with the case and ending with Pyrrhus himself (3.40–76). Some flaws in his arguments have already been discussed, but rhetorically it is to be noted how apparently he conducts an extensive examination of all possible angles if Phile was legitimate, leading to the inevitable conclusion that she was not.[16] The speech concludes with a recapitulation of the arguments and repetition of the questions asked at the start, but there is none of the emotional appeal to the jurors that is common in epilogues. Rather, the speaker continues his arguments to the end and directs them on the questions they should be asking Nicodemus. Use of questions, indeed, is one of the most notable fea-

---

[14]With probability argument (3.14) and depositions.

[15]It is introduced by a form of concession (*synchōrēsis*). See Usher 1999: 164.

[16]See Usher 1999: 166. Note the extended *hypophora* in 3.72–73.

tures of the speech, as are the frequent (almost tedious) repetitions[17] that help make this the longest speech in the Isaean corpus.

The date of the speech is entirely uncertain. Two of the witnesses mentioned in 3.22 are known from events in the late 340s,[18] but these are not relevant to the dating of the trial. Using statistical analysis, Wevers (1969: 21) suggests ca. 389.

3

[1] Gentlemen of the jury, my mother's brother Pyrrhus, having no legitimate children,[19] adopted my brother Endius as his son. Endius inherited his estate and lived on for over twenty years, and in all this time that he held the estate nobody ever claimed it or disputed his inheritance. [2] But since my brother died last year, Phile has come forward, ignoring the last heir and claiming to be our uncle's legitimate daughter, and her legal representative[20] Xenocles of Coprus made a claim to the estate of Pyrrhus, who had been dead for over twenty years, entering its value at three talents. [3] When our mother, Pyrrhus' sister, disputed this claim,[21] the representative (*kyrios*) of the woman claiming the estate had the audacity to make a declaration[22] that her brother's estate could not be claimed by our mother because Pyrrhus, its original owner, had a legitimate daughter. We formally contested[23] this declaration and brought before

---

[17]Note, for example, the repeated assertion that Phile's mother was a prostitute available to anybody (3.13, 15) and she herself was the child of a prostitute (3.6, 24, 45, 48, 52, 52bis, 55, 55bis, 70, 71).

[18]See below, 22n.

[19]Apparently another *petitio principii* (on which see above, Speech 1, n. 4), since the speaker's opponents claimed that Phile was Pyrrhus' legitimate daughter. But the Greek (*apais*) may be taken to mean without *male* children.

[20]A woman had to be represented at law by her *kyrios* ("legal representative"), a male relative who was normally her husband (as here), father, brother, or paternal uncle.

[21]As the sister of Pyrrhus, not as the mother of Endius.

[22]By a *diamartyria,* which asserted a preemptory claim to the estate; see the Introduction to Speech 2.

[23]By *episkēpsis,* a formal undertaking to prosecute a witness.

you²⁴ the man who had dared make it, [4] and by proving mani-festly that he had given false testimony, won from you a verdict of false witness. At the same time, we proved before the same jurors that Nicodemus here was completely shameless in the testimony he gave, since he had the audacity to testify that he had given his sister in marriage to our uncle as his wife in accordance with the laws.²⁵ [5] But the condemnation of the witness²⁶ on that occasion very clearly proves that Nicodemus' testimony in the previous trial was thought to be false. For if it had not been thought that Nicodemus gave false testimony on that occasion, clearly Xenocles would have left court acquitted in the suit concerning the declaration, and the woman who was declared to be a legitimate daughter would have become the heiress to our uncle's property instead of our mother. [6] But since the witness was condemned and the woman who claimed to be Pyr-rhus' legitimate daughter relinquished the estate, it's an absolutely unavoidable conclusion that the testimony of Nicodemus also has been condemned: he made a declaration and was tried for false wit-ness about this same matter, whether the woman who claimed our uncle's estate was the child of a lawfully wedded wife or a *hetaira*.²⁷ And you too will see this when you've heard our sworn affidavit,²⁸ Nicodemus' deposition, and the declaration that was rejected by the court. [7] Take these and read them to the jurors.

[AFFIDAVIT. DEPOSITION. DECLARATION]

---

²⁴Since the speaker had won the previous case, it is in his interest to employ a common tactic in Athenian litigation and associate the present jurors with the earlier ones (and some may have sat in both trials), but he could not rely on the first verdict being repeated here.

²⁵Except in the case of heiresses (in which marriage had to be ratified by a court hearing, *epidikasia*), marriage consisted of a betrothal (*engyē*), followed by the handing over (*ekdosis*) of the bride by her *kyrios* to the bridegroom, with or without a dowry (see below, 28n). The wedding itself (*gamos*) seems to have had no legal significance, despite the speaker's arguments about the wedding feast (*gamēlia*) at 3.79. Further on marriage, see the Introduction to this volume.

²⁶I.e., Xenocles.

²⁷A *hetaira* was a high-class courtesan, such as Neaera in Dem. 59.

²⁸The *antōmosia* ("counter-oath") sworn by the opposing parties at the pre-liminary hearing (*anakrisis*) to the truth of their pleas.

It has been shown that everyone on that occasion immediately decided, without hesitation, that Nicodemus had given false testimony; but, as is proper, his testimony must also be proved false before you, who are about to give your verdict on this same matter. [8] First, I want to learn what dowry he claims he provided,[29] when (as he testified) he gave his sister in marriage to the owner of an estate worth three talents; next, whether this lawfully wedded wife left her husband while he was alive or left his house when he died;[30] and from whom the defendant recovered his sister's dowry when the man he has testified he betrothed her to had died, [9] or if he didn't recover it, what action he saw fit to bring for maintenance[31] or for the actual dowry in twenty years against the man in possession of Pyrrhus' estate; or whether in all this time he proceeded to make a claim against the heir for his sister's dowry in the presence of any witness. I would be pleased to learn the reason why none of these things has happened when the woman was (so the defendant has testified) a lawfully wedded wife, [10] and in addition whether anybody else has taken the defendant's sister as his lawfully wedded wife, either any of those who were involved with her before our uncle knew her, or those who had relations with her when he did know her, or those who did so later after his death. After all, her brother has clearly married her in the same way to everybody who has had relations with her. [11] If we had to list these people one by one, it would certainly be no small task. So if you command it, I'll mention some of them; but if it's as distasteful to some of you to hear about this as it is for me to say anything about it, I'll produce for you the depositions from the previous trial, none of which my opponents saw fit to contest. Yet when they themselves have admitted that the woman was available to anybody who wanted her, how could one reasonably believe that this same woman was a lawfully wedded wife? [12] Indeed, since they've never contested the

---

[29]See below, 28n.

[30]On her husband's death, a widow might remain in his house (if she had children or was pregnant) or return to the house of her guardian, who would also recover her dowry, if necessary by legal action (cf. 3.9).

[31]The *dikē sitou*, a private suit to recover maintenance from a dowry. For this and the *dikē proikos*, an action to recover the dowry itself, cf. [Arist.], *Ath. Pol.* 52.2.

depositions on this very point, they have admitted it. And when you too have heard the actual depositions, you will know that the defendant has clearly given false testimony, and the men who judged the case decided correctly and in accordance with the laws that the woman who was not born legitimately was not entitled to the estate. Read, and you, stop the water.[32]

[DEPOSITIONS]

[13] You've heard the testimony of Pyrrhus' other friends and neighbors that the woman whom the defendant has testified he betrothed to our uncle was a *hetaira* available to anybody who wanted her and was not his wife. They have testified that the defendant's sister was the subject of fights, revelry, and frequent disorder whenever she was at Pyrrhus' house. [14] But I don't suppose that anybody would dare to sing songs about a married woman, and married women do not go with their husbands to dinner parties or see fit to dine with strangers, especially chance visitors. But our opponents did not see fit to challenge any of those who have testified. And to prove I'm telling the truth, read the deposition to the jurors again.

[DEPOSITION]

[15] Read as well the depositions about the men who had relations with her, so they may know that she was both a *hetaira* available to anybody who wanted her and clearly never bore the child of any other man.[33] Read to the jurors.

[DEPOSITIONS]

[16] You should remember how many people have testified to you that the woman whom the defendant has testified he betrothed to our uncle was available to anybody who wanted her, and that clearly she was never betrothed to or lived with anybody else. But let us also consider under what circumstances a proper marriage might conceivably have taken place with such a woman, to see if anything like this happened to our uncle. [17] After all, some young men have

---

[32]See 2.34 and n.

[33]The innuendo is that Phile was not even the daughter of Pyrrhus' mistress.

before now fallen in love with women like her and, unable to control themselves, have been led in their folly to ruin themselves like this. So how could we get a clearer picture about this matter than from considering the depositions made on our opponents' behalf in the previous trial and from the probabilities of the case itself? [**18**] Consider the impudence of what they are saying. The man who was about to give his sister in marriage to a man with an estate worth three talents, as he says, when arranging such an important matter claimed that a single witness was present on his behalf, Pyretides, and our opponents produced his absentee deposition (*ekmartyria*)[34] at that trial, a deposition Pyretides has disavowed, and he refuses even to admit that he gave any deposition or knows whether any of it is true. [**19**] And here is a strong proof that the deposition our opponents produced was a manifest forgery. You all know that whenever we are embarking on a matter that we are aware must take place in front of witnesses, we usually take our closest friends and most intimate acquaintances with us to business of this kind, whereas with unforeseen matters that occur on the spur of the moment, we all procure as witnesses anybody we chance to meet. [**20**] For actual depositions we are obliged to use as witnesses the people who were actually present, whoever they are. But when procuring an absentee deposition from people who are ill or about to go abroad, each of us summons above all the most reputable citizens and the ones best known to us, [**21**] and we all obtain absentee depositions in the presence not of one or two people but of as many as possible, to prevent the person who testified *in absentia* from denying the deposition afterwards and to make you all the more confident in the unanimous testimony of a large number of gentlemen (*kaloi kagathoi*). [**22**] So, when Xenocles went to Besa[35] to our factory at the mine works, he didn't think he should rely on the people who just happened to be there as witnesses to the eviction, but took with him from Athens Diophantus of Sphettus, who

---

[34]The deposition of a witness who was ill or abroad at the time of the trial, confirmed by witnesses (cf. 3.20–21).

[35]A deme near Laurion in southern Attica, the main silver mining area for Athens. Xenocles presumably went to Besa to take possession of the factory there and, anticipating that he would need to evict some people, took witnesses with him.

presented his case at his previous trial, Dorotheus of Eleusis and his brother Philochares,[36] and numerous other witnesses, summoning them to that place nearly three hundred stades[37] away. [23] But in the matter of the marriage of his own children's grandmother, when he was obtaining an absentee deposition in the city (as he claims), he evidently summoned none of his own friends but instead Dionysius of Erchia and Aristolochus of Aethalidae.[38] Our opponents say they obtained the absentee deposition there in the city in the presence of these two men—such an important deposition in the presence of these individuals whom nobody else would trust in any matter whatsoever! [24] Perhaps it was a trivial, unimportant matter on which they say they obtained the absentee deposition from Pyretides, and so it's not surprising that they took the matter lightly. But how can that be, when the trial in which Xenocles was prosecuted for false witness turned on this very issue, whether his own wife was the child of a *hetaira* or a lawfully wedded wife? And if this deposition were true, wouldn't he have seen fit to summon all his own friends? [25] Yes, he would, by Zeus, or so I would have thought, if the claim were true. He clearly did not, but Xenocles gave this absentee deposition before two passersby, while Nicodemus here says he summoned only one witness to go with him when he betrothed his sister to the owner of an estate worth three talents! [26] The defendant pretended the only one there with him was Pyretides, though he denies it, whereas Lysimenes and his brothers, Chaeron and Pylades, say they were summoned by Pyrrhus when he was about to marry a woman of this kind and were present at the betrothal, even though they were the bridegroom's uncles.[39] [27] So it's a matter for you now to con-

---

[36]Diophantus, a well-known political figure, is connected with the Embassy trial of 343 (cf. Dem. 19.198). Dorotheus was a trierarch in 366/5 and 357 and owned property in Athens ca. 343 (Dem. 59.39); see further Davies 1971: 174. His brother is otherwise unknown.

[37]One stade was approximately 202 yards (185 meters); hence the journey was about 34 miles (55.5 kilometers).

[38]Dionysius is otherwise unknown; Aristolochus, also unknown, is not the Aristolochus of 6.33.

[39]The speaker implies that close relatives would never be called to witness a marriage to a *hetaira*. For the uncles, see the stemma.

sider whether the affair seems credible. To judge from the probabilities, I think it's far more likely that Pyrrhus would have preferred to keep all his friends in the dark if he was preparing to make some agreement or do something unworthy of his family than to summon his own uncles as witnesses to such an enormous mistake.

[28] Furthermore, I'm amazed that neither the giver nor the receiver made any agreement about having a dowry for the woman.[40] If he did give one, the people who claim they were present would probably have testified also to the gift, whereas if our uncle had contracted a marriage with a woman of this kind out of desire, clearly the man who gave her away was far more likely to make the groom agree that he had taken money with the woman, so that it would not have been so easy for him to get rid of her whenever he wished. [29] And the one giving her in marriage would probably have summoned many more witnesses than the man who was marrying a woman of this kind, for none of you is unaware that few unions of this kind usually last. So now the man who claims to have betrothed his sister says he did so before one witness and without an agreement about a dowry to a man with an estate of three talents, and the uncles have testified that they were present as witnesses for their nephew when he took in marriage a woman of this kind without a dowry.

[30] These same uncles have testified to being present by their nephew's invitation at the tenth-day ceremony,[41] when the child was presented as his daughter. And I am utterly outraged that the husband, claiming his wife's paternal inheritance on her behalf, entered the girl's name as Phile, while Pyrrhus' uncles, who say they were present at the tenth-day ceremony, testified that her father named

---

[40] The bride's father was not legally obliged to give a dowry (*proix*) with her, though this was the usual practice, especially when the families were wealthy. The sum was agreed upon at the betrothal (*engye*), and the husband was expected to use the money as capital for investment, the proceeds going towards the maintenance of his wife and children. The capital was returnable if the marriage ended without male issue; hence the dowry served as a protection to the woman. The speaker here implies that, since Pyrrhus was wealthy, he might have agreed to provide a fictitious dowry to afford Phile some protection (cf. 3.35–36).

[41] A family religious celebration at which the father formally acknowledged paternity and the child was named.

her Cleitarete after her grandmother.[42] [31] I'm amazed that a man who had already lived with her for more than eight years did not know the name of his own wife! Couldn't he have discovered it earlier from his own witnesses? Didn't his wife's mother in all that time tell him the name of her own daughter, or didn't her uncle, Nicodemus? [32] No, instead of her grandmother's name (if anybody really knew this was the name her father gave her), her husband Xenocles entered her name as Phile, and he did so when claiming her paternal inheritance for her. Why did he do that? In order that the husband might deprive his own wife of her claim to her grandmother's name given her by her father? [33] Isn't it obvious, gentlemen, that the events that these men testify happened a long time ago were invented by them much later to strengthen their claim to the estate? Otherwise those who (as they say) were invited to the tenth-day ceremony for Pyrrhus' daughter, the defendant's niece, could never have come to court with an accurate recollection from that day, whenever it was, that her father named her Cleitarete at the ceremony, [34] while the closest of all her relatives, her husband and her uncle and her mother, did not know the name of the child they say is his daughter. They most certainly would know it, if their story were true. But there will be an opportunity to speak about these uncles again later.[43]

[35] As for Nicodemus' testimony, it is not difficult to decide simply from the laws that he clearly gave false testimony. For if a man gives an unspecified sum of money, according to the law, if the wife leaves her husband or if the husband divorces his wife,[44] the giver is not entitled to claim back anything he had not specified in giving the dowry; surely then, by saying that he gave his sister in marriage without any agreement at all about a dowry, the defendant is clearly shown to be shameless. [36] What did he stand to gain from the marriage if

---

[42]The speaker's argument about the daughter's name is not compelling, since there were no birth certificates in Athens; e.g., Neaera's daughter was called Strybele as a child, but Phano as an adult (Dem. 59.50, 121). It should be noted, however, that Neaera was also attacked as being a prostitute.

[43]Cf. 3.63–71.

[44]A husband could simply "send away" (ekpempein) his wife to terminate their marriage, whereas a wife had to go to the Archon and give him written notice (cf. 3.78; Dem. 30.17, 26). The story goes that Alcibiades was then able to intervene and carry his wife home (And. 4.14; Plut., Alcibiades 8.5–6).

the bridegroom could divorce his wife whenever he wished? And he clearly could do this, gentlemen, if he had not agreed that he should receive any dowry with her. Again, would Nicodemus have betrothed his sister to our uncle on these terms, even though he knew she had been childless all her life and the agreed dowry by law would be his if anything happened to the woman before she had children? [37] Does any of you really think that Nicodemus cares so little about money as to overlook any of these possibilities? I don't think so. Furthermore, would our uncle have seen fit to marry the sister of this man who was prosecuted for noncitizenship by a member of the phratry to which he said he belonged and retained his rights by only four votes?[45] And to prove I'm telling the truth, read the deposition.

[DEPOSITION]

[38] So Nicodemus has testified that he betrothed his sister to our uncle without a dowry, even though the dowry would devolve to him if anything happened to the woman before she had children. Now take and read these laws to the jurors.

[LAWS]

[39] Do you think Nicodemus would care so little about money that, if what he says were true, he would not have paid close attention to his own interests? Yes, by Zeus, of course he would, in my opinion, since even men who give their women as concubines always reach prior agreement about the sums to be given to the concubines.[46] But when Nicodemus, as he says, was about to betroth his sister, did he carry out the betrothal only in accordance with the legal requirements?[47] A man who is eager to be dishonest for the paltry sum of money that he hopes to receive for speaking to you?[48]

---

[45]See 2.14n.

[46]Concubinage (*pallakia*) was a long-term but informal union, regularly between a citizen male and noncitizen female. It is tempting to view the relationship between Pyrrhus and Phile's mother in this way (though there is no hint that she was not a citizen woman).

[47]I.e., a dowry was not strictly a legal requirement but was normal practice; see above, 28n.

[48]As a reward for giving false testimony.

[40] As for his dishonesty, most of you know about it without my having to say anything, so I really don't lack witnesses to whatever I say about him. But I wish first to prove from the following considerations that he was utterly shameless in his testimony. Tell me, Nicodemus, if you had betrothed your sister to Pyrrhus and if you knew he was leaving a legitimate daughter by her, [41] how come you allowed our brother to claim the estate by adjudication[49] without regard to the legitimate daughter you say our uncle left behind? Did you not realize that as a result of the claim to the estate by adjudication, your own niece was being made a bastard? For when he claimed the estate by adjudication, he was making the daughter of the man who left it a bastard. [42] And still further back, Pyrrhus' adoption of my brother as his son—nobody is entitled to dispose of or leave any of his property to anybody without regard to the legitimate daughters he leaves behind on his death.[50] You will understand this when you hear the actual laws being read out. Read these laws to the jurors.

[LAWS]

[43] Do you think that the man who has testified to the betrothal would have allowed any of these things to happen? When Endius made his claim to receive the estate by adjudication, would Nicodemus not have claimed to receive it on his niece's behalf and made a declaration that her paternal estate was not adjudicable to Endius? Yet to prove that our brother did indeed claim the estate by adjudication and nobody contested his claim, read the deposition.

[DEPOSITION]

[44] When this claim by adjudication was made, then, Nicodemus did not dare to claim the estate or make a declaration that his niece was a legitimate surviving daughter of Pyrrhus.

---

[49]An uncontested claim to the estate (*epidikasia*); a contested claim led to a *diadikasia* (inheritance claim), as in Speech 1. If Pyrrhus' will made provision for the future marriage of the young Phile, there was no reason for Nicodemus to contest Endius' claim; see the Introduction.

[50]Cf. 3.68. This is regularly interpreted to mean that fathers with a daughter were obliged when adopting a son to stipulate that he marry the daughter, but this clearly did not happen on every occasion. See Rubinstein 1993: 95–96.

[45] Now, with regard to Endius' claim by adjudication, somebody might offer you a false excuse; he could pretend they knew nothing about it or even accuse us of lying. Let's ignore this. But when Endius was betrothing your niece to Xenocles, Nicodemus, did you allow the daughter born to Pyrrhus of a lawfully wedded wife to be betrothed as if she were his child by a *hetaira*?[51] [46] And did you not bring an impeachment (*eisangelia*) before the Archon for maltreatment of an heiress (*epiklēros*), when she was being so insulted by the adopted son and deprived of her patrimony, especially since these suits alone carry no risk to the plaintiff and anybody who wishes is entitled to help heiresses?[52] [47] No fine can be imposed for impeachments before the Archon, even if the prosecutors fail to win a single vote, and there are no deposits or court fees[53] in any impeachments. But whereas the prosecutors are entitled to impeach without risk, the severest penalties are imposed on people who are convicted in the impeachments. [48] So if his niece was our uncle's child by a lawfully wedded wife, would Nicodemus have allowed her to be betrothed as if she were the child of a *hetaira*? And when it happened, wouldn't he have brought an impeachment before the Archon that the heiress was being abused by the man who betrothed her in this way? And if what you[54] have now dared to depose were true, you

---

[51]If Phile was illegitimate even though she was the daughter of an Athenian citizen, this raises much-disputed questions about the validity of her marriage to Xenocles and the status of their children. See Todd 1993: 178–179.

[52]An ordinary public suit (*graphē*) could be brought by "anybody who wishes" (*ho boulomenos*), and the rewards for successful prosecutions were higher than in a private suit (*dikē*). But those who failed to win twenty percent of the votes were heavily fined (1,000 drachmas) and suffered partial disfranchisement (the loss of the right to bring further cases of the same kind). The main exception to this rule, until about 330, was a public suit tried by the procedure *eisangelia* ("impeachment"), used, e.g., in cases concerned with the maltreatment of orphans (as in Speech 11) and heiresses (as here). Further on heiresses, see the Introduction to this volume.

[53]The litigants in many cases had to pay a deposit (*prytaneia*), and the losing party had to reimburse his opponent, while plaintiffs in certain public suits had to pay a fee (*parastasis*).

[54]Note the striking, abrupt shift to the second person here, and the equally abrupt shift back to the third person in 3.49. The speaker has previously addressed Nicodemus by name in 3.40 and 45.

would immediately then have had the wrongdoer punished. Or will you pretend you weren't aware of this either? [49] Then weren't you made suspicious by the dowry that was given with her? Surely for this reason alone you should have been outraged and induced to impeach Endius, if he himself was claiming as his right an estate worth three talents but saw fit to marry Pyrrhus' legitimate daughter to another man with a dowry of a thousand drachmas.[55] Wouldn't this have outraged the defendant and made him impeach Endius? By Zeus, of course it would, if his story were true. [50] I don't think for one moment that he or any other adopted son would be so naïve or negligent of the established laws that when there existed a legitimate daughter of the man who left the estate, he would give her to another instead of himself.[56] He knew perfectly well that the whole of their grandfather's estate belongs to the children born of a legitimate daughter. Knowing this, then, would anybody hand his own property over to another, especially if it were as valuable as they claimed? [51] Do you think that any adopted son would be so shameless or brazen as to give a legitimate daughter in marriage with a dowry of not even a tenth of her patrimony? And when this happened, do you think it would have been allowed by her uncle, who has testified that he gave away her mother in marriage? I don't think so; rather, he would have claimed the estate, made a declaration, and brought an impeachment before the Archon, and if there were any stronger measures than these, he would have taken them all. [52] Endius, then, married off the woman Nicodemus says is his niece as if she were the child of a *hetaira,* and the defendant did not dispute the claim to Pyrrhus' estate with Endius or, when Endius betrothed his niece as if she were the child of a *hetaira,* impeach him before the Archon, nor was he at all upset at the dowry bestowed on her, but he let all these things happen. But the laws are precise on all these points. [53] So first the clerk will read to you once again the deposition concerning Endius' claim to the estate by adjudication, then the one about the woman's betrothal. Read them to the jurors.

---

[55]The manuscripts read 3,000 drachmas, but the estate was valued at 3 talents (18,000 drachmas), while the dowry was "not even a tenth" of this (3.51). In giving a dowry of 1,000 drachmas with a bastard child, Endius might be viewed as being generous.

[56]Cf. 3.68 and n.

[DEPOSITIONS]

Now read the laws as well.

[LAWS]

Now take the defendant's deposition too.

[DEPOSITION]

[54] How could any plaintiff prove false witness more clearly than by demonstrating it from the behavior of the defendants themselves and from all our laws?

I've now said almost everything about the defendant. But consider too whether the behavior of his niece's husband also provides proof that Nicodemus' testimony is false. [55] Proof and testimony have been presented that he took her in marriage for his wife as if she were the child of a *hetaira,* and for a long time now Xenocles himself has testified to the truth of this testimony by his conduct.[57] For clearly if he did not receive her in marriage from Endius as the child of a *hetaira,* once he had children by her, who are now growing up,[58] on behalf of a legitimate daughter he would have claimed her patrimony from Endius while he was still alive, [56] especially since he was prepared to deny that Endius had been adopted by Pyrrhus. It was because he denied it that he formally contested the evidence of the people who have testified they were present when Pyrrhus made his will. And to prove I'm telling the truth, the clerk will read to you the deposition that was made. Read it to the jurors.

[DEPOSITION]

[57] Another proof that they deny Endius' adoption by Pyrrhus took place is that they would not have ignored the last heir to the property and decided to make a claim to Pyrrhus' estate on behalf of the woman. Pyrrhus had already been dead for over twenty years,

---

[57]A commonplace argument. Cf. 2.38 and n.

[58]Xenocles and Phile had been married for over eight years (3.31), and if Phile was Pyrrhus' legitimate daughter, their children stood to inherit their grandfather's estate on reaching maturity.

but Endius died in *Metageitnion*[59] last year, and these people immediately made their claim to the estate two days later. [58] The law prescribes that claims for an estate must be made within five years of the heir's death. Therefore, the woman had two alternatives, either to claim the patrimony while Endius was still alive or, when the adopted son had died, to make a claim to her brother's estate by adjudication, especially if, as our opponents say, he had betrothed her to Xenocles as his legitimate sister. [59] We all know perfectly well that we all have the right to make a claim to a brother's estate by adjudication, but if he has legitimate children fathered by himself, no child needs to claim his patrimony by adjudication.[60] And there is no need for any discussion of this, for all of you, like every other citizen, possess your patrimonies without having to go to law. [60] Our opponents, then, have become so bold that they denied that the adopted son needed to claim what had been bequeathed to him by adjudication, but then decided to make a claim for the award of her father's estate to Phile, who they say was a legitimate surviving daughter of Pyrrhus. And yet (as I've just said), when men leave legitimate children of their own, the children do not need to claim their patrimony by adjudication, whereas when they adopt children by will, these must claim by adjudication the property bequeathed to them. [61] Nobody I imagine would contest the patrimony against the former, since they are born to the deceased, but all blood relations see fit to claim patrimony left to adopted sons. So to prevent claims to estates being made by any chance person and to stop people daring to claim estates by adjudication, alleging they are vacant, all adopted sons make claims by adjudication. [62] Therefore, none of you should think that, if he thought his wife was legitimate, Xenocles would have made a claim for her patrimony on her behalf; on the contrary, the legitimate daughter would have entered directly into possession of her father's estate, and if anybody tried to deprive her of it or use force against her, he would have been ejecting her from her patrimony, and if he used force, he not only would have been subject to

---

[59]Early August to early September.
[60]See the Introduction to Speech 2.

private prosecution but also would have been impeached publicly before the Archon, risking his life and all his property.[61]

[63] But even before Xenocles, if Pyrrhus' uncles knew their nephew had left a legitimate daughter and none of us wanted to marry her, they would never have allowed Xenocles, who was not in any way related by birth to Pyrrhus, to marry the woman who by kinship belonged to themselves.[62] That would have been extraordinary. [64] As for women given in marriage by their fathers and living with their husbands (and who better to judge their interests than their father?), the law prescribes that if their father dies without leaving them legitimate brothers, even women who have been given in this way are adjudicable to their next of kin; and many husbands in the past have been deprived of their own wives.[63] [65] So women who have been given in marriage by their fathers must necessarily be adjudicable as a result of the law; but if Pyrrhus had left a legitimate daughter, would any of his uncles have allowed Xenocles to marry and keep the woman who belonged to them by kinship and make him the heir[64] of such a large estate instead of themselves? Don't believe it, gentlemen. [66] No man hates his own advantage or puts the interests of strangers ahead of his own. So if they pretend that because of Endius' adoption the woman was not adjudicable and say that is why they did not claim her, the first question you should ask them is why, if they admit Endius' adoption by Pyrrhus, they have formally contested the evidence of the people who have testified it took place? [67] Second,

---

[61]By a *dikē exoulēs* (suit for ejectment) and by an *eisangelia kakōseōs epiklērōn* (impeachment for maltreatment of heiresses).

[62]The argument assumes that if Phile had been legitimate, she would have been an heiress. But after Pyrrhus adopted Endius as his son and heir, she would not have had this status until after Endius died without children.

[63]Cf. 10.19. The law prescribed that the nearest relative (*ankhisteus*) should marry the heiress, but he might decline his claim, in which case the right to claim her descended in the order of a statutorily defined group of kin (*ankhisteia;* cf. 3.74). The right to claim a married heiress was probably restricted if she already had a son.

[64]Isaeus uses the word *klēronomos,* or "heir," even though strictly speaking neither Xenocles nor the uncles would have been heirs to Pyrrhus' estate but would merely have controlled it until Phile's son or sons reached maturity.

why did they decide to make an unlawful claim to Pyrrhus' estate, ignoring the last heir to the property? And in addition, ask them if any legitimate child thinks to enter a claim to his own estate. Ask these questions in response to their impudence.

That the woman was adjudicable, if she really was a legitimate daughter left by Pyrrhus, one may very clearly discover from the laws. [68] The law expressly states that if a man does not leave legitimate male children, he is entitled to dispose of his property in whatever way he chooses, but if he leaves daughters, he must dispose of them together with it.[65] So a man can leave and dispose of his property along with his daughters, but he cannot either adopt or leave any of his property to anybody without including his legitimate daughters. [69] So if Pyrrhus adopted Endius as his son without including his legitimate daughter, the adoption would have been invalid according to the law, but if he intended to give his daughter in marriage and left her after adopting him on this condition, how could you, Pyrrhus' uncles, have allowed Endius to put in a claim to Pyrrhus' estate without his legitimate daughter (if he had one), especially since you testified that your nephew solemnly charged you with taking care of this girl? [70] My good men, can you really claim that you did not even notice this? But when Endius betrothed the woman and gave her in marriage, did you, his uncles, allow your own nephew's daughter to be betrothed to Xenocles as if she were the child of a *hetaira,* especially since you claim you were present when your nephew formally agreed to take this woman's mother as his wife in accordance with the laws, and furthermore that you were invited to and attended the feast on her tenth-day ceremony?[66] [71] Above all (and this is dreadful), although you claim that your nephew solemnly charged you to take care of this girl, did you take such good care of her that you allowed her to be betrothed as the child of a *hetaira,* despite her bearing the name of your own sister, as you testified?

[72] From these arguments, gentlemen, and from what actually happened, it's easy to see that these are the most shameless of men. Why, if our uncle left a legitimate daughter, did he adopt my brother and make him his son and heir? Did he have other closer relatives

---

[65]See above, 42n.

[66]See above, 30n.

than us whom he wanted to deprive of their claim to his daughter when he adopted my brother as his son? But if he had no legitimate sons, then he didn't and doesn't have any single relative closer than us: for he had no brother or brother's sons, while we were the sons of his sister. [73] Well, by Zeus, he might perhaps have adopted some other relative and given him possession of the estate and his daughter. Yet why should he have openly offended any of his relatives when, if he really had married Nicodemus' sister, he could have introduced the daughter who has been presented as his child by her to the phratry as his own legitimate child,[67] left her to be claimed with his entire estate, and solemnly charged that one of her sons be introduced as his son? [74] Clearly by leaving her as the heiress he would have been certain that she faced one of two futures: either one of us, his closest relatives, would claim her and take her as his wife, or if none of us wanted to take her, one of these uncles who are testifying, or if not them, then one of the other relatives in the same way would claim her with the whole property and take her as his wife in accordance with the laws. [75] So then, he would have accomplished this by introducing his daughter to his phratry without adopting my brother as his son; but by adopting him without introducing her, he made her a bastard, as was fitting, and disinherited her, and left my brother heir to his estate. [76] Furthermore, to prove our uncle neither gave a wedding feast nor saw fit to introduce to the phratry the woman our opponents say was his legitimate child, even though they have a rule to this effect, the clerk will read to you the deposition of the members of his phratry. Read it; and you, stop the water.

[DEPOSITION]

Now also take the deposition proving that he adopted my brother as his son.

[DEPOSITION]

---

[67]It is very unlikely that daughters were registered on any phratry list of members as were sons, but there is no reason to doubt the speaker's claim that they might be "introduced."

[77] Will you, then, consider Nicodemus' testimony more credible than the absentee depositions from our uncle himself,[68] and will anybody attempt to persuade you that our uncle took this woman, who was available to anybody who wanted her, as his lawfully wedded wife? But I don't think you'll believe it, unless he proves to you, as I said at the beginning of my speech, [78] first, what the dowry was when, as he says, he betrothed his sister to Pyrrhus; second, before what Archon this lawfully wedded wife left her husband or his household;[69] next, from whom he recovered her dowry, when the man died to whom he says he betrothed her; or if he demanded it back but couldn't recover it in twenty years, what action he brought for maintenance or for her dowry on behalf of the lawfully wedded wife against the man in possession of Pyrrhus' estate. [79] And on top of all this, let him show the one he betrothed his sister to before or afterwards and if she has had children by some other man. These are the things you should seek to learn from him, and don't forget about the wedding feast in his phratry. This is one of the strongest proofs against the defendant's testimony, for clearly if Pyrrhus was induced to marry her, he would also have been induced to give a wedding feast for her in his phratry and to introduce the child who has been presented as this woman's daughter as his own legitimate child. [80] In his deme, moreover, since he owned property worth three talents, if he had been married, he would have been compelled on behalf of his wedded wife both to host a feast for the women at the Thesmophoria[70] and to perform for her the other public services in his deme that someone who possessed a property of this size was obliged to do. But it's clear that none of these things has ever happened. The members of his phratry have testified to you; now take the deposition of his fellow demesmen too.

[DEPOSITION]

---

[68]On the *ekmartyria* (used figuratively here), see 18n.

[69]See above, 35n.

[70]A three-day women's festival in honor of Demeter, celebrated in the autumn, from which men were excluded.

4. ON THE ESTATE
OF NICOSTRATUS:
SUPPLEMENTARY SPEECH

Nicostratus died while serving abroad as a mercenary, after being away from Athens for eleven years. He left an estate of two talents, which was claimed by a number of people. All of them eventually desisted, with the exception of the brothers Hagnon[1] and Hagnotheus, whose claim was challenged by Chariades. Chariades alleged that he had served as a mercenary with Nicostratus and was his business partner (4.18, 20, 26), and he also produced a will to the effect that he had been adopted by Nicostratus as his son and heir. Hagnon and Hagnotheus disputed the genuineness of the will and claimed the estate in a *diadikasia* (inheritance claim).[2] They argued that, as the sons of Thrasippus, the brother of Nicostratus' father Thrasymachus, they were his first cousins and thus his next of kin. The brothers were young (4.26); Hagnon is always mentioned first (4.1, 2, 24, 27) and may have been the elder of the two, and he apparently delivered the main speech.[3] The present supporting (or "supplementary") speech, which is much briefer than Speech 2 and contains far fewer details of the case, was delivered by a more experienced advocate (*synēgoros*), who was a friend of the now deceased Thrasippus (4.1, 27). The author of the Argument[4] found in the manuscripts seems to have misunderstood the first sentence of the speech and names the speaker as Isaeus himself; not only were Athenian juries deeply suspicious of

---

[1]A Hagnon son of Thrasippus is named as lessee of a silver mine in ca. 338/7; see Davies 1971: 257–258. Hagnotheus and Chariades are otherwise unknown.

[2]On this process, see the Introduction to this volume.

[3]He is twice described as being present in court (4.1, 2).

[4]For a translation of the Argument (*Hypothesis*), see the Appendix.

Stemma

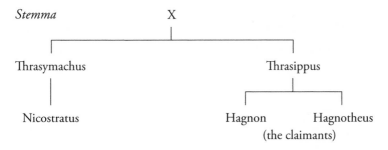

logographers, however, but Isaeus will have had no legal competence if he was a metic.

The task confronting Hagnon and Hagnotheus was twofold: to prove that they were themselves the next of kin and to cast doubt on the genuineness of the will. Chariades had produced witnesses both to the genuineness of the will (4.23) and to the allegation that Nicostratus' father was named Smicrus, not Thrasymachus (4.3–6, 24–25). Hagnon may have dealt adequately with these points in the main speech; he also produced witnesses to Nicostratus' parentage (4.2, 26) and to show that Nicostratus and Chariades were not close friends and business partners (4.18, 20, 26) and that Chariades had not performed Nicostratus' funeral rites (4.19–20, 26). But the present speaker does little to further Hagnon's case beyond restating these points and asserting that Chariades' witnesses to the will were unreliable because they were his friends (4.23). Much of the speech consists of rhetorical commonplaces (especially 4.11–23), with the regular attack on the character of the opponent (*diabolē*) and the eulogy of Hagnon and Hagnotheus and their father (4.27–31).

From a rhetorical point of view, the speech is well constructed. The briefest of proems justifying the speaker's appearance (4.1) is followed by a preliminary attack on Chariades (4.1–6). Cleverly dismissing events abroad, which the brothers would have had great difficulty contesting, the speaker concentrates on Chariades' actions in Athens, in particular how he confused the issue by inventing a different name for Nicostratus' father, as part of a conspiracy to prevent the brothers from easily discrediting the will (4.5). This leads neatly into a narrative that locates Chariades among a number of false claimants, who "swooped down" like vultures on Nicostratus' estate (4.7–10). This section of the speech comes to a climax with Chariades' alleged motive of attempting to have his illegitimate son recognized as a citizen through the claim, a strategy that he then abandoned.

The matter of the will is tackled next, with commonplace arguments on the conflict between wills and claims of kinship (4.11–23). Having highlighted the superiority of kinship over wills, the speaker has to return to the problem of the opponents' claim that Hagnon and Hagnotheus were not in fact kinsmen of Nicostratus (4.24–25). He turns this on its head by arguing that if Chariades' witnesses really were relatives of Nicostratus, it would not be in their interest to back Chariades. The epilogue begins with a recapitulation of the arguments put forward by the brothers (4.26), followed by character comparison, with commonplace arguments on the performance of public services by Thrasippus and his sons contrasted with Chariades' criminal behavior (4.27–30). The speech concludes with an appeal to the jurors in a long periodic sentence in the form of an hypothetical inversion, that the brothers are not vexatious, and so Chariades is not on trial for his life as he might have been, and it is up to the jurors to ensure that justice is done.

As to the date of the trial, most editors have accepted Valckenaer's ingenious textual emendation at 4.7 of *hexakis* ("six times") to *ex Akēs*, whereby the speaker says that the two talents that made up Nicostratus' estate "came from Ace" (modern Akko in Israel). An army was assembled there by the Persian satrap Pharnabazus for an invasion of Egypt in 374, and it is assumed that Nicostratus was intending to serve as a mercenary but died, and his money was returned to Athens. I follow Wevers (1969: 21–23) in defending *hexakis* and altering the verb, and I here translate my proposed emendation *eisēlthetēn*.[5] There is then no internal evidence for the date of the speech, which Wevers' statistical analysis puts at ca. 350.

4

[1] Hagnon here and Hagnotheus, gentlemen, happen to be close friends of mine, as was their father before them. I therefore think it reasonable to speak in their support as best I can.

---

[5]See M. J. Edwards, "A Note on Isaeus 4.7," *Mnem.* 55 (2002), 87–88.

When events take place abroad, it's not possible to discover witnesses,[6] nor is it easy to prove whether our opponents are telling any lies, because neither of my friends has ever been to that place. But what has happened here I think should be sufficient proof for you that all the people who are claiming Nicostratus' property as a bequest want to deceive you. [2] First, gentlemen, it is right to examine the names that are entered and consider which side made their claim more simply and more naturally. Hagnon here and Hagnotheus entered Nicostratus' name as the son of Thrasymachus, present themselves as his first cousins, and produce witnesses to these facts; [3] whereas Chariades and his supporters say that Nicostratus was the son of Smicrus, yet claim the estate of the son of Thrasymachus. My friends make no claims either to know that name or to have anything to do with it; they simply say Nicostratus was the son of Thrasymachus, and similarly they claim the estate of this person. [4] If they agreed about Nicostratus' patronymic and were disputing about the estate alone, you would have to consider only whether the Nicostratus about whom they both agreed made a will or not; but as it is, how is it possible to enter two fathers for the same man? This is what Chariades has done: he claimed the estate of Nicostratus son of Smicrus, and when my friends claimed the estate of the son of Thrasymachus, he paid his deposit[7] as if it was the same man. [5] All this is an insult and a plot. They think that, if the matter is simple and they do not introduce some confusion into it, my friends will easily prove that Nicostratus made no will; but if they say that Nicostratus' father is not the same and claim the estate just the same, they know perfectly well that my friends will have to advance a longer argument to show that Nicostratus was the son of Thrasymachus than that he made no will. [6] Furthermore, even if they admit that Nicostratus was the son of Thrasymachus, they wouldn't be able to prove that my friends are not his cousins; but by inventing another father for the deceased, they have introduced an argument not only about the will but also about his parentage.

---

[6]Though the brothers did produce some such witnesses (cf. 4.18–20, 26).

[7]Not the court fee of 3.47, but the fee paid by those claiming an inheritance (*parakatabolē*). The sum was one-tenth of the estimated value of the estate and was forfeited to the state by the losing party.

[7] You can see that the men who are carrying out these plots against my friends are strangers not only from these considerations but also because of what has happened since the beginning. For who did not cut his hair[8] when the two talents came into dispute six times?[9] Who did not wear black clothing, as if mourning would cause them to inherit the estate? How many relatives and sons claimed Nicostratus' property on the ground of bequest? [8] Demosthenes said he was his nephew but relinquished his claim when he was proved a liar by my friends. Telephus said Nicostratus had bequeathed him all his property; he too desisted not long after. Ameiniades produced Nicostratus' son who was not yet three to the Archon, even though Nicostratus had not been in Athens for eleven years.[10] [9] Pyrrhus of Lamptrae said the money had been dedicated to Athena by Nicostratus but had been bequeathed to him by Nicostratus himself.[11] Ctesias of Besa and Cranaus first said that they had secured a verdict in a suit against Nicostratus for one talent; but when they couldn't prove this, they pretended that he was their freedman,[12] and they were still unable to prove their claim. [10] These were the men who at the start immediately swooped down on Nicostratus' property. Chariades made no claim at the time but came forward later, trying to insert into the family not only himself but also his child by his *hetaira*.[13] It was the same to him whether he was going to inherit the money or make the child a citizen. But when he too realized that he would be defeated over the parentage, he dropped the child's claim and paid the deposit on his own claim to the estate as a bequest.

---

[8]In mourning.

[9]Or, on the commonly printed text, "when the two talents came from Ace." See the Introduction.

[10]I.e., Ameiniades pretended to be acting as the boy's guardian.

[11]The speaker's brevity heightens the apparent absurdity. Pyrrhus may have claimed that Nicostratus left the money to him for the duration of his life, then it was to be dedicated to Athena; or that it was dedicated to the goddess on condition that payments were made to Pyrrhus during his lifetime.

[12]And so, since he had died without issue, his property should revert to his former masters. Cranaus may have been Ctesias' son (cf. Athen. 10.416d–f).

[13]A courtesan; see 3.6 and n.

[11] It ought to be the case, gentlemen, that anyone who enters a claim for money as a bequest and loses his case should not be fined at the current rate [14] but should pay a fine to the state equal to what he set out to obtain. In this way the laws would not be flouted and families would not be insulted, and above all, nobody would invent lies about the dead. But since everybody is entitled to claim the whole estate even of a stranger, just as he pleases, it's your duty to examine their claims as carefully as possible and as far as you can to overlook nothing. [12] It seems to me that it's only in cases concerning estates that we should put more trust in circumstantial evidence than witnesses. In other transactions it is not particularly difficult to prove who are the ones giving false testimony, since they testify against the agent when he is alive and present. But in the case of wills, how can one know who are the ones not telling the truth, unless the inconsistencies are particularly great, since the man they are testifying against is dead, the relatives know nothing about what happened, and the means of refutation are not at all clear? [13] Further, gentlemen, many men who do make wills do not even tell those who are present what is in the will,[15] but summon them as witnesses solely to one thing, that they are leaving a will, and it can easily happen that a document is substituted or rewritten to say the opposite to what the deceased willed. For the witnesses will not know any better whether the same will is being produced as the one they were called on to attest. [14] But since it's possible to deceive even those who were admittedly present, how much more readily might somebody attempt to mislead you who know nothing of the matter?

Furthermore, gentlemen, the law also prescribes that a will is valid not merely if somebody makes one, but if he does so when of sound mind.[16] So you must first consider whether a man made a will and then whether he was of sound mind when he did so. [15] But since we deny that any will at all was ever made, how could you decide if somebody was out of his mind when he made his will before you are sure that a will was made? You see, then, how difficult it

---

[14]I.e., his deposit of one-tenth of the estimated value (see 4n).

[15]Cf. 7.1–2; Dem. 46.28; but contrast the argument at 9.12. On the untrustworthiness of wills, cf. 1.41–43.

[16]See the Introduction to Speech 2.

is to determine whether those who claim by bequest are telling the truth; whereas those who claim by right of kinship first do not need to produce any witnesses that the estate is theirs (for everyone agrees that the property of the deceased belongs to his next of kin), [16] and second not only do the laws dealing with kinship favor relatives but so too do those dealing with bequests. The law does not allow a man to bequeath his own property to anybody if he is not in his right mind through old age, illness, or the other causes that you also know about, but by right of kinship the next of kin receives the property of the deceased, whatever his mental state, without dispute. [17] Apart from this, you must secure trust in a will through witnesses, but it's possible also to be deceived by them (otherwise there wouldn't be any prosecutions for false witness), whereas you trust kinship on your own authority, since relatives claim in accordance with the laws that you enacted.[17] [18] Additionally, gentlemen, if the men who are claiming by will were admitted to be close friends of Nicostratus, even then it would not be certain, although there would be a greater likelihood that the will would be regarded as genuine. Before now, men who were not on good terms with their relatives have favored friends outside the family above those who were very closely related. But Nicostratus and Chariades were neither messmates nor friends nor in the same company,[18] and we have produced witnesses to you of all these facts. [19] And consider this point, which is very important and is the clearest evidence of Chariades' impudence: when he neither took up the body of his adoptive father after he died nor cremated it nor collected the bones but left all this to be done by complete strangers, how would he not be utterly impious in thinking he should inherit the deceased's money even though he performed none of the customary rites over him? [20] Well, by Zeus, after not doing any of this, did he administer Nicostratus' property?[19] But you have heard testimony about this too, and even he doesn't deny most

---

[17]A commonplace type of remark, equating the jurors with the people as a whole, who in turn are identified with the citizens who had passed the laws originally (many of which were proposed by Solon).

[18]Some words are missing from the text at this point.

[19]The speaker apparently answers an imaginary objection, though he later refers to business dealings between Nicostratus and Chariades (4.26).

of it. Makeshift excuses have of course been found for each of his actions—for what is left when someone openly admits the facts?

[21] So you can clearly see, gentlemen, that there is no legal support to these people's assault on Nicostratus' property, but they want to deceive you and deprive my friends, who are his relatives, of what the laws have granted them. Chariades is not the only person who has done this; many others before now have claimed the property of men who have died abroad, sometimes without even knowing them. [22] They reckon that if they win they will secure somebody else's property, and if they lose the risk is small. Some are even willing to give false testimony, and any refutation involves matters unknown. In short, there is a world of difference between a claim based on kinship and one based on bequest. But you, gentlemen, must first consider whether in your view the will was made; this is what the laws instruct and is the most just course. [23] But when you yourselves do not know the truth for certain and the witnesses were friends not of the deceased but of Chariades, who wants to take somebody else's property, what could be more just than to vote to award the property of a relative to his relatives? Indeed, if anything had happened to my friends, their property would have passed to none other than Nicostratus, since he would have claimed it by the same right of kinship, as their first cousin born of their father's brother.[20] [24] But by Zeus, I forgot, gentlemen, neither Hagnon nor Hagnotheus is a relative of Nicostratus, according to our opponents' assertion, but he has other relatives. And then are these relatives testifying for a man who claims the estate on the ground of bequest, but are not claiming it themselves by right of kinship? Surely they are not so mad as to have complete confidence in the will and relinquish so much money so readily! Again, even from what our opponents themselves say, it is more to the advantage of the relatives themselves that my friends succeed in their claim to Nicostratus' property rather than Chariades. [25] For if my friends, who claim by right of kinship, gain control of the estate, these men will also be entitled in the future to

---

[20]Implying that Hagnon and Hagnotheus had no children, sisters, or other relatives who took precedence over their first cousin. For a similar hypothetical argument based on who would have inherited in the case of the death of the claimants, cf. 1.44–46.

make a claim whenever they wish by right of kinship, and prove to you that they were themselves closer relatives of Nicostratus and he was the son of Smicrus not Thrasymachus. But if Chariades inherits the estate, it will not be possible for any relative to bring a suit for the property of Nicostratus—for when he is in possession of the property on the ground that it was adjudicated as a bequest, what will those who claim by right of kinship in fact say? [21]

[26] So confirm for these young men the same rights as each of you would expect for yourselves. They produced witnesses, first that they are first cousins of Nicostratus by his father's brother; second that they were never in dispute with him; furthermore that they buried Nicostratus; in addition that Chariades here was never close to Nicostratus either in Athens or on campaign; and finally that the business partnership on which our opponent especially relies is a fiction.

[27] Even apart from this, gentlemen, it is right for you to examine the characters of each side. Thrasippus, the father of Hagnon and Hagnotheus, has before now performed public services for you [22] and paid war taxes, [23] and he was generally an excellent citizen. My friends themselves have never gone anywhere abroad unless you ordered them, nor in staying here are they useless to the state, but they serve in the army, pay war taxes, and perform all their other prescribed duties, and they conduct themselves (as everybody knows) in a law-abiding manner. [28] So they could far more fittingly claim Nicostratus' money as a bequest than could Chariades. He, when he lived here, was first of all arrested in the act as a thief and led off to prison, then released with some others by the Eleven, all of whom you publicly condemned to death; [24] and when he was again denounced to

---

[21]They might say that the will was a forgery or was in some other way invalid, for a period of five years after Chariades' death (cf. 3.58).

[22]"Liturgies" (*leitourgiai*) performed by wealthy citizens; see the Series Introduction, p. xxiii.

[23]These special taxes (*eisphorai*) were levied on the wealthy in times of need; see the Series Introduction, p. xxiii.

[24]Common criminals (*kakourgoi*, lit. "evildoers"), such as thieves and muggers, if caught in the act could be arrested and brought before the Eleven, the officials responsible for the prison and executions. The implication is that this board of Eleven was executed for misconduct in office, but we know nothing else about such an incident, which seems, on the face of it, unlikely.

the Council as a common criminal (*kakourgos*), he absconded and failed to appear.[25] [29] He didn't return to Athens for seventeen years after that, until Nicostratus died. He has never served in the army on your behalf or paid any war tax, except perhaps since he claimed Nicostratus' property, nor has he performed any other public service for you. And then, such as he is, he is not content to avoid punishment for his crimes, but he actually claims other people's property! [30] If my friends were fond of quarreling or were like other citizens, perhaps he would not be claiming Nicostratus' money but would be on trial for his life;[26] as it is, gentlemen of the jury, somebody else will punish him, if he wishes to do so. [31] But you must help my friends and not prefer those who seek to possess other people's property unjustly to those related by birth to the deceased, who apart from this have before now been of service to him.[27] Remember the laws and the oaths you swore, and in addition the testimony that we produced, and vote according to justice.

---

[25]This allegation may indicate that the Council investigated the affair of the Eleven and summoned Chariades to appear to give evidence, rather than that he was tried as a *kakourgos* before the Council. If he was, in fact, due to be tried but absconded, we would expect that when he claimed this inheritance in Athens he would have been arrested and executed as an exile who had illegally returned to Athens.

[26]I.e., they would be prosecuting him on a capital charge.

[27]I.e., by burying him (4.26).

5. ON THE ESTATE OF DICAEOGENES

Dicaeogenes II, the son of Menexenus I, was killed in a sea battle off Cnidus, probably in 411.[1] The wealth and prominence of his family are reflected in his service as the commander of the Paralus, one of the state triremes (5.6), but he had no sons or brothers to inherit his large estate. He did, however, have four sisters, all of whom were married and stood to share the estate, but Proxenus, a descendant of the tyrant slayer Harmodius who was married to the sister of Menexenus I,[2] produced a will whereby Dicaeogenes II adopted his son, Dicaeogenes III,[3] and left him one-third of the estate, the other two-thirds to be shared by the sisters.

The will was not challenged, and the arrangement lasted for twelve years. At this point, Dicaeogenes III produced another will, whereby he was left the entire estate. By now, one of the sisters' husbands, Theopompus, was dead and another, Democles, was either dead or divorced; the other two husbands, Polyaratus and Cephisophon, were still alive, and it was Polyaratus who appears to have contested the validity of the second will (5.9). He lost the case, and Dicaeogenes III enjoyed the whole estate for another ten years. Polyaratus, who had threatened to prosecute Dicaeogenes III's witnesses for bearing false

---

[1] Cf. Thuc. 8.42.

[2] Davies (1971: 476–477) suggests that Dicaeogenes I's daughter was Proxenus' mother, since Proxenus' son Harmodius was still active in 371. This does not, however, rule out the possibility that he was born in the 440s and his mother in the 460s, just before her father's death.

[3] Named after his maternal grandfather, indicating that he was the younger son.

Stemma

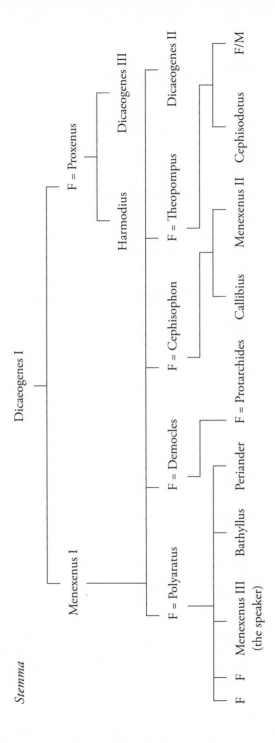

testimony, died soon after the trial, and Cephisophon may also have died about this time, because it was his younger son, Menexenus II, who successfully prosecuted one of Dicaeogenes III's witnesses, Lycon. To forestall further prosecutions, Dicaeogenes III bought off Menexenus II by offering to restore his mother's share of the estate, but he failed to keep his word. Menexenus II, therefore, joined with his cousins, Menexenus III and Cephisodotus, in claiming the whole estate as next of kin, on the ground that both wills were now shown to be invalid and so Dicaeogenes II had died intestate.

Dicaeogenes III responded with a declaration (*diamartyria*) lodged by his friend Leochares that the estate was not adjudicable.[4] Leochares was then prosecuted for false witness, and the votes were about to be counted when Dicaeogenes III again offered to compromise by promising to surrender two-thirds of the estate. Leochares and Mnesiptolemus were to act as sureties, and the deal was sanctioned by the court. But a further dispute arose over the interpretation of the agreement. In the twenty-two years since the death of Dicaeogenes II, his successor had suffered financial problems and had sold or mortgaged much of the estate. He also claimed compensation for expenditures he had incurred on public services and on building and repair work. With little left to recover, the cousins sued Leochares as surety, and after a failed attempt at arbitration, Menexenus III prosecuted Leochares by the present speech.[5]

As Wyse (1904: 404) observed, it is easy to forget that Leochares, not Dicaeogenes III, was the defendant in this suit, since little of the speech is concerned with his acting as surety (5.19–21, 25–26). This does not indicate that the speech was a secondary speech (*synēgoria*)[6] but rather that Menexenus III had good reason for adopting this approach. The prosecution case turns on the wording of the agreement, with Menexenus III claiming that Dicaeogenes III agreed to hand over two-thirds of the estate "without dispute" (5.1, 18, 20, 21), that is, free from claims and liabilities, and so he should recover and re-

---

[4]Presumably on the ground that Dicaeogenes III had been recognized as Dicaeogenes II's adopted son.

[5]Cephisodotus was in court (cf. 5.2, 12), but Menexenus II does not appear to have been. The case may be classified as a *dikē engyēs*.

[6]See Speech 2, n. 2.

store everything he had sold or mortgaged. Leochares denied that this stipulation was written down (5.25) and will have argued that Dicaeogenes III had handed over all he could (cf. 5.3).

The prosecution's response is to claim that in the hasty drafting of the document in court not all of the agreed conditions were written down, but additional undertakings were made orally in front of witnesses, whom they can produce (5.20). They do not, however, produce the document itself, and the weakness of their case is apparent.[7] Menexenus III therefore concentrates on attacking the character of Dicaeogenes III, who callously shows no mercy to a widow and orphans (5.9–11), does not perform his public duties (5.35–38) or military service (5.46), and is a disgrace to his family (5.39–44). This is in stark contrast to the behavior of the cousins, who despite his wickedness allowed him to retain his share of the property and more besides (5.29–30).[8] It is clear that Menexenus III is no inexperienced litigant (cf. 5.33), and as a piece of character assassination, the speech is excellent. We do not, however, know the outcome.

The structure of the speech reflects Isaeus' versatility as a logographer. The proem (5.1–5) contains none of the conventional appeals to the jurors[9] but opens with a statement of the case followed by nontechnical proofs (*atechnoi pisteis*)[10] and closes with anticipation (*procatalepsis*) of what Leochares will say in his narrative. The speaker's own, extended narrative follows (5.5–18), which damns the character of Dicaeogenes III (note the attack on his hybris, 5.10–11). The proofs may be divided into three main sections, each of which contains snippets of narrative: the lies and deceptions perpetrated by Dicaeogenes III and Leochares (5.19–30) contrasted with the veracity and honesty of their opponents, with narratives of the attempted ejection

---

[7]Though perhaps not as decisive as modern scholars have imagined, given the greater importance of witnesses over documents in most legal transactions.

[8]On the other hand, they did originally claim the whole estate, arguing that he had no right to any share in it (5.14–17).

[9]Though, as Usher notes (1999: 134), the first section takes the conventional form of a hypothetical inversion (on which, see Speech 2, n. 8).

[10]I.e., evidential proofs, consisting here of documents and a witness deposition, as opposed to argumentative and rhetorical proofs (*entechnoi pisteis*); see Arist., *Rhetoric* 1.2, 15.

of Micion from the bathhouse (5.22–24) and the swindling of Protarchides (5.26–27); the injustice of Dicaeogenes III and Leochares,
as evidenced by the affair of the arbitration (5.31–34); and the meanness and cowardice of Dicaeogenes III, as demonstrated by his public and private actions, in contrast to the record of the speaker's ancestors (5.35–47). Isaeus pulls out the rhetorical stops[11] as the speech
reaches its climax in a comparison of Dicaeogenes III with his ancestors, the tyrant slayers, ending it forcefully with a direct address to
him and so dispensing with an epilogue.

About twenty-two years had elapsed between the death of Dicaeogenes II and the trial (cf. 5.7, 35). If Dicaeogenes II died in 411
(see above), this dates the trial to ca. 389, which is consistent with the
claim that Dicaeogenes III sent Cephisodotus to Corinth (5.11, i.e.,
during the Corinthian War of 395–386) and with the references to
the capture of Lechaeum (5.37) and the long war being fought by the
Olynthians and islanders (5.46). Wevers' dating system also favors
389 (Wevers 1969: 16).

5

[1] We thought, gentlemen, that in our dispute with Dicaeogenes
the agreement we reached in court would be valid; and so, when
Dicaeogenes relinquished two-thirds of the estate and provided sureties who pledged that he would give us this part without dispute,[12]
we renounced our claims against one another. But since, gentlemen,
Dicaeogenes is not carrying out his agreement, we are suing Leochares, as Dicaeogenes' surety, in accordance with our sworn affidavit.[13]
[2] Please read the affidavit.

[AFFIDAVIT]

Cephisodotus here knows our affidavit is true, and we'll produce
witnesses first that Dicaeogenes renounced two-thirds of the estate

---

[11]Note, e.g., the sudden apostrophe, rich and emotive vocabulary in 5.43
("wickedly and shamefully squandered"), and the *hypophora* in 5.45–46.

[12]On the meaning of "without dispute," see the Introduction.

[13]See 3.6n.

in our favor, and then that Leochares went surety for him. Please read the deposition.

[DEPOSITION]

[3] You have heard the witnesses, and I don't believe even Leochares himself would claim that their testimony was not true; but he will perhaps resort to the argument that Dicaeogenes has done everything he agreed he would do, and he himself has fulfilled his duty as surety. If he says this, he will be lying and will easily be refuted. The clerk will read you the inventory of what Dicaeogenes, the son of Menexenus, left behind in his estate and the money Dicaeogenes received.

[INVENTORY]

[4] If they deny that our uncle Dicaeogenes possessed this property in his lifetime and bequeathed it to us on his death, let them prove it; but if they say he did leave it and we have recovered it,[14] let somebody testify to this on their behalf. We are producing witnesses that Dicaeogenes agreed to give us the two-thirds of what the son of Menexenus left and that Leochares went surety for his doing this; this is the basis of our suit and is affirmed in our affidavit. Please read the affidavit.

[AFFIDAVIT]

[5] If, gentlemen, these were the only points on which Leochares or Dicaeogenes were going to defend themselves, what I have said would be enough; but since they are prepared to talk about the estate from the beginning, I want you to learn the facts from me as well, so that you may vote as seems best to you in full knowledge of the truth, without being deceived.

Our grandfather Menexenus[15] had one son, Dicaeogenes, and four daughters, one of whom was married to Polyaratus,[16] my father,

---

[14]The speaker admits to recovering some of the property in 5.22.

[15]Menexenus I was killed at Spartolus in 429 (cf. 5.42).

[16]Polyaratus of Cholargus was Assessor (Paredros) of the Hellenotamiae in 410/9 and Secretary of the Council in 405/4; he had two daughters and three sons. See Dem. 40.6, 24–25; Davies 1971: 461.

another to Democles of Phrearrhioi,[17] the third to Cephisophon[18]of
Paeania, while the fourth was the wife of Theopompus,[19] the father
of Cephisodotus. [6] Dicaeogenes sailed out as trierarch of the Paralus[20] but was killed in action at Cnidus.[21] He died childless, and
Proxenus,[22] the father of Dicaeogenes here, produced a will that our
fathers relied on when dividing up his estate.[23] According to the will,
Dicaeogenes here became the adopted son of our uncle Dicaeogenes,
the son of Menexenus, and inherited a third of the estate; and each
of the daughters of Menexenus was adjudicated a share of the rest.
For this I'll produce witnesses who were present at the time.

[WITNESSES]

[7] When they had divided up the estate, swearing not to violate
the agreement, they each possessed their share for twelve years; and
in all this time, although there were courts in session, none of them
thought of saying that what had been done was unjust until the time
when the city was faring badly and civil strife arose.[24] Then Dicaeogenes here was persuaded by Melas the Egyptian, whom he trusted
in everything else as well, to claim the entire estate from us, alleging
that he'd been adopted as sole heir by our uncle. [8] We thought he
was mad in making this claim, never imagining the same man could

---

[17]Democles was dead or divorced in 399 (cf. 5.9).

[18]Cephisophon was Secretary of the Council in 403/2 and Treasurer of Athena in 398/7; see Davies 1971: 148.

[19]Theopompus was dead by 399 (cf. 5.9).

[20]The Paralus and Salaminia were the sacred state triremes. As trierarch,
Dicaeogenes would have paid for the ship's outfitting and crew for a year.

[21]In 411; see above, n. 1.

[22]Proxenus of Aphidna was a Hellenotamias in 410/9; see Davies 1971: 476–
477.

[23]Menexenus III is speaking on behalf of himself and his two cousins, Menexenus II and Cephisodotus. Possibly, as Wyse (1904: 414) argued, Proxenus
came to an arrangement with the sisters' husbands, since Dicaeogenes III was
still a minor, but when Dicaeogenes became an adult, he insisted on the full
terms of the will being implemented.

[24]A reference to Athens' defeat in the Peloponnesian War and the rule of
the Thirty in 404/3, though the case did not in fact come to court until 399 (if
Dicaeogenes II died in 411).

at one time state that he'd been adopted as heir to one-third of the estate and at another time that he'd been adopted as sole heir, and that you would believe he was telling the truth. But on coming to court, even though we had far more to say and the juster case, we were wronged, not by the jurors but by Melas the Egyptian and his friends, who thought that the city's misfortunes gave them the license to possess other people's property and testify falsely for one another; and by acting in this way they deceived the jurors. [9] We became victims of false witness and lost our property, for my father died not long after the trial, before prosecuting the witnesses he had indicted. Dicaeogenes, after winning the verdict he wanted against us, on the very same day drove out of her share the wife of Cephisophon of Paeania, the sister of Dicaeogenes who left the money,[25] robbed the former wife of Democles of what her brother Dicaeogenes had left her, and also robbed the mother of Cephisodotus and Cephisodotus himself of everything they had.[26] [10] He was at the same time the guardian, legal representative (*kyrios*), and opponent of these people,[27] and yet he showed not the slightest degree of pity for them despite their relationship, but they became orphans, unprotected and penniless, and lacking all life's daily necessities. This is how Dicaeogenes here, their next of kin, behaved as their guardian; he handed over to their enemies what their father Theopompus left them and robbed for himself before any trial what my maternal uncle and my grandfather gave them. [11] Worst of all, while they were children, he bought their ancestral house and demolished it, turning it into a garden next to his own townhouse. And although he was receiving an income of eighty minas from the property of our uncle Dicaeogenes,

---

[25]The text here is much disputed, and I have adopted Buermann's emendations (which were rejected by Wyse). The manuscript reading "the daughter of Cephisophon of Paeania, the niece of Dicaeogenes II" would imply among other things that this girl's mother was dead in 399, but 5.18 and 20 suggest that she was alive then, while 5.16 implies that she was still alive at the time of the present trial. See further Edwards 2002.

[26]5.10–11 indicate that Cephisodotus was not an only child, and some words may have fallen out of the text here.

[27]I.e., of Cephisodotus and however many brothers or sisters he had.

he sent that man's nephew Cephisodotus to Corinth[28] with his own brother Harmodius in place of a servant; such was his insolence and brutality. And adding insult to injury, he criticized and derided him for wearing cheap shoes and a coarse woolen cloak, as if he were being wronged in some way by Cephisodotus wearing cheap shoes and had not wronged him by robbing him of his property and leaving him penniless.

[12] But that's enough about these matters; I'll now return to the point where I left off.[29] Menexenus, the son of Cephisophon and cousin to Cephisodotus here and me, had a right to the same share of the estate as I,[30] so he prosecuted the men who had testified falsely against us and him.[31] He first took Lycon to court and secured a conviction against him for testifying that the Dicaeogenes who is still alive had been adopted by our uncle as heir to the entire estate. [13] This was his testimony, and he was convicted of false witness. Then, since Dicaeogenes, gentlemen, could no longer deceive you, he persuaded Menexenus, who was acting for our sake as well as his (I'm ashamed but am forced by his depravity to mention it), to do—what? To take the share of the estate that was due him and to betray us, for whom he was acting, and release those witnesses who hadn't yet been convicted. And though we were treated like this by our friends and enemies, we took no action. I'll produce witnesses of this.

[WITNESSES]

[14] Now Menexenus got what he deserved for his behavior and was deceived by Dicaeogenes. He released the witnesses and betrayed us but received no reward for his services. Then, wronged by Dicaeogenes, he joined our side again. We now decided that Dicaeogenes no longer had the right to keep any part of the property from the estate, since his witnesses had been convicted, so we claimed the whole estate from him on the ground of kinship. And I can easily show

---

[28]I.e., during the Corinthian War.

[29]At the end of 5.9.

[30]Since Menexenus II had one brother and Menexenus III had two brothers, their individual shares were not in fact equal.

[31]Carrying out the intention of the speaker's father Polyaratus (5.9), between ca. 399 and ca. 389.

that we made the correct decision and Dicaeogenes no longer has any right to the estate. [15] Two wills were produced, one made long ago, the other much later; and under the old will that Proxenus, the father of Dicaeogenes here, produced, Dicaeogenes was to be the adopted son and heir to one-third of our uncle's estate, but under the will that Dicaeogenes himself produced, he was to be heir to the entire estate. Of these two wills Dicaeogenes persuaded the jurors that the one Proxenus produced was not genuine; but the men who testified that our uncle made the other one, which Dicaeogenes produced, were convicted of false witness. [16] Since both the wills were invalid and it was agreed that no other will existed, nobody had any claim on the estate as a bequest, but a claim on the ground of kinship was open to the sisters of the deceased Dicaeogenes, among whom are our mothers.[32] We therefore decided to claim the estate on the ground of kinship, and we each claimed our share. But when we were about to swear our affidavit,[33] Leochares here made a declaration[34] that the estate was not adjudicable to us.[35] [17] We in turn indicted Leochares, and the claim to the estate was struck off the case list, and the action for false witness was set for hearing. In court we made all the arguments that we are now making and Leochares defended himself at length, and the jurors decided that Leochares had given false testimony. When this became clear after the votes had been poured out of the urns,[36] I don't know what I need say about Leochares' appeals to the jurors and to us, or about the penalties we

---

[32]Those of Menexenus II, Menexenus III, and Cephisodotus.

[33]See 3.6n.

[34]By a *diamartyria*, on which, see the Introduction to Speech 2.

[35]On the ground that Dicaeogenes III had been adopted in his uncle's will, whose validity was challenged by his opponents.

[36]This seems to indicate that at the time of this trial, an older method of voting was still being used, in which there were two urns (one for acquittal, the other for condemnation). The juror placed his voting pebble in the desired urn, and it is hard to see how this can have been a secret vote. Later, the juror had two voting pebbles, bronze discs with a rod through the center that was either hollow (for condemnation) or solid (for acquittal). He cast his vote in a bronze urn, covering the ends of the rod with his thumb and forefinger for secrecy, and discarded the unwanted disc in a wooden urn.

could have exacted then, but listen to what we agreed. [18] We agreed
with the Archon that he would not count the votes but would mix
them together; Dicaeogenes relinquished two-thirds of the estate
to the sisters of Dicaeogenes and agreed to hand over these shares
to us without dispute; and Leochares here went surety for him that
he would carry out his agreement.[37] He was not the only surety,
but there was also Mnesiptolemus of Plotheia. And I'll produce witnesses of this.

[WITNESSES]

[19] After suffering this treatment by Leochares, although we could
have punished him with disfranchisement since we had won a verdict of false witness, we did not want this but were content to recover what belonged to us and be rid of him. But after acting in this
way towards Leochares and Dicaeogenes, they deceived us, gentlemen; for neither did Dicaeogenes give us the two-thirds of the estate, though he'd agreed to do this in court, nor does Leochares
admit that he went surety on that occasion. [20] And yet if he had
not gone surety before the jurors, five hundred of them, and before
the bystanders who were watching, I don't know what he would have
done.[38] To prove, then, that they are manifestly lying, we are producing as witnesses men who were present when Dicaeogenes relinquished the two-thirds of the estate and agreed to hand it over without dispute to the sisters of Dicaeogenes, and Leochares went surety
that he would actually carry out his agreement. And we beg of you
too, gentlemen, if any of you happened to be present then, to recol-
lect whether we are telling the truth and help us; [21] since, gentlemen, if Dicaeogenes is telling the truth, what did we gain by our
victory and what penalty did my opponent pay for his defeat? If he
merely relinquished the two-thirds of the estate (as he says) but did
not agree to hand it over without dispute, what penalty did he pay by
relinquishing property whose value he was still holding? Before he
lost the case he was not even in possession of the property we are suing him for, but the men who bought it from him or held it on mort-

---

[37]Dicaeogenes III (5.21) and Leochares (5.25) denied that they agreed on the
condition "without dispute."

[38]To avoid being punished for his false testimony.

gage, whom he should have paid off and then given us our share. [22] This is why we took sureties from him, because we didn't believe he would carry out his agreement. And we've recovered nothing except for two small buildings outside the walls and sixty *plethra* of land in the Plain,[39] but the men who mortgaged or bought it from him have possession. We are not trying to eject them, because we are afraid of losing our suits. We tried to eject Micion from the bathhouse when Dicaeogenes urged us to and assured us that he would not guarantee his title,[40] and we were fined forty minas, all on account of Dicaeogenes, gentlemen.[41] [23] We thought that he would not guarantee the title to any of the property that he relinquished to us in court, and so we pressed the case against Micion before the jurors, ready to face any consequences if Dicaeogenes guaranteed to him the title to the bathhouse, because we never thought that he would do the opposite to what he had agreed to do, for the sole reason that we had received the sureties. [24] But after relinquishing this share of the property, which he even now admits he relinquished to us, Dicaeogenes guaranteed Micion's title to the bathhouse. I was then in the miserable position of not only receiving nothing from the estate but of losing in addition forty minas, and I left court having been thoroughly abused by Dicaeogenes. And I'll produce witnesses of this.

[WITNESSES]

[25] This is the treatment we have received from Dicaeogenes, gentlemen; Leochares, the man who went surety for him and is to blame for all our troubles, denies that he went surety to the extent that the witnesses testified, claiming that it is not included in the document drawn up in court. At the time, gentlemen, we were in a hurry on

---

[39]The Plain of Athens, the valley of the Cephissus river. A *plethron* was the equivalent of something under 10,000 square feet (929 square meters); hence this figure is approximately equal to thirteen acres (55,740 square meters).

[40]As vendor, Dicaeogenes III will have guaranteed the title of the property and had an obligation to answer if the purchaser was evicted. We know nothing more about Micion or this affair.

[41]This may indicate that Menexenus III had lost a suit for ejectment (*dikē exoulēs*).

the platform,[42] wrote down some things and secured witnesses to others, but our opponents confirm the validity of only those parts of that agreement that are in their own interest, even if they are not in writing, and deny the validity of what is not in their interest, unless it is in writing. [26] But I, gentlemen, am not surprised that they deny their verbal agreements, since they are not even willing to carry out their written ones. And we'll provide yet another proof that we are telling the truth. Dicaeogenes gave his cousin's daughter[43] in marriage to Protarchides of Potamus with a dowry of forty minas, but instead of paying it in cash, he gave him his apartment block in the Ceramicus.[44] This woman, the wife of Protarchides, has a right to exactly the same share of the estate as my mother.[45] [27] Now when Dicaeogenes relinquished the two-thirds of the estate to the women, Leochares suggested that, as he was surety, Protarchides should hand over to him the apartment block he possessed in lieu of the dowry and receive from him his wife's share of the estate on her behalf. He then took over the apartment block but did not hand over the share. And I'll produce Protarchides as a witness of this.

[WITNESS]

[28] As for the repairs to the bathhouse and the building costs, Dicaeogenes has said previously and will perhaps say now again that we agreed to reimburse him his expenses but did not do so, and for this reason he cannot discharge his creditors or hand over what he owes us. [29] But, gentlemen, when we compelled him in court to relinquish this property, in consideration of his public services[46] and the

---

[42]The *bēma* from which litigants and witnesses addressed the court.

[43]This passage is obscure. It is uncertain which Dicaeogenes (II or III) was giving which woman, though she was almost certainly either the former wife of Democles (5.5, 9) or her daughter (as translated here). Nor is it clear how Leochares was able to persuade Protarchides to give up his wife's dowry (5.27), which was independent of her share in the estate. Was he in need of ready cash? See further Edwards 2002.

[44]The potters' quarter in northwest Athens.

[45]If the daughter of the former wife of Democles is meant, this remark implies that her mother was now dead.

[46]See 4.27n.

expenses he'd incurred on the buildings, we released him from paying the revenues from it, according to the decision of the jurors. Later, under no compulsion but of our own free will, we gave him the townhouse as a special gift on top of his third share of the estate in consideration of the repairs he'd carried out, and he sold this to Philonicus for 5,000 drachmas. [30] We gave it not because of Dicaeogenes' honesty, gentlemen, but to prove that we do not value money above our relatives, even if they are complete scoundrels. Even before, when we had the chance to punish Dicaeogenes by depriving him of what he had, we didn't want to acquire any of his property but were content merely to recover our own.[47] But when he had us in his power, he robbed us of everything he could and tried to ruin us, as if we were his enemies rather than his relatives.

[31] And we'll also provide strong proof of our ways compared with this man's injustice. When the suit against Leochares was about to be heard, gentlemen, in the month of Maemacterion,[48] Leochares and Dicaeogenes asked us to postpone the suit and submit the case to arbitration.[49] We agreed to this, as if we'd only suffered minor wrong, and submitted the case to four arbitrators, two of whom we nominated and two, they. And in the presence of these men we agreed to abide by their decision and took an oath. [32] The arbitrators said that if they could reconcile us without taking an oath, they would do so, otherwise they would take an oath themselves and declare what was in their view just. When the arbitrators had questioned us at length and learned the facts, the two I had proposed, Diotimus and Melanopus, were ready to declare either under oath or not what they regarded as the truest of the statements, but the ones Leochares had proposed refused to do so. [33] And yet Diopeithes, one of these two arbitrators, was the brother-in-law of Leochares here and was my enemy and opponent in other contract cases;[50] and his colleague Demaratus was a brother of Mnesiptolemus, who

---

[47]But cf. 5.14.

[48]Roughly, November.

[49]I.e., private arbitration, on which see Todd 1993: 123–125.

[50]This statement suggests that Menexenus III was no stranger to the courts. If so, he may have been born before 420. He was still active in 356, when he served as syntrierarch. See Davies 1971: 461–462.

acted as surety for Dicaeogenes with Leochares.[51] Even so, these men refused to make a declaration, although they had made us swear to abide by their decision. And I'll produce witnesses of this.

[WITNESSES]

[34] Isn't it extraordinary, gentlemen, if Leochares should beg you to acquit him when Diopeithes, his brother-in-law, condemned him?[52] So how can it be right for you to acquit Leochares of these charges, when not even his relatives acquitted him? I beg you therefore to condemn Leochares, so that we may recover what our ancestors left us and possess not only their names but also their property. Leochares' private property we do not covet.

[35] You have no just grounds, gentlemen, either to pity Dicaeogenes for suffering misfortune or poverty or to benefit him for providing some benefits for the city; he has no claim to either of these, as I will show, gentlemen. I'll prove that he is at the same time rich and the most wicked of men in dealing with the city, his relatives, and his friends. Through your verdict he acquired the estate, which brings in a yearly revenue of eighty minas,[53] and after enjoying it for ten years, he will not admit to saving any money nor can he show where he spent it, gentlemen. But you should think about this. [36] He was *chorēgos*[54] for his tribe at the Dionysia and came fourth, and was last in the tragic contest and Pyrrhic dances.[55] These were the only public services he performed, under compulsion, and he acted as *chorēgos* in this fine fashion despite his great wealth.[56] Moreover,

---

[51]Cf. 5.18.

[52]By not declaring in his favor.

[53]A suspiciously high sum.

[54]Another liturgy, so too the trierarchy below. See the Series Introduction, p. xxiii.

[55]The speaker refers to the tribal dithyrambic contests (where Dicaeogenes III came fourth out of ten), tragic choruses (last out of three), and the Warrior Dance at the Panathenaic festival (for which the number of competitors is unknown).

[56]The implication is that Dicaeogenes III's lack of success indicates he was miserly in the performance of his liturgies, but this does not necessarily follow.

although so many trierarchs were appointed, he neither acted as trierarch himself nor has he jointly contributed to a trierarchy with anybody else in these times of crisis,[57] while others with less capital than he has income have acted as trierarchs.[58] [37] And yet, gentlemen, it was not his father who left him his large fortune, but you gave it to him by your verdict, so that even if he were not a citizen, he would have been duty bound for this reason to benefit the city. Then, even though all the citizens have paid so many taxes for the war and the safety of the city,[59] Dicaeogenes hasn't contributed anything,[60] except that after the capture of Lechaeum,[61] when called on by another citizen, he pledged three hundred drachmas in the Assembly, less than Cleonymus the Cretan.[62] [38] He pledged this sum but didn't pay it, and his name was posted up on a most shameful list in front of the statues of the Eponymous Heroes,[63] headed "these men voluntarily promised the people to contribute money for the deliverance of the city but did not pay." So how can you be surprised, gentlemen, that he deceived me, a single person, when he acted in this way towards all you gathered together in the Assembly? And I'll produce witnesses of this.

[WITNESSES]

[39] These, then, are the number and kind of public services Dicaeogenes has performed for the city out of so large a fortune; with

---

[57]The Corinthian War.

[58]This seems to be an exaggeration. It is unlikely that a man whose property was worth less than three talents (180 minas) was subject to liturgies. See Davies 1971: xx–xxiv.

[59]See 4.27n.

[60]It is hard to believe that a man of Dicaeogenes III's wealth could have escaped paying *eisphorai* during the Corinthian War. Was he in financial difficulties, which might explain why parts of his estate were sold or mortgaged (5.21–22)?

[61]One of Corinth's harbors, captured by the Spartans in 392.

[62]And so not even an Athenian citizen.

[63]The heroes after whom the ten tribes were named. The statues stood near the Council chamber (Pausanias 1.5.1).

respect to his relatives, he's the kind of man you see: he robbed some of us of our property, because he was stronger; others he allowed to enter paid employment through lack of daily necessities.[64] Everybody saw his mother sitting in the temple of Eileithyia[65] and charging him with acts I am ashamed to mention, but he was not ashamed to perform. [40] Of his close friends he deprived Melas the Egyptian,[66] who had been his friend from boyhood, of money he'd received from him and is now his bitterest enemy; and of his other friends, some have not recovered money they lent him, others were deceived and never received what he'd promised to give them if the estate were adjudicated to him. [41] And yet, gentlemen, our ancestors who acquired and bequeathed this property performed all the choregic offices, contributed large sums of money to your war expenses, and never stopped acting as trierarchs. And as evidence of these services they set up dedications in the temples out of their remaining property as monuments to their civic virtue,[67] such as tripods in the sanctuary of Dionysus,[68] which they had received as winning *chorēgoi,* and others in the sanctuary of Pythian Apollo.[69] [42] Further, they dedicated on the Acropolis the first fruits of their goods and so have adorned the shrine with bronze and marble statues, a large number indeed, considering they are from a private fortune. They themselves died fighting for their country: Dicaeogenes, the father of Menexenus my grandfather, who was a general in the battle at Halieis;[70] Menexenus his son, a cavalry commander at Spartolus in the territory of Olyn-

---

[64]Hired laborers were at the bottom of the social scale, working alongside slaves and freedmen. It was not the manual labor itself that was despised, so much as the dependence on another, as a slave on a master.

[65]The goddess of childbirth. The implication seems to be that the mother was giving birth after an incestuous relationship with her son.

[66]Cf. 5.8.

[67]The surviving example of such a monument, which supported the tripod won as a prize, is the Choregic Monument of Lysicrates, dedicated in 335/4.

[68]Beside the theater.

[69]For prizes given at the Thargelia festival.

[70]I accept Dobree's emendation of "at Eleusis" (an unrecorded battle). The battle of Halieis took place in 460/59 (Thuc. 1.105.1).

thus;[71] Dicaeogenes, the son of Menexenus, in command of the Paralus at Cnidus.[72] [43] It's the estate of these men, Dicaeogenes, that you inherited and have wickedly and shamefully squandered, and after liquidating it you plead poverty. What did you spend it on? You obviously have not spent any of it on the city or your friends. You've certainly not spent it keeping horses—you've never owned a horse worth more than three minas—or keeping racing teams—since you've never even owned a pair of mules, despite your many farms and estates. Nor did you ever ransom a prisoner of war. [44] You have not even fetched the dedications to the Acropolis that Menexenus commissioned for three talents and died before setting them up[73] but they're still hanging around in the sculptor's workshop; and you yourself claimed possession of money that didn't belong to you at all but did not render to the gods the statues that were theirs. [45] On what grounds, then, do you think the jurors should acquit you, Dicaeogenes? Because you've performed numerous public services for the city and enhanced the majesty of their city by spending a lot of money? Or because as trierarch you've inflicted heavy losses on the enemy and by contributing taxes for the war bestowed great benefits on your country when it was in need? But you have done none of these things. [46] Or because you are a good soldier? But you haven't served in the course of this great long war, during which Olynthians and islanders are dying fighting the enemy in defense of this land, but you, Dicaeogenes, have not served at all, even though you are a citizen.[74] But perhaps you will claim to have an advantage over me through your ancestors, because they killed the tyrant.[75] I honor them, but I don't think you share one bit of their valor. [47] First, you chose to possess our property instead of their glory, and you were willing to be called son of Dicaeogenes rather than of

[71] In 429.

[72] Cf. 5.6.

[73] Dicaeogenes II, not Dicaeogenes III, ought to have set up these statues.

[74] The implication is that Dicaeogenes III was a draft dodger, but he would surely have been prosecuted if this were really the case.

[75] Dicaeogenes III's brother was named Harmodius (5.11), and their ancestor was one of the legendary tyrant slayers Harmodius and Aristogeiton, who assassinated Hipparchus in 514.

Harmodius, disdaining the right to dine in the Prytaneum and despising the seats of honor and tax exemptions granted to their descendants.[76] Further, the great Aristogeiton and Harmodius were honored not through their birth but through their bravery, in which you do not share at all, Dicaeogenes.

---

[76]The dining right was established by a decree, possibly passed in the 430s, but was restricted to the oldest living male descendants of each tyrannicide. Since it is probable (from the names of the brothers, the elder being named after his paternal grandfather) that Dicaeogenes III was the younger son of Proxenus, he would not have been entitled to share these privileges anyway. Michael Gagarin points out to me that Isaeus seems to be suggesting Dicaeogenes III chose to be adopted by Dicaeogenes II but had the choice of being adopted by Harmodius (we would then have to assume that Harmodius was much older than his brother and childless).

6. ON THE ESTATE OF PHILOCTEMON

❧❧❧

Euctemon of Cephisia, a wealthy landowner, had three sons, Philoctemon, Ergamenes, and Hegemon, and two daughters. The daughters were both married with children, but none of the sons had any offspring, and all three predeceased their father. Philoctemon was the last to survive, and before his death in action off Chios (6.27), probably during the 370s, he allegedly made a will in which he adopted his nephew Chaerestratus, the son of Phanostratus and one of his sisters. Chaerestratus, however, did not have the will recognized by a court, and when he claimed the estate on Euctemon's death at the age of ninety-six in 365/4 or 364/3, a rival claim was made by one of Euctemon's collateral relatives, Androcles (6.46, 55, 57). Androcles at some point tried to claim in marriage Euctemon's daughter, whose husband Chaereas had also died, on the basis that she was an heiress[1] and he was her next of kin. More crucially, he entered a declaration (*diamartyria*) that the estate was not liable to adjudication,

---

[1] It is unclear whether Androcles claimed the widow as the heiress to Euctemon or Philoctemon. If to the latter, it has been disputed whether she was technically classed as an *epiklēros*. Wyse (1904: 655–656) thought the title applied only to daughters; Harrison (1968: 138) conjectured that a sister was regarded as the heiress to her father, not her brother; but Menander's *Aspis* (ll. 138–143, 183–187, 269–273) suggests that a sister could become the *epiklēros* to her brother's estate. See MacDowell 1982: 48; V. J. Hunter, "Agnatic Kinship in Athenian Law and Athenian Family Practice: Its Implications for Women," in B. Halpern and D. W. Hobson (eds.), *Law, Politics and Society in the Ancient Mediterranean World* (Sheffield, 1993), 100–121 (esp. 108–110). This has implications for the legal position of the alleged heiress in Speech 10.

Stemma

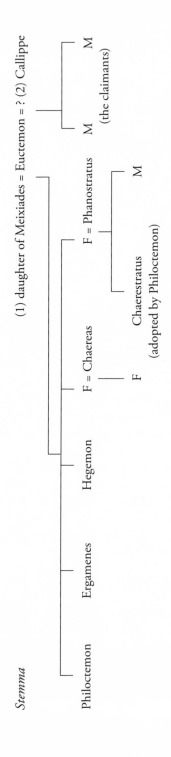

(1) daughter of Meixiades = Euctemon = ? (2) Callippe

Philoctemon   Ergamenes   Hegemon   F = Chaereas   F = Phanostratus

M   M
(the claimants)

M

F   Chaerestratus
(adopted by Philoctemon)

because Euctemon had had two other legitimate sons by a woman named Callippe, and these were alive; and he challenged the existence of Philoctemon's will. The older of Callippe's boys was no more than twenty (6.14), and so if Euctemon was his father, he would have been at least seventy-six when his son was born, but Euctemon had introduced him to his phratry as his legitimate son (6.21–24). Chaerestratus was therefore forced to prosecute Androcles and his associate Antidorus (6.39, 47) for false witness by a *dikē pseudomartyriōn,* and the present speech was delivered in support of this action by a friend of Chaerestratus' family (6.1–2), acting as an advocate (*synēgoros*). It is possible that his name was Aristomenes, by which he will be called here for the sake of convenience.[2]

Aristomenes adduces evidence to show that Philoctemon made a will (6.5–7) and has the law read out to the court demonstrating that Philoctemon had the right to make it (6.8–9). But Aristomenes concentrates on trying to disprove the legitimacy of Euctemon's two sons by Callippe (6.10–26), arguing that they were in fact the children of a prostitute named Alce by the freedman Dion. Alce, he claims, had seduced the old man when he visited the apartment block in Piraeus, which she managed for him, and collected the rent. She gained such a hold over him that he not only went to live with her, but she managed to persuade him to recognize the boys as his own. The members of Euctemon's phratry refused, however, to accept the older of the two when he tried to introduce him. Not surprisingly, his son Philoctemon also opposed the introduction, but he was maneuvered into agreeing to it on condition that the boy receive only a single farm. Thus, on his reintroduction the boy was admitted to the phratry.

A document, which Aristomenes calls a will (6.27), was drawn up ratifying Euctemon's arrangement with Philoctemon after the latter's death, but about two years later Androcles and Antidorus, on Alce's prompting, persuaded the old man to revoke the will. They further induced him to sell over three talents' worth of his property and plotted to secure the remainder of the estate by pretending to be the boys' guardians. They eventually succeeded in plundering more than half of Euctemon's fortune, and even went so far as to strip his house

---

[2]See Davies 1971: 564.

while he was lying dead in it. Among their other machinations, Aristomenes notes that Androcles' attempt to claim Euctemon's daughter as an heiress was inconsistent with his assertion that Euctemon had two sons. Finally, the characters of Alce and Androcles are attacked, in contrast to the public spiritedness of Chaerestratus and his father Phanostratus.

Aristomenes makes out a persuasive case on Chaerestratus' behalf, and this speech is a good example of effective Isaean rhetoric. But the potential weaknesses of the case are evident: it was Euctemon's estate that was in dispute, not Philoctemon's (despite the manuscript title of the speech), and Chaerestratus had never been legally recognized as Philoctemon's adopted son. By making two statements, that Euctemon had legitimate sons and that Philoctemon had not made a will, Androcles safeguarded his position (as the speech indicates at 6.52, 56–57): if Chaerestratus won this case, he would still have to establish his own exclusive claim to the estate; Androcles would contest the will and, as a relation of Euctemon, demand Chaereas' widow in marriage along with her share of the estate. There is also the interesting question as to why the fact that Euctemon's wife, the daughter of Meixiades (6.10), survived her husband (6.39–40) is not used to demonstrate that Euctemon cannot have married Callippe. Some have taken this to indicate the existence of "lawful concubinage" or even the possibility that polygamy was permitted after the Peloponnesian War. But it was not in Aristomenes' interest to admit that Euctemon had divorced his first wife (though 6.22 indicates his single status), thus opening up the possibility of a second marriage to Callippe.

Aristomenes opens with a brief proem (6.1–2), in which he explains his relationship with Chaerestratus' family (with a pathetic paradox in 6.2). Much of the speech is taken up with narrative, broken into sections, with facts stated simply and briefly and punctuated by sections of proof. The preliminary narrative (6.3–9) concerns Philoctemon and his will and is to some extent a diversionary tactic, concealing that Chaerestratus did not make his claim for some twenty years after Philoctemon's death, and when he did, the claim was to the estate of Euctemon.

The real issue is the legitimacy of Euctemon's two alleged sons, and this is dealt with in an extended main narrative, the longest in Isaeus (6.10–42). Aristomenes has already begun to show Androcles in a bad light (6.5), and the thrust of his argument is that if he would lie about the will, he would also lie about the two boys. Aristomenes immediately brings forward witnesses from unnamed relatives that Euctemon had never remarried or had more children by a second wife (6.10–11). The story of the opposition's inability to name the mother at the first hearing before the Archon follows, and to this suspicious ignorance is added the rough calculation that Callippe must already have been over thirty when she gave birth to the older of the two boys. Aristomenes turns next to his version of the boys' parentage, which centers on Euctemon's relationship with Alce. A friend telling the story to some extent spares the blushes of the family (cf. 6.17), and he narrates the first part of it in a tragic manner (6.18–24).[3]

The story is tested by a series of searching questions in apostrophe (6.25–26) and supported by witnesses, before the second part is told of how, after Philoctemon's death, Euctemon made his will and deposited it with Pythodorus but was then persuaded by the opponents (under Alce's influence) to revoke the document and began selling off his assets (6.27–34). More witnesses are summoned, then the third part of the story relates "the most dreadful scheme of all" (6.35): the opponents' plot to secure the rest of the by now incapacitated Euctemon's property by having the boys posthumously adopted as sons of Philoctemon and Ergamenes and themselves appointed as guardians; and their attempt to have Euctemon's properties leased to themselves, which was foiled by the intervention of some unnamed persons (6.35–37). After a further set of witness statements, the final stage of the narrative describes the opponents' appalling behavior in the emotional time after Euctemon's death, when they prevented the slaves from announcing the news of his demise, stripped his house of its furniture, and refused his wife and daughters entry (6.38–42): all this with Euctemon lying dead in the house—a vivid detail that is repeated (6.39, 41) and designed to make a deep impression on the jurors of the opponents' callousness. Witnesses are again adduced to round off this emotive narrative.

Some proofs follow that highlight the inconsistencies in Androcles' claim: after trying to register Alce's sons as the children of

---

[3] As Usher 1999: 151.

Philoctemon and Ergamenes, he now declares that they are the sons of Euctemon, contrary to the law[4] and to the previous decision of the jurors (which is not, of course, binding on this case; 6.44–45), and Androcles' claim to the widow of Chaereas runs counter to his testimony that Euctemon had a legitimate son (6.46). Isaeus paints the picture of a man who is desperate to get his hands on the property in any way he can, backed up by a shameless woman who treated Athens' religious ceremonies with contempt (6.48–50). Aristomenes concludes his proofs (6.51–61) with a series of arguments that are made more persuasive by numerous rhetorical devices: a comparison of the relative merits of the claimants and the precarious position of Chaereas' widow; confirmation of the validity of Philoctemon's will, with imaginary direct speech, rhetorical questions and emotive vocabulary ("shameless," "bitterest enemy," "depravity"); an attempt to arouse the jurors' indignation, with repetition of previous points, more rhetorical questions, appeals to the gods, a pathetic paradox and, most notably, a rare reference in the orators to the opponent's own rhetoric ("rhetorical digressions," 6.59); and finally a regular list of public services. In the epilogue (6.62–65) Aristomenes employs the tactic of trying to dictate, through the jurors, what the opponent must argue in his speech (note the repeated "order" in 6.62, 65): the issues are the opponents' declaration against the validity of Philoctemon's will and the legitimacy of the claimants. To the end, the emphasis on witnesses and the law is paramount.

The date of the speech is indicated by the remark in 6.14 that fifty-two years had passed since the departure of the Sicilian expedition (in summer 415): the trial must therefore have taken place (on Greek inclusive reckoning) in 365/4 or 364/3. A mid-fourth-century inscription with the name "Chaerestratus son of Phanostratus" (*IG* II².2825.11), not "son of Philoctemon," if it is indeed later than this speech,[5] indicates that despite Isaeus' skills, Chaerestratus lost the case.

6

[1] I think most of you know, gentlemen, that I am the closest of friends with Phanostratus and Chaerestratus here, but for those who

---

[4]But see below, 6.44n.
[5]For this view, see Thompson 1970: esp. 2–4.

do not know I will give sufficient proof. When Chaerestratus[6] set sail for Sicily as trierarch, I knew in advance from sailing there previously myself all the dangers there would be, but nevertheless at their request I sailed out with him and shared his misfortune, as we were captured by the enemy. [2] It would be strange if at that time I endured those things despite the foreseen dangers because I was close to them and considered them my friends, but now did not try to speak in their support to ensure that you will vote according to your oath and they will be treated justly. I beg you, therefore, to indulge me and listen with goodwill: the suit is no minor matter for them but is of the utmost importance.

[3] Philoctemon of Cephisia was a friend of Chaerestratus here and died leaving him his property and adopting him as his son.[7] Chaerestratus claimed the estate in accordance with the law.[8] But any Athenian who wished could make a claim, enter a direct action (*euthydikia*) before you and, if he should seem to be making the juster case, gain possession of the estate. [4] Androcles here thus made a declaration[9] that the estate was not adjudicable, so depriving my friend of his claim and you of your authority to decide who should be the heir to Philoctemon's property. And he thinks that by a single verdict and a single suit he will make men who are not related to Philoctemon at all into his brothers, will possess the estate himself without having to go to law, will become the legal representative (*kyrios*) of the deceased's sister,[10] and will make the will invalid. [5] Androcles

---

[6]Many editors read Phanostratus, taking this as a reference to the Sicilian expedition of 415–413. But since Chaerestratus is still young (6.60) and it is fifty-two years since the beginning of the expedition (6.14), he cannot have asked the speaker to sail there with Phanostratus (cf. "at their request"). Some other expedition must be referred to (perhaps in 366/5; see Davies 1971: 564), and Chaerestratus' acting as trierarch is confirmed by 6.60.

[7]If Philoctemon died in the 370s, Chaerestratus (born ca. 390) will have been in his mid to late teens when he was adopted.

[8]By a *diadikasia* (inheritance claim) in the case of a testamentary adoption.

[9]By a *diamartyria,* on which see Introduction to Speech 2.

[10]I.e., the widow of Chaereas (6.6, 51), who had reverted to the control of her father on her husband's death. Androcles would become her *kyrios* only if the two boys were both minors, but cf. 6.14.

has made a number of extraordinary declarations, but I will prove this point to you first, that Philoctemon made a will and adopted Chaerestratus here as his son. Since Philoctemon had no child by the woman he was married to and since he faced considerable danger because it was wartime and he was both serving in the cavalry and frequently sailing as a trierarch,[11] he thought he should dispose of his property by will, so as not to leave his family without an heir if anything should happen to him. [6] He had two brothers who both died childless, and of his two sisters, one, who was the wife of Chaereas, had no male child and had never had one in many years of marriage, but the other, who was the wife of Phanostratus here, had two sons. The older of these, Chaerestratus here, he adopted as his son; [7] and he wrote in the will that if he should have no child by his wife, this man was to inherit his property. He then deposited the will with his brother-in-law Chaereas, the husband of his other sister. And this will will be read to you and those who were present will testify. Please read.

[WILL. WITNESSES]

[8] You've heard that he made a will and on what conditions he adopted this man as his son. To prove that he was entitled to do this, I'll produce to you the actual law, which in my opinion is the most correct place to learn about such matters. Please read it.

[LAW]

[9] This law, gentlemen, is common to everybody and entitles a man to dispose of his own property by will, providing he has no legitimate male children, and providing he does so when he is neither insane nor senile nor out of his mind through any of the other reasons listed in the law.[12] That Philoctemon was not in any of these conditions, I'll show you in a few words. For how could anybody dare to say that a man who all his life showed himself to be such a

---

[11]The war against the Thebans (378–371) may be meant. The Athenian cavalry fought in Boeotia in 377/6 (Diod. 15.32.2), but the naval operations referred to are unknown.

[12]See the Introduction to Speech 2.

good citizen that through your esteem he was chosen for command, and who died fighting the enemy, was not of sound mind?

[10] It has been proved to you, then, that he was of sound mind when he made a will and adopted a son, as he was entitled to do, and consequently it has been proved that Androcles gave false testimony on this point. But since he has further stated in his declaration that my opponent is a legitimate son of Euctemon, I will prove that this too is false. Gentlemen, the real sons of Philoctemon's father Euctemon, Philoctemon, Ergamenes, and Hegemon, and his two daughters and their mother, Euctemon's wife, the daughter of Meixiades of Cephisia, are known to all their relatives and members of his phratry and to most of his demesmen, and they will testify to you. [11] But nobody at all knows or ever heard during Euctemon's lifetime that he married some other wife, who became mother of my opponents by him.[13] And yet it's reasonable to think these people are most trustworthy witnesses, since relatives ought to know such things. So please call these people first and read their depositions.

[DEPOSITIONS]

[12] Next, I'll prove that even my opponents have by their actions testified to this point.[14] When the preliminary hearings were being held before the Archon and my opponents had paid the deposit on their claim that these were legitimate sons of Euctemon,[15] when we asked them the names of their mother and of her father, they couldn't say, although we protested, and the Archon ordered them to reply in accordance with the law. And yet it was strange, gentlemen, that they entered a claim alleging they were legitimate sons and made a declaration but could not say who their mother was or name any of their relatives. [13] At the time they alleged she was a Lemnian[16] and secured an adjournment; later, when they returned to the pre-

---

[13]But Euctemon had introduced the older boy to his phratry (6.21–24), and so must have named the mother and claimed that she was his wife.

[14]For this type of argument, cf. 2.38 and n.

[15]See 4.4n.

[16]I.e., the daughter of an Athenian *cleruch* (settler) on the island of Lemnos, and so an Athenian citizen. This would provide a reason why they did not know much about her or her family.

liminary hearing, even before anybody could ask a question, they immediately said that Callippe was the mother, and that she was the daughter of Pistoxenus, as if it were enough for them merely to produce the name Pistoxenus. When we asked who he was and if he was alive or not, they said that he had died on military service in Sicily, leaving behind this daughter at Euctemon's house, who had the children by her when she was his ward, an invented tale going beyond shamelessness and quite untrue, as I'll prove to you first from the answers they themselves gave. [14] It's now fifty-two years since the expedition set sail for Sicily in the archonship of Arimnestus,[17] but the older of these alleged sons of Callippe and Euctemon is not yet more than twenty years old. If we deduct these, more than thirty years remain since the Sicilian expedition, and so Callippe should no longer have been a ward, if she was thirty years old, nor should she have been unmarried and childless but long since married, either betrothed in accordance with the law or assigned by adjudication.[18] [15] Furthermore, she must necessarily have been known to Euctemon's relatives and slaves, if she really had been married to him or lived for such a long time in his house. It's not enough merely to provide these facts at the preliminary hearing, but their truth must be made clear, and testimony must be given by the relatives. [16] Again, when we demanded that they state who of Euctemon's family knew of any Callippe who was married to him or was his ward, and that they interrogate our servants or hand over to us any of their slaves who said they knew about this, they refused to take any of ours or hand over to us any of theirs.[19] Now please take their reply and our depositions and challenges.

[REPLY. DEPOSITIONS. CHALLENGES]

[17] My opponents, then, avoided so decisive a test; but I will show you who these men are and where they're from, whom my opponents

---

[17]This remark serves to date the speech; see the Introduction.

[18]A reasonable calculation and inference, as long as the opponents really mean that Pistoxenus died on the Sicilian expedition of 415–413. Athenian girls normally married in their teens.

[19]The challenge to torture slaves was a standard procedure whose equally standard refusal was used to make rhetorical gain.

have declared to be legitimate and are seeking to establish as heirs to Euctemon's property. It's perhaps distasteful to Phanostratus, gentlemen, to make Euctemon's misfortunes manifest, but a few things must be said, so that knowing the truth you may more easily vote for what's just.

[18] Euctemon lived till he was ninety-six, and for most of this time he seemed to be quite happy—he had a considerable fortune, children, and a wife, and in other respects fared reasonably well. But in his old age he suffered a great misfortune that ruined his entire household, cost him a great deal of money, and set him at odds with his closest relatives. [19] How and where this started I'll show you as briefly as I can. He had a freedwoman, gentlemen, who managed an apartment block of his in Piraeus and kept prostitutes. One of those she acquired was named was Alce, and I think many of you know her. After her purchase this Alce lived in the brothel for many years but retired from the profession when she became too old. [20] While she was living in the brothel, a freedman by the name of Dion slept with her, and she said he was the father of these boys; and Dion did indeed bring them up as his own children. Some time later Dion committed a crime and fearing for himself departed for Sicyon; and Euctemon set up this woman Alce as manager of his apartment block in Ceramicus,[20] near the back gate where wine is on sale. [21] Her establishment there was the start of many evils, gentlemen. Euctemon regularly went there for the rent and would spend much of his time in the apartment block; sometimes he even dined with the woman, abandoning his wife and children and the house he lived in. Despite the protests of his wife and sons, he not only didn't stop going there but in the end he lived there completely, and he was reduced to such a state either by drugs or disease or something else that she persuaded him to introduce the older of the two boys to the members of his phratry under his own name. [22] But when his son Philoctemon would not agree to this and the members of his phratry would not admit the boy, and the sacrificial victim was removed from the altar, Euctemon was angry with his son and wanted to insult him. So he became engaged to a sister of Democrates of Aphidna,[21] with the in-

---

[20]See 5.26n.
[21]A well-known politician and wit (cf. Aesch. 2.17; Hyp. 2.2–3).

tention of recognizing her children and bringing them into his family, unless Philoctemon agreed to allow this boy to be introduced. [23] His relatives, knowing that he would not have any more children at his time of life, but that they would appear in some other way and as a result there would be still greater disputes, persuaded Philoctemon, gentlemen, to allow the introduction of this boy on the terms that Euctemon sought, giving him a single plot of land. [24] And Philoctemon, ashamed at his father's folly but at a loss how to cope with the problem he faced, made no objection. But when this agreement was made and the child was introduced on these terms, Euctemon got rid of the woman, showing that he had not been planning to marry to produce children but to introduce this child. [25] For why did he need to marry, Androcles, if these were his children by an Athenian woman (*astē*), as you have testified? Who could have prevented him from introducing them if they were legitimate? And why did he introduce him on set conditions, when the law prescribes that all the legitimate sons have an equal share in their patrimony? [26] And why did he introduce the older of the two boys on set conditions but not say a word to Philoctemon while he was alive or to his relatives about the younger one, even though he was already born? Yet you have now expressly testified that they are legitimate and heirs to Euctemon's property. To prove I'm telling the truth in this, read the depositions.

[DEPOSITIONS]

[27] After this, then, Philoctemon was killed by the enemy while serving as trierarch off Chios.[22] Some time later Euctemon told his sons-in-law that he wanted to write down the arrangement he'd made with his son and deposit it for safekeeping. Phanostratus was about to set sail as trierarch with Timotheus,[23] his ship was anchored at Munichia,[24] and his brother-in-law Chaereas was there saying goodbye to him. Euctemon took some people with him and came

---

[22]See the Introduction.

[23]Usually dated to 376/5 or 374/3 (see, e.g., Develin 1989: 238–239, 244), but due to the young age of the boy, perhaps rather in 367/6. See Thompson 1970: 1–2.

[24]One of Athens' harbors, on the east of the peninsula at Piraeus.

to where the ship was anchored, and after drawing up a will[25] detailing the conditions under which he introduced the boy, deposited it in the presence of these men with his relative Pythodorus of Cephisia. [28] And this very action is sufficient proof, gentlemen, that Euctemon was not acting as with legitimate children, as Androcles has testified, since nobody records in a will any bequest of anything to his own natural sons, because the law itself assigns a father's property to his son and does not even allow someone who has legitimate children to make a will.[26]

[29] When the document had been deposited for almost two years and Chaereas had died, my opponents fell under the influence of that woman and, seeing that the estate was going to ruin and that Euctemon's old age and folly afforded them an ideal opportunity, made a concerted attack. [30] First they persuaded Euctemon to annul the will on the ground that it was not advantageous to the boys; for nobody would have a right to the visible property[27] when Euctemon died other than his daughters and their offspring; but if he sold part of the property and left a sum of money, they would get a secure hold on it. [31] Euctemon listened and immediately demanded the document back from Pythodorus and served him a summons for the discovery of objects.[28] When Pythodorus appeared before the Archon, Euctemon said that he wanted to annul the will. [32] Pythodorus agreed with him and Phanostratus, who was present, that it should be annulled, but since Chaereas, who had been one of the depositaries, had an only daughter, he thought it should not be annulled until her legal representative had been appointed, and the Archon so decided. Euctemon, after making this agreement in the presence of

---

[25]Aristomenes uses the word *diathēkē*, which regularly means "will" but here seems in fact to be an agreement between Euctemon and his sons-in-law. Hence, after Chaereas' death (6.29) Pythodorus required the agreement of a representative of Chaereas' daughter before the document's destruction (6.32).

[26]Cf. 10.9. This may have been the letter of the law, but fathers with legitimate sons did make dispositions. See Harrison 1968: 151–152; Rubinstein 1993: 83–85.

[27]I.e., the real estate.

[28]For the *dikē eis emphanōn katastasin,* cf. Lost Speech III. Further on this procedure, see Harrison 1968: 207–210.

the Archon and his assistants, called numerous witnesses to see that his will was no longer deposited and went away. [33] In a very short space of time—the reason why my opponents persuaded him to destroy the will—he sold a farm at Athmonon[29] for seventy-five minas to Antiphanes and the bathhouse at Serangion[30] for 3,000 drachmas to Aristolochus; and he arranged a mortgage of forty-four minas on a house in the city with the hierophant.[31] Further, he sold some goats with their goatherd for thirteen minas and two pairs of mules, one for eight minas, the other for 550 drachmas, and all the slave craftsmen he had. [34] In all, more than three talents' worth was sold as quickly as possible after the death of Philoctemon. And to prove I'm telling the truth in this, I'll first call the witnesses for each of my statements.

[WITNESSES]

[35] This part of his property was handled in this way; and then they immediately began plotting about the rest, and they came up with the most dreadful scheme of all, to which you should pay close attention. Seeing that Euctemon was completely debilitated by old age and could not even get out of bed, they began looking for a way to get their hands on his property when he died. [36] So what did they do? They registered these two boys with the Archon as being adopted by the deceased sons of Euctemon,[32] putting themselves down as their guardians, and they asked the Archon to lease out the houses as belonging to orphans, so that some of the property might be leased in their names and some might stand as security with mortgage stones placed on it, while Euctemon was still alive, and that they themselves might become lessees and obtain the income. [37] And the first time the courts sat, the Archon put the lease up for auction, and they offered to take it on. But certain persons present reported the plot to the relatives, who came and revealed the affair to the jurors, and so they voted not to lease out the houses. If

---

[29]About seven miles northeast of Athens.

[30]At Munichia. The baths have been discovered.

[31]An official at the Eleusinian Mysteries who displayed the sacred symbols and figures.

[32]Philoctemon and Ergamenes (cf. 6.44).

the plot had not been uncovered, the whole property would have been lost. Please call those who were present as witnesses.

[WITNESSES]

[38] Now, before my opponents made the woman's acquaintance and plotted with her against Euctemon, Euctemon and his son Philoctemon possessed such a large fortune that both of them at the same time performed the most expensive public services for you without selling any of their assets and even saved some of their income, so that their wealth continually increased. But when Philoctemon died, the fortune was managed in such a way that less than half the capital remained and all the income had vanished. [39] And they were not even content with plundering this much, gentlemen, but when Euctemon also died, they had the effrontery to shut in the slaves, while he was lying dead inside, so that none of them could announce the news to his two daughters or his wife or any of his relatives; and with the woman's help they moved the furniture that was inside to the house next door, which one of these people, that man Antidorus, was leasing and living in. [40] And not even when the daughters and wife arrived after hearing the news from others, not even then did they allow them to enter but shut the door on them, declaring it was none of their business to bury Euctemon. They were only able to enter with considerable difficulty about sunset. [41] On entering, they found that he was lying inside dead for the second day, as the slaves said, and that everything in the house had been removed by these people. So the women, as was right, attended to the deceased, while my friends immediately showed the men who'd accompanied them the state inside the house and, in the presence of our opponents, first asked the slaves where the furniture had been taken. [42] When they said our opponents had carried it off to the next house, my friends immediately claimed the legal right to search it and demanded the surrender of the slaves who had carried out the removal, but they refused to accede to any of their just demands. And to prove I'm telling the truth, take and read these depositions.

[DEPOSITIONS]

[43] So then, they removed all this furniture from the house, sold all this property keeping the proceeds, and in addition plundered the

income that accumulated in that period, and now they think they will gain control of the rest as well. They are so shameless that although not daring to proceed by a direct action (*euthydikia*), they made a declaration (*diamartyria*) as if the children were legitimate, which was at once false and contrary to their own previous actions: [44] for although they registered the boys with the Archon, one as the son of Philoctemon, the other of Ergamenes, they have now made a declaration that they are both Euctemon's. Yet even if they were legitimate sons of Euctemon and had been adopted, as our opponents said, even so they cannot be called the sons of Euctemon, since the law does not allow an adopted son to return to his original family unless he leaves behind a legitimate son in his adoptive family.[33] So even on the basis of their own actions their testimony is necessarily false. [45] And if they had contrived on that occasion to have the houses leased, my friends would no longer have been able to claim them; but as it is, the jurors voted against them, deciding that they did not have the right to do this, and they have not even dared to enter a claim, but instead they cap their shamelessness by now testifying that the men you rejected are his heirs.

[46] Furthermore, consider the effrontery and shamelessness of the actual witness, who has claimed for himself the daughter of Euctemon,[34] alleging that she is an heiress,[35] and that a fifth[36] of Euctemon's estate should be adjudicated to her, but has also testified that Euctemon has a legitimate son. And yet how does he not clearly convict himself of giving false testimony? For obviously if Euctemon had a legitimate son, his daughter would not be an heiress, nor would the estate be adjudicable. To prove, then, that he made these claims, the clerk will read you the depositions.

[DEPOSITIONS]

---

[33]In this case, of course, the boys were not in fact being adopted out of their family into another one, but the adoption would make them Euctemon's grandsons instead of his sons.

[34]I.e., the widow of Chaereas (cf. 6.51).

[35]See above, n. 1.

[36]There is no legal reason why he should have claimed a fifth, and editors agree that the text is corrupt here.

[47] The opposite has happened, then, to what the law prescribes: by law no male or female bastard has had any right based on kinship to share in a family's cults or property since the archonship of Eucleides,[37] but Androcles and Antidorus think they have a right to deprive Euctemon's legitimate daughters and their offspring and to possess the estate of both Euctemon and Philoctemon. [48] And the woman who destroyed Euctemon's mind and got her hands on a great deal of property is so insolent with the complete support of these men that she treats not only Euctemon's relatives with contempt but the whole city. You have to hear only one example and you'll easily realize the woman's disregard of the law. Please take this law.

[LAW] [38]

[49] These are the terms, gentlemen, so solemn and revered, in which you framed the law, attaching great importance to behaving with reverence towards these goddesses[39] and the other gods. But although the mother of these young men was admittedly a slave who'd lived her whole life in shame [50] and should never have gone into the temple or seen any of the activities inside, she had the audacity to accompany the procession when a sacrifice was being made to these goddesses, enter the temple, and see what she was not entitled to see. You will learn that I'm telling the truth from the decrees that the Council passed about her. Take the decree.

[DECREE]

[51] You must consider then, gentlemen, whether this woman's son should be heir to Philoctemon's estate and go to the tombs to pour libations and offer sacrifices, or my friend, the son of his sister and the one he himself adopted; and whether the sister of Philoctemon, who was married to Chaereas but is now a widow, should fall into the power of our opponents either to be married to anybody they wish or to be allowed to grow old a widow, or whether as a

---

[37] 403/2. Pericles' citizenship law of 451/0 similarly restricted bastards; it is not clear why a new law was enacted in 403/2.

[38] Presumably the law that excluded slaves and immoral women from participating in the Thesmophoria (on which cf. 3.80 and n).

[39] Demeter and Persephone (Kore).

legitimate daughter she should be assigned by your adjudication to marry whomsoever you think fit.⁴⁰ [52] This is what your verdict is about today. Their declaration (*diamartyria*) has the purpose of putting all the risk on my friends, while even if our opponents lose the case today and the estate is deemed adjudicable, they may enter a counter-claim and contest the same property twice. Yet if Philoctemon made a will when he was not entitled to, they should have made a declaration on this very point, that he was not legally entitled to adopt this man as his son.⁴¹ But if he was entitled to make a will and our opponent's claim is that he made no bequest or will, he should not have obstructed proceedings by a declaration (*diamartyria*), but should have proceeded by a direct action (*euthydikia*). [53] As it is, how could he be more clearly convicted of giving false testimony than if somebody were to ask him, "Androcles, how do you know that Philoctemon did not make a will or adopt Chaerestratus as his son?" It is right, gentlemen, in cases in which a person was present, for him to give evidence, and in cases in which he was not present but heard from somebody else, for him to give hearsay evidence; [54] but you, though not present, have expressly given evidence that Philoctemon did not make a will but died childless. But how can he possibly know this, gentlemen? It's as if he said he knew everything you all do even though he was not present. Shameless as he is, surely he's not going to say he was present at everything and knows everything Philoctemon accomplished in his life? [55] Philoctemon regarded him as his bitterest enemy, both because of his general depravity and because he alone of his relatives, along with that woman Alce and in concert with this man⁴² and the others, plotted against Euctemon's property and contrived the kinds of things I've described to you.

---

⁴⁰But if Chaerestratus should secure the estate as the adopted son of Philoctemon, Chaereas' widow would not be an heiress or subject to the court's control.

⁴¹Philoctemon was, of course, perfectly entitled to adopt Chaerestratus, since he had no children. He could not, however, leave him the whole estate if the two boys were legitimate.

⁴²I.e., Antidorus. According to 6.27–29, 38, the plotting started after Philoctemon's death.

[56] But what upsets me the most is when our opponents abuse the name of Euctemon, my friend's grandfather. If, as they claim, Philoctemon was not entitled to make a will and the estate is Euctemon's, who has a better right to inherit Euctemon's property, his daughters who are admitted to be legitimate and we who are their sons[43] or those who are in no way related, [57] who are proved so not only by us but also by their own actions as guardians? I beg and earnestly supplicate you to remember, gentlemen, what I described to you just now, that Androcles here says he's the guardian of our opponents whom he alleges are the legitimate sons of Euctemon but has himself claimed for himself Euctemon's estate and his daughter as heiress; and you have heard testimony to this effect. [58] But by the Olympian gods, isn't it extraordinary, gentlemen, that if the children are legitimate, their guardian should claim Euctemon's estate and his daughter as heiress for himself, and if they are not legitimate, that he should have testified just now that they are? This is self-contradictory. Therefore, he is proved to have given false testimony not only by us but by his own actions. [59] Moreover, nobody is making a declaration against him that the estate is not adjudicable, but although this man was entitled to proceed by a direct action, he is now depriving everybody else of their claim. He expressly testified that the children are legitimate, and he thinks you will be content with rhetorical digressions, and that if he doesn't even attempt to prove this or only mentions it briefly, but abuses us in a loud voice and says that my friends are rich while he is poor, this will make you think that the children are legitimate. [60] But my friends' fortune, gentlemen, is being spent more on the city than on themselves. Phanostratus has already been trierarch seven times; he's performed all the public services and has in most cases won victories. Chaerestratus here, despite his youth, has been trierarch, *chorēgos* in tragic contests and gymnasiarch at the torch race. Both have paid all the war taxes as members of the three hundred.[44] For a while only the two paid, but now the younger son here is also *chorēgos* in tragic contests, has been registered among the three hundred, and pays the war taxes.

---

[43]Aristomenes is only a friend of Chaerestratus (cf. 6.1), but (if the text is sound) he associates himself with the two brothers.

[44]The wealthiest citizens (cf. Dem. 18.171).

[61] So you should not begrudge them, but far rather these people, by Zeus and Apollo, if they get what does not belong to them. If Philoctemon's estate is adjudicated to my friend, he will manage it in your interests, performing the requisite public services as he does now and still more; but if these people get it, they will squander it and then plot against others.

[62] I therefore beg you, gentlemen, to pay close attention to the declaration you are going to vote on, so that you won't be misled. Order him to make his defense on this declaration just as we have based our prosecution on it. It is written in the declaration that Philoctemon made no bequest or will: this has been proved to be false, as the people who were present testify that he did. [63] What else do they say? That Philoctemon died childless. How was he childless when he adopted his own nephew as his son and was survived by him, to whom the law gives the same right of inheritance as children born of him? Indeed, it is expressly written in the law that if children are later born to a man who has adopted, each takes his share of the property and both kinds of children inherit equally. [64] So let Androcles prove that these children are legitimate, as each of you would have to do. Just by stating a mother's name he does not make them legitimate, but he must prove that he's telling the truth by producing the relatives who know she was married to Euctemon and his demesmen and phratry members, to testify if they have ever heard or know anything about Euctemon performing public services on her behalf, and further where she is buried, in what tomb, [65] and who saw Euctemon performing the customary rites. Where, moreover, her sons still go to offer sacrifices and pour libations, and which citizen or slave of Euctemon saw these things. All this is proof, but abuse is not. And if you order him to prove the matter he actually made the declaration about, you will pass a verdict that accords with your oath and the laws, and justice will be done for my friends.

7. ON THE ESTATE OF APOLLODORUS

〰〰〰

The brothers Eupolis, Mneson, and Thrasyllus I jointly inherited a large estate from their father, who was probably named Apollodorus.[1] Mneson died childless, and Thrasyllus died on the Sicilian expedition of 415–413, leaving a son, Apollodorus II, who was a minor and therefore came under the guardianship of his uncle, Eupolis. According to the speaker, Eupolis misappropriated the whole of Mneson's estate, half of which belonged by law to Apollodorus, and embezzled his nephew's property. Meanwhile, Apollodorus' mother had remarried, and her second husband, Archedamus, brought him up in his own house. When Apollodorus reached the age of majority, Archedamus helped him win two lawsuits against Eupolis, securing his share of Mneson's estate and the restoration of three talents. In return, Apollodorus aided Archedamus after the latter had been taken prisoner of war; later, when he was himself about to serve in the Corinthian War (395–386), Apollodorus made a will leaving his estate to his half-sister, Archedamus' daughter, and arranging her marriage. But this will did not come into effect, because Apollodorus survived the war and in due course had a son of his own. The son died the year before this trial, however, and since Apollodorus was by now at least sixty, he determined to adopt a son.

The obvious choice, given his enmity towards Eupolis' family, was his half-sister's son, Thrasyllus II (the speaker). Apollodorus presented Thrasyllus to his *genos* (descent group) and phratry at the Thargelia festival of 355,[2] but he died before Thrasyllus had been registered in

---

[1]Since both Eupolis and Thrasyllus so named their sons.

[2]On this procedure, see Andrewes 1961: 5–6.

Stemma

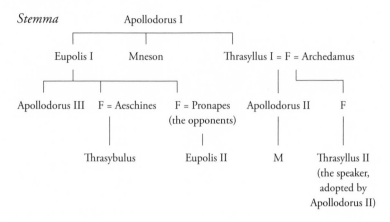

his deme though the demesmen subsequently admitted him to the list, against the protests of Apollodorus' first cousin, the daughter of Eupolis who was married to Pronapes. Through her husband she challenged the validity of the adoption and claimed Apollodorus' estate by a *diadikasia* (inheritance claim). Another potential claimant was Thrasybulus, the son of Eupolis' other daughter (who was also now dead); but he did not make a claim, because (according to Thrasyllus) he was satisfied that the adoption was legal (7.21) or because (according to the opponents) he had lost his rights through being adopted into another family (7.23).

The cousin's claim seems, on the face of it, to be a piece of opportunism, an attempt through a technicality to get her hands on the sizeable fortune of a man who had long been at odds with her side of the family. It is hard to imagine that Pronapes will have disputed in court that Apollodorus had fully intended to go through with the adoption; he may have argued that the old man had come under the influence of a woman and so the adoption was invalid, though Thrasyllus makes no direct mention of this (he perhaps hints at it at 7.36). Nevertheless, it is clear that the proper formalities of adoption had not been completed when Apollodorus died, and Pronapes may well have entered a claim immediately. Thrasyllus was left in an awkward position: he could not enter a declaration (*diamartyria*) that the estate was not adjudicable because there was a legitimate son; and he had not been adopted by a will, nor was he the next of kin (since in Athenian law kin on the father's side took precedence over kin on the mother's side, and Thrasyllus was in any case only Apollodorus' half-nephew, being the son of his half-sister, not his nephew). He therefore emphasizes the affection between the families of Apollodorus and Archedamus and the hostility between Apollodorus and Eupolis; and he describes at length the measures that Apollodorus took to adopt him before his death. He also highlights how his opponents had allowed the family of Apollodorus III, the son of Eupolis and brother of Pronapes' wife, to become extinct, a danger he claims was now threatening the house of Apollodorus II as well. It seems, then, that the law favored the wife of Pronapes, but equity favored Thrasyllus. We do not know how the jurors decided.

Isaeus' main rhetorical strategy in this speech is to give the strong impression that Thrasyllus was Apollodorus' regularly adopted son, papering over that the formalities of the adoption had not actually been completed. In the proem (7.1–4) he immediately contrasts adoption *inter vivos* ("between living people") with testamentary adoption, noting that disputes normally arose only in the latter, and he flatters the jurors by pretending that he could have entered a *diamartyria* but has decided instead to put the full facts to them. Before the *topoi* of asking for the jurors' goodwill and promising to be brief, he inserts a prothesis: that he will prove that there was enmity between the two sides of the family and that Apollodorus had adopted him. This twin approach forms the basis of his subsequent main narrative. In the earlier phase of the story the wickedness of Eupolis is contrasted with the kindness of Archedamus, for which he is in turn repaid by the kindness of Apollodorus; and this part of the narrative ends by returning to Eupolis, who gave neither of his daughters in marriage to Apollodorus, thus demonstrating their enmity (7.5–12).

The continuing enmity then forms a link with the second phase of the narrative, as Thrasyllus describes his adoption by Apollodorus in great detail (7.13–17). The importance of registration in the *genos* and phratry is magnified, and Thrasyllus stops short of saying that he was not introduced into the deme before Apollodorus died, but instead emphasizes that his name was entered in the public register as "Thrasyllus son of Apollodorus." Before broaching the tricky subject of his deme registration, Thrasyllus inserts a long (and dubious) comparative argument (7.18–26): Thrasybulus has a stronger entitlement to the estate than Pronapes' wife but has not claimed it; she should therefore accept the validity of Thrasyllus' adoption.

The complex discussion of the law demonstrates not only Isaeus' command of its intricacies but also, almost certainly, how to interpret them misleadingly.[3] It is only now, while the jurors are wrestling with these legalities, that Thrasyllus tells the crucial part of the story in a brief third narrative (7.27–28), how his registration in Apollodorus' deme took place while he was away at the Pythaid festival at Delphi. This time there is less detail, so as not to highlight that the formalities were not completed, but Thrasyllus nevertheless boldly brings forward witnesses from the deme. He naturally does not dwell on this potentially fatal flaw in his case but moves swiftly on to argue that even without the hostility that existed, Apollodorus would not have left his estate to Pronapes' wife (7.29–32): the sisters of Apollodorus III had done nothing to preserve his estate and would act no differently with respect to Apollodorus II's estate. Thrasyllus' own good character was, however, well known to Apollodorus, who furthermore was of sound mind (7.33–36); and this proof by character naturally leads into the conventional praise of the public spiritedness of Apollodorus himself (in contrast to Pronapes) and his father, before Thrasyllus recaps his own services and promises that the right verdict will ensure further benefits for the city (7.37–42). In the epilogue (7.43–45) Thrasyllus reminds the jurors of his arguments, contrasting the claims of both parties and reaffirming that he had a better legal and moral right to the estate.[4]

The case will have been heard after 357/6, the earliest year in which joint trierarchies (cf. 7.38) are known.[5] The speech may be dated to the spring of 354 by the reference in 7.27 to a recent Pythaid festival; see H. W. Parke, "The Pythais of 355 B.C. and the Third Sacred War," *JHS* 59 (1939), 80–83. But if, with some editors, we read "Pythiad"

---

[3]See Wyse 1904: 560–563; Harrison 1968: 147–148 n. 2. Thrasybulus' adoption by Hippolochides (7.23) may well explain why he did not put in a claim for Apollodorus' estate.

[4]On the effectiveness of the rhetoric here, see Usher 1999: 162–163.

[5]See, e.g., P. J. Rhodes, *A Commentary on the Aristotelian Athenaion Politeia* (Oxford, 1981), 680.

in 7.27, that is, the Pythian festival that was held in the third year of the Olympiad, since 357/6 was the fourth year of Olympiad 105, the speech will have been delivered in Olympiad 106.3 (i.e., 354/3) or possibly Olympiad 107.3 (i.e., 350/49).

7

[1] I thought, gentlemen, that there could not be any dispute over adoptions of the kind made by a man personally, in his lifetime and when of sound mind, when he has taken the adopted son to the temples, presented him to his relatives, and entered him in the public registers,[6] carrying out all the proper formalities himself, though there might be when a man who is about to die has disposed of his property to another, in case anything should happen to him, and has sealed his wishes up in a document and deposited it with others. [2] By the former method the adopter makes his wishes clear, ratifying the whole business as the laws allow him; but by sealing his wishes in a will, the adopter keeps them secret and consequently many decide to enter a claim against the adopted sons, alleging the will is a forgery. But it seems that in this case it doesn't matter, since even though I was openly adopted, nevertheless my opponents have come on behalf of the daughter of Eupolis and entered a claim against me for Apollodorus' property. [3] If I saw that you preferred a declaration (*diamartyria*)[7] to a direct action (*euthydikia*), I would have produced witnesses that the estate is not adjudicable, since Apollodorus adopted me as his son in accordance with the laws. But since I realize that you would not understand the rights of the matter in that way, I have come forward myself to tell you the facts, so they cannot possibly accuse us of not wanting to put the matter to trial. [4] I will prove not only that Apollodorus did not leave his estate to his next of kin because of the many terrible wrongs they did him but also that he legally adopted me, his nephew, after receiving great kindnesses from my family. I beg you, gentlemen, all equally to show your goodwill

---

[6]Of the phratry, possibly also of the *genos* or deme.

[7]I.e., a direct action to claim the estate, rather than a declaration with witnesses that a rival's claim was invalid. Further on *diamartyria,* see the Introduction to Speech 2.

towards me, and if I prove that my opponents are going after the estate shamelessly, to help me obtain my rights. I'll make my speech as brief as I possibly can, showing you the facts from the beginning.

[5] Eupolis, gentlemen, Thrasyllus, and Mneson were brothers with the same mother and father. Their father left them a large fortune, which allowed each of them, in your view, to perform public services for you. The three divided this fortune among themselves. Two of them died at about the same time, Mneson here, unmarried and childless; Thrasyllus in Sicily[8] where he served as a trierarch, leaving behind a son, Apollodorus, who has now adopted me. [6] Eupolis, the sole survivor of the three, decided that he should enjoy not just a small part of the fortune, but he appropriated the whole of Mneson's estate, half of which belonged to Apollodorus, alleging that his brother had given it to him. Moreover, as guardian he managed Apollodorus' property so badly that he was condemned to pay him three talents. [7] This was because my grandfather Archedamus, after marrying Apollodorus' mother, my grandmother, saw him being deprived of all his money and brought him up as his own child. And when Apollodorus became an adult, he helped him go to law and secured the half-share of the estate Mneson left him and whatever Eupolis had embezzled as guardian, winning two lawsuits, and so enabled him to recover his whole fortune. [8] Consequently, Eupolis and Apollodorus have always been hostile towards one another, while my grandfather and Apollodorus naturally were close friends. But Apollodorus' actions would be the best evidence that he was treated in a way he thought he should reciprocate to his benefactors. When my grandfather met with disaster and was captured by the enemy,[9] Apollodorus was willing to contribute money for his ransom and act as hostage for him until he could raise the money.[10] [9] With Archedamus reduced from affluence to poverty, Apollodorus helped him look after his affairs and shared what he had with him. And when he was about to leave for Corinth on military service,[11] in case anything should happen to him, he disposed of his property in a

---

[8] I.e., during the expedition of 415–413.
[9] Presumably during the Peloponnesian War.
[10] I.e., even swap places with him.
[11] During the Corinthian War of 395–386.

will, leaving it to Archedamus' daughter, my mother and his own sister, and giving her in marriage to Lacratides,[12] who has now become hierophant.[13] This, then, is how he treated us, because we saved him to begin with. [10] To prove what I'm saying is true, that he won two lawsuits against Eupolis, one over his guardianship, the other over the half-share of the estate, that my grandfather helped him go to law and spoke for him in court, and that he recovered his money through our help and reciprocated these favors, I wish first to provide witnesses on these points. Please call them here.

[WITNESSES]

[11] These, then, are the many important benefits he received from us; but towards Eupolis his hostility concerned such large sums of money that it's impossible to pretend they resolved their differences and became friends. Strong evidence of their hostility is that Eupolis had two daughters, but he gave neither of them to Apollodorus in marriage even though he and Apollodorus were born of the same family and he could see Apollodorus had money. [12] And yet intermarriages are thought to reconcile serious disputes not only between relatives but also between ordinary acquaintances, when they entrust one another with what they value most. So whether Eupolis was at fault for not wishing to give his daughter or Apollodorus for being unwilling to receive her, this fact makes clear that their hostility persisted.

[13] I think I've said enough already about their dispute: I know that the older men among you remember that they were opponents, because the importance of the lawsuits and the fact that Archedamus won heavy damages against Eupolis caused a sensation. So now please pay close attention, gentlemen, to these points: that Apollodorus

---

[12]This implies that Apollodorus, by the testamentary adoption of his uterine half-sister, assumed the further right of a father to arrange for the marriage of his daughter, to prevent her being claimed as an heiress by Eupolis' family. Two other female adoptees appear at 11.8 and 41; it is unclear how common a practice such adoption was, or how common it was to nominate a husband for an heiress without adopting him. On the latter, see Rubinstein 1993: 97. Of course the will, and so the marriage, never came into effect.

[13]See 6.33 and n.

himself adopted me as his son during his lifetime, put me in control of his property, and registered me among the members of his *genos* and phratry. [14] Apollodorus had a son he educated and cared for, as was only fitting. While this boy was alive, he hoped to make him heir to his property, but when he fell ill and died in Maemacterion last year,[14] Apollodorus, depressed by all his troubles and complaining about his advanced age, did not forget those he had been well treated by originally, but came to my mother, his own sister whom he valued above all others, and said he thought he should adopt me; he asked her permission and received it. [15] He was determined to do this as quickly as possible, and so he immediately took me home with him and entrusted me with the management of all his affairs, saying that he could no longer do any of this himself, but I would be able to do all of it. And when the Thargelia[15] came, he took me to the altars before the members of his *genos* and phratry. [16] They share the same rule, that when a man introduces his son, whether natural or adopted, he swears an oath with his hand on the sacrificial victims that he is introducing the child of an Athenian mother (*astē*) and born in wedlock, whether it's his natural son or an adopted one; and even after he has introduced him in this way, the others still have to vote, and if they agree, then they enter him in the public register, and not till then. Such is the precision with which their procedures are carried out. [17] This being their rule, then, since the members of his phratry and *genos* had full confidence in Apollodorus and knew that I was his sister's son, they voted unanimously and entered me in the public register, after Apollodorus had sworn the oath with his hand on the victims. And so I was adopted by a living man and entered in the public register as Thrasyllus son of Apollodorus, after he'd adopted me in this way, as the laws have entitled him to do. To prove I'm telling the truth, please take the depositions.

[DEPOSITIONS]

[18] Now I imagine, gentlemen, that you would be more likely to believe these witnesses if some who are just as closely related as my opponent have clearly testified by their actions that Apollodorus

---

[14]Roughly, November.

[15]A festival celebrated in the month of Thargelion, at the beginning of June.

did these things correctly and in accordance with the laws.[16] Now Eupolis left two daughters, this one who is the present claimant and is married to Pronapes, and another who was the wife of Aeschines of Lusia. She has died but left a son, Thrasybulus, who is now an adult. [19] There is a law that provides that, if a brother by the same father dies childless and intestate, his property is to be divided in equal shares between his sister and any nephew born of another sister. My opponents themselves are well aware of this, as they have made clear by their conduct: when Eupolis' son Apollodorus died childless, Thrasybulus received half his property, which easily amounted to five talents. [20] The law, then, grants the sister's son and the sister an equal share of their father's or brother's estate, but for the estate of a cousin or more distant relative, the share is not equal, but the law gives the right of succession to the male relatives in preference to the female. It says, "The males and the descendants of males who have the same origin shall have preference, even if they are more distantly related."[17] This woman, therefore, was not entitled to claim any share of the estate, while Thrasybulus was entitled to all of it, if he thought my adoption was not valid.[18] [21] But neither has he claimed against me from the start nor has he now brought a suit over the estate, but he has agreed that everything is fine; whereas my opponents have dared to claim the whole estate on this woman's behalf, such is their shamelessness. Take the clauses of the law that they have broken and read them to the court.

[LAW][19]

---

[16]For this type of argument, cf. 2.38 and n.

[17]"Same origin" here means same common ancestor; "more distantly related" means more generations removed. Thus a man's nephew (brother's son) would have a stronger claim to his estate than the man's sister.

[18]Isaeus' argument is that although Thrasybulus and his aunt divided the estate of Apollodorus III (her brother and his uncle), if Apollodorus II, a more distant relative, had no direct heir, Thrasybulus would be entitled to claim his entire estate. Isaeus very probably misrepresents the law here (cf. 11.1–2): the principles of succession applied both to the direct line and to collateral relatives. See Wyse 1904: 560–563.

[19]The law is quoted at Dem. 43.51. Isaeus has it read out in three parts.

[22] Here sister and nephew have equal shares under the law. Now take this one and read it to them.

[LAW]

If there are no first cousins or children of first cousins, or any relatives on the father's side, then the law gave the right of inheritance to relatives on the mother's side, specifying the order of succession. Now take this law and read it to them.

[LAW]

[23] This is what the laws prescribe, yet Thrasybulus, a male relative, has not even claimed a part of the estate, whereas my opponents have claimed all of it on behalf of this woman; so they don't consider shamelessness a stigma. And to prove they should be awarded the whole estate, they will even dare to use arguments like this: that Thrasybulus has been adopted out of his family into that of Hippolochides. This is a true statement with a false conclusion.[20] [24] Why was he any the less entitled to this right of kinship? It was not through his father but through his mother that not only did he receive his share of the estate of Apollodorus, the son of Eupolis, but if he thought my adoption was not valid, he was also entitled to claim this estate by this right of kinship, his claim being prior to this woman's. But he is not so shameless. [25] Nobody is removed from his mother's family by adoption, but the fact remains that he has the same mother whether he remains in his father's house or is adopted out of it. Therefore, he was not deprived of his share of Apollodorus' fortune but has received half of it, sharing it with this woman. And to prove I'm telling the truth, please call the witnesses to this.

[WITNESSES]

[26] So not only have the members of the *genos* and phratry been witnesses to my adoption, but also Thrasybulus himself, by not entering a claim, has shown by his conduct that he considers the act of Apollodorus valid and in accordance with the laws; otherwise he would never have failed to claim such a large amount of money.

---

[20]We do not know what relationship (if any) existed between Thrasybulus and Hippolochides or whether Isaeus' argument on this point is valid.

But there have been other witnesses to these facts as well. [27] Before I returned from the Pythaid festival,[21] Apollodorus told his demesmen that he had adopted me as his son, had registered me among the members of his *genos* and phratry, and had entrusted his property to me; and he urged them, if anything should happen to him before I returned, to enter me in the deme register as Thrasyllus son of Apollodorus and not to fail in this. [28] The demesmen listened to this, and, even though our opponents complained at the deme elections that he had not adopted me as his son, based on what they heard and what they knew, they swore the oath with hands on the victims and registered me, just as he had asked them to, so well known amongst them was my adoption. To prove I'm telling the truth, please call the witnesses to this.

[WITNESSES]

[29] My adoption took place, gentlemen, before all these witnesses, when there was a longstanding hostility between Apollodorus and my opponents, but he felt a close friendship and kinship existed with us. But I think it will also be easy to prove to you that even if he felt neither of these things—neither hostility towards my opponents nor friendship towards us—Apollodorus would never have left this estate to them. [30] All men who are soon to die take precautions not to leave their families without heirs and to ensure that there will be somebody to offer sacrifices and perform all the customary rites over them. And so even if they die childless, they at least adopt children and leave them behind. And not only do they decide to do this for themselves, but the city too has publicly so decided, since by law it enjoins on the Archon the duty of ensuring that families are not left without heirs. [31] Now it was quite clear to Apollodorus that if he left his estate in the control of these people, he would render his family extinct. For what did he see before him? That these sisters of Apollodorus inherited their brother's estate but did not give him a son for adoption, even though they had children, that their husbands sold the land he left and his possessions for five talents and split the

---

[21]Held at Delphi in the summer; it would have taken place after the Thargelia (cf. 7.15 with n). The reference helps to date the speech; see the Introduction.

money, and that his house was thus left shamefully and disgracefully without heirs. [32] Since Apollodorus knew their brother had been treated in this way, how could he himself have expected, even if he was on friendly terms, to receive the customary rites from them, when he was only their cousin, not their brother? Surely there was no hope of this. And now please call the witnesses to the fact that they disregarded their brother's childlessness, possessed his fortune, and allowed a family to die out that could clearly support a trierarchy.

[WITNESSES]

[33] If this was how they were naturally disposed towards one another, then, and if they felt such great hostility towards Apollodorus who adopted me, what better course of action could he have taken than he did? He could have chosen a child to adopt from the family of one of his friends and given him his property. But because of his age, even the child's parents would not have known whether he would turn out an excellent man or a worthless one. [34] But he knew me from experience and had tested me enough. He knew exactly how I behaved towards my father and mother, that I was attentive to my relatives and knew how to look after my own affairs; and he was well aware that in my position as Thesmothete[22] I was neither unjust nor greedy. So it was not in ignorance but with full knowledge that he was putting me in control of his property. [35] Further, I was no stranger but his nephew, and had done him services that were not small but great; nor again did I lack public spirit, nor was I going to sell his possessions as my opponents have done with the property of that estate[23] but would be keen to serve as trierarch, in the army and as *chorēgos,* and perform all the duties you prescribed, as he himself had done. [36] And so, if I was his relative, friend, and benefactor, a public-spirited man who had been put to the test, who could claim that this adoption was made by a man who was not of sound mind? Indeed, I have already performed one of the services approved of by him, as I have acted as gymnasiarch[24] at the festival of Prometheus

---

[22]One of the six junior Archons.

[23]By converting real estate into cash, one would have less "visible" property and could more easily avoid public services, which were shared among the wealthy.

[24]Providing a team for the torch race.

this year[25] with a public spirit recognized by all the members of my tribe. To prove I'm telling the truth, please call the witnesses to this.

[WITNESSES]

[37] These are the just grounds on which we claim we can properly keep the estate, gentlemen; and we beg you to help us for the sake of both Apollodorus and his father. You will find that they were not useless citizens but as devoted as possible to your interests. [38] His father performed all the other public services and also acted as trier-arch the whole time, not in a group[26] as they do now but at his own cost, not jointly with another but by himself alone; nor did he take a break for two years,[27] but he served continuously and did not dis-charge his duties perfunctorily but provided the best possible equip-ment. In return, you remembered his actions and honored him, and saved his son when he was being deprived of his fortune, compelling the men who were in possession of his property to give it back to him. [39] Further, Apollodorus himself did not act like Pronapes, who assessed his property at a low valuation, but since he paid taxes as a knight, thought he should hold the appropriate offices, and who seized other people's property by force but thought you should not benefit at all. Instead, he openly declared the value of his property to you and performed all the services you enjoined on him. He did no wrong to anybody but tried to live with public spirit on his own fortune, thinking he ought to be moderate in his personal expendi-ture and save the rest for the city, so it could cover its costs. [40] As a result of this attitude, what public service did he not completely discharge? What war tax was he not among the first to pay? What duty has he ever neglected? He was victorious when acting as *chorēgos* to a boys' chorus, and the well-known tripod stands as a memorial to his public spiritedness. So what is the duty of a respectable citizen? Is it not, while others are using force to take what doesn't belong to them, to do no such thing but try to save what is one's own? Is it not, when the state needs money, to be among the first to contribute and not to conceal any part of one's fortune? [41] Such a man, then, was Apollodorus. In return, you would justly repay him for this service

---

[25]October 355. See Davies 1971: 45.
[26]See the Introduction.
[27]As the law permitted.

by approving his wishes concerning his own property. And as for myself, as far as my age allows, you will not find me a bad or useless citizen. I have served the city on its campaigns, and I perform my duties: this is what men of my age should do. [42] Thus, for their sake[28] and ours, you would reasonably take care, especially since our opponents have allowed a family worth five talents that supported the trierarchy to die out, have sold the estate, and made it extinct, whereas we have already performed public services and will do so in the future, if you approve Apollodorus' wishes by restoring this estate to us.

[43] So that you don't think I am wasting time by speaking on these matters, before I step down I wish to remind you briefly of the issues on which each side bases its claim. My claim is that my mother was Apollodorus' sister and a close affection existed between them, and no hostility ever arose; that I am his nephew and was adopted by him as his son when he was alive and of sound mind, and was registered among the members of his *genos* and phratry; that I possess the estate he gave me; and that my opponents should not be able to render his family extinct. But what does Pronapes claim on behalf of the claimant? [44] That he should possess a half-share of the estate of his wife's brother, valued at two and a half talents, and also receive this estate, even though there are others more closely related to Apollodorus than his wife, even though he did not give him a son for adoption but has left the house without heirs, nor would he give Apollodorus a son for adoption, and he would similarly leave this family too without heirs. And he makes the claim even though great hostility existed between them and no reconciliation ever took place afterwards. [45] You must consider these facts, gentlemen, and also remember that I am the deceased's nephew, but she is only his cousin; that she is asking to possess two estates, but I claim only this one into which I was taken by adoption; that she was not on good terms with the man who left the estate, but I and my grandfather have been his benefactors. Consider all these points and weigh them up in your own minds, and then pass your verdict for what is just.

I don't know that I need say any more: I think you are fully aware of what's been said.

---

[28]I.e., that of Apollodorus and Eupolis.

8. ON THE ESTATE OF CIRON

~~~~~~

Ciron died at an advanced age (8.37), leaving a daughter but no son. The daughter (according to the speaker) was the child of his first marriage to his first cousin, the daughter of his mother's sister. This wife died after four years (8.7); their daughter was married first and without issue to Nausimenes of Cholargus, and after his death she was married to an unnamed husband (also deceased) by whom she had two sons, the elder of whom is the speaker (8.8, 31, 36). Ciron's second marriage was to the half-sister of Diocles of Phlya, who survived him, but their two sons had both died (8.36). As soon as Ciron died, the speaker sought to establish his claim to the estate by performing the funeral rites (8.21–27), but he was opposed by a second claimant, the son of Ciron's brother (8.31, 38); and their bitter rivalry spilled over into a dispute at the funeral (8.27). At the subsequent hearing of the inheritance claim (*diadikasia*), the nephew argued that the speaker's mother was not Ciron's legitimate daughter, since Ciron never had a daughter (8.1), and the speaker's mother was not even Athenian (8.43). The Argument attached to the speech states (on what grounds is unclear)[1] that the nephew also argued that, even if the speaker's mother were legitimate, a brother's son had a stronger legal claim to an estate than a daughter's son, under the law that the descendants of males took precedence over those of females. This law is probably not applicable here, and the speaker

---

[1]Forster (1927: 283) thinks it is "clear from the speech"; *contra* Wyse 1904: 585–586, 609. See further the Argument to Speech 8 in the Appendix.

Stemma

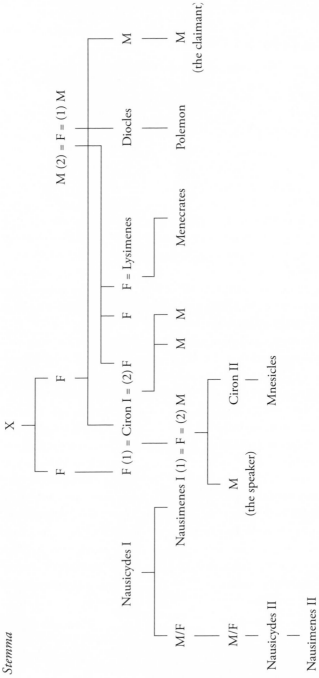

ignores it, concentrating on the argument that descendants have a stronger claim than collaterals (8.30–34).

It is clear that the main issue, as Isaeus saw it, was to establish the legitimacy of the speaker's mother. An immediate problem for the speaker then is that the alleged marriage between Ciron and his grandmother will have taken place some forty years earlier, and so he could not find any witnesses to it but had to rely on hearsay evidence (8.14, 29). Similarly, he could not prove that Ciron's daughter was regularly introduced to his phratry. He has therefore to base his arguments on her treatment by Ciron (he formally betrothed her to both her husbands, 8.8–9)[2] and by her husband (he gave a wedding breakfast and wedding feast to the phratry, 8.18), as well as that afforded her by the wives of the demesmen (8.19). Further, her children were enrolled in their father's phratry without objection (8.19). Other circumstantial evidence is adduced, of Ciron's conduct towards the boys (8.15–17) and that of Diocles (8.21–27); and the opponents' refusal to allow the examination under torture of Ciron's slaves is taken as further evidence for his case (8.9–14).

The arguments are weighty but fall short of proving the speaker's legitimacy: he distracts attention from this by a classic attack (*diabolē*) on the character not of his opponent but of Diocles, Ciron's second wife's half-brother, who was the subject of two other Isaean speeches (Lost Speeches VIII and IX). One of these was presumably delivered in the suit for hybris that was pending during this trial (8.41), perhaps by the speaker. The second indicates that the younger of the two half-sisters of Diocles mentioned at 8.41 (the full sisters of Ciron's second wife) was married to Lysimenes, who allegedly was murdered; Diocles became the guardian of his son Menecrates and deprived him of some land (cf. 8.42), which led to further litigation. Diocles, whose third half-sister (8.40) was probably the wife of Ciron, is not heard of again, but the name of his son, Polemon, is recorded.[3]

The attack on Diocles had some justification, since it appears that he is in control of the estate (8.37) and therefore is to all intents and purposes the opponent. It begins early (8.3) but reaches a climax

---

[2]A procedure that is not accepted as proof of Phile's legitimacy in Speech 3.

[3]Cf. *IG* II2.1590.9–10; Davies 1971: 314.

towards the end of the speech in 8.40–44: Diocles is violent (see the nickname "Orestes" at 8.3, repeated at 8.44) and a murderer (8.41); he is dishonest (8.40, 42) and an adulterer (8.44, 46). The speaker will be taking further legal action against him (8.44): since his influence lies behind his opponent's claim (8.3), the jurors could only vote one way. We do not know, however, if they agreed (but see below).

Whatever the outcome, this speech is recognized as one of Isaeus' finest pieces of rhetoric. The proem (8.1–5) is one of the longest in the corpus, responding to the opponent's case by the adoption of an indignant tone, accompanied by emotive vocabulary: "dare," "do away with rights," "insult" (8.1); "greed," "force," "dare" again (8.2). Added to this is the *petitio principii*[4] that the speaker and his brother were "the sons of [Ciron's] legitimate daughter" (8.1); and given that Ciron was the grandfather, their opponent has been "enlisted" by the violent Diocles (8.3). Commonplace elements of proems follow, including the opponents' "plotting" (8.4), the importance that the jurors vote in full knowledge of the facts after paying close attention to the speech (8.4), the inexperienced speaker fighting against the "fabrications" of his opponent (8.5), and flattery of the jurors and a plea for their goodwill (8.5). The prothesis follows (8.6), in which the speaker sets out the two main points he will demonstrate: that his mother was Ciron's legitimate daughter and that he and his brother had a better legal claim to the estate than their opponents.

The first of these topics is dealt with in 8.7–29, with a short narrative of the history of the speaker's side of the family (8.7–8), followed by a series of proofs. The first concerns the speaker's mother and how her treatment by Ciron, which demonstrates that she was legitimate, could have been confirmed by the evidence of the household slaves (8.9–14). But slave evidence could only be heard in court if it had been given under torture, and, as is the case throughout the orators,[5] the opponents had refused the demand to torture them. This leads in turn to commonplace arguments over the implications of the refusal and the trustworthiness of torture evidence. The witnesses that the speaker does have are then produced, and a series of rhetorical

---

[4]See Speech 1, n. 4.

[5]See Todd 1993: 96; M. Gagarin, "The Torture of Slaves in Athenian Law," *CP* 91 (1996), 1–18.

questions builds an argument from probability (*eikos*) over the reliability of the witnesses on both sides. The speaker juxtaposes to this the circumstantial evidence that Ciron's behavior towards his grandchildren was further proof of their mother's status (8.15–17);[6] again, the testimony of the free witnesses produced serves to highlight how important the slaves' testimony would have been. The conduct of the boys' father and of the wives of his demesmen is an additional indication of their mother's legitimacy (8.18–20); and the grandsons' legitimacy is also demonstrated by their involvement in Ciron's funeral rites and the contrasting behavior of their opponents (8.21–27). This again commonplace argumentation permits the reintroduction of Diocles, with a narrative of his actions concerning the funeral (8.21–24). Diocles' dishonesty in monetary matters is emphasized; so too his tacit acceptance of the speaker's position, which is highlighted by imaginary direct speech (8.24). Finally, the arguments supporting the speaker's first contention are recapitulated (8.28–29), with an effective opening series of rhetorical questions in the form of *hypophora*.

The speaker's second main contention, that of the precedence of descendants over collateral relatives, is the subject of 8.30–34. Scholars have mostly accepted the speaker's claims here, though he does not cite a specific law (if indeed one existed), but puts forward two clever arguments. The first (8.32) is that direct descendants are responsible for the maintenance of their parents and grandparents— how, then, is it right that, if the parents are indigent, their children are liable to be prosecuted for neglect, but if they are wealthy, others might inherit the estate? This law, which concerned the care of aged relatives, not inheritance, *is* read out (8.34). The second is a comparative argument (8.33): again using a series of rhetorical questions, the speaker argues that if Ciron's daughter is more closely related to him than his brother, and her children are nearer kin than the brother, then *a fortiori* her children are more closely related to Ciron than the brother's children.

Having addressed his two main points, the speaker returns in the remainder of the speech to the attack on Diocles. A third narrative

---

[6]Usher (1999: 142) notes how the speaker stirs the jurors' emotions in 8.16.

details the estate's wealth and the intrigues whereby Diocles had secured it (which he now denied existed). His patience during Ciron's lifetime, preparing a bogus rival claimant, contrasts with his immediate actions on his death, as he tried to prevent the speaker from involvement in Ciron's funeral rites (8.35–39). A fourth narrative describes Diocles' corruption and murderous intentions with regard to his half-sisters' inheritance (8.40–42) and is followed by a pathos-inducing argument over the consequences that a victory for the opponents would have on the status of the grandsons (8.43–44), rounded off with a final attack on Diocles' character: his nickname Orestes is recalled from 8.3, and now he is branded a serial adulterer. The speaker moves swiftly into his epilogue (8.44–46), with a last appeal to the jurors and commonplace reminder of their duty to judge according to their dicastic oath, capped by the masterstroke of ending the speech with a deposition testifying to Diocles' adultery.

Upper and lower limits for the date of the speech can be roughly determined. The speaker and his brother were born after the archonship of Eucleides in 403 (8.43), and so the speech will not have been delivered until the speaker reached the minimum age of twenty for bringing an action, in 383. Then, several passages in the speech are adapted by Demosthenes in his prosecutions of his guardians Aphobus and Onetor, giving a lower limit of 363.[7] Wevers' method (1969: 21) suggests ca. 365. Davies (1971: 315–316) suggests that the speaker (who does not mention his youth) was probably nearer thirty than twenty and also that his name was Ciron, since his father was probably from Pithus (an inference from 8.19), and the name Mnesicles son of Ciron of Pithus is found in an inscription of ca. 330 (IG II².2385.101). But since the elder son is more likely to have been named after his father's father, and the younger after his mother's father, this Ciron was more probably the speaker's younger brother. Either way, the continuance of the name and, it seems, this Ciron's ability to be a creditor for 600 drachmas,[8] might be indicators that the speaker won his case.

---

[7] The passages in question are 8.5, 12, 28–29, 45, for which cf. Dem. 27.2–3, 30.37, 27.47–48 and 29.55–57, 28.23.

[8] See M. I. Finley, *Studies in Land and Credit in Ancient Athens, 500–200 BC* (New Brunswick, NJ, 1952), 134, no. 53; Davies 1971: 316.

8

[1] One cannot but feel indignant, gentlemen, against the kind of people who not only dare to claim the property of others but even hope by their arguments to do away with rights conferred by the laws. This is exactly what our opponents are trying to do now. Although our grandfather Ciron did not die childless but has left us behind him, the sons of his legitimate daughter, our opponents are claiming the estate as next of kin, and they insult us by alleging that we are not the children of his daughter and that he never even had a daughter at all. [2] The reason for their acting like this is their greed and the value of the property that Ciron has left and that they hold by force and are controlling; and they dare both to say that he has left nothing and at the same time to lay claim to the estate. [3] But you must not imagine that this case today is directed against the man who has brought the suit over the estate; no, it is against Diocles of Phlya, nicknamed Orestes.[9] It is he who has enlisted our opponent to cause us trouble by embezzling the fortune our grandfather Ciron left us when he died and forcing us to risk this trial, so that he will not have to give any of it back if you are deceived into believing this man's words. [4] Since this is what they are plotting, you must learn all the facts, so that you may cast your vote with full awareness and clear knowledge of what's happened. If, then, you have ever paid close and careful attention to any other case, I beg you to pay similar attention to this one, as indeed is only just. Although many lawsuits are heard in the city, it will be clear that nobody has claimed the property of others more shamelessly or brazenly than these people. [5] It's a difficult task, gentlemen, to conduct a case on such important matters against fabrications and perjurious witnesses when one has absolutely no experience of the lawcourts. Still, I have great hopes that I shall obtain my rights from you and speak well enough at least on the matter of justice, unless something should happen to me such as I now happen to expect.[10] I therefore beg you, gentlemen, both to

---

[9]Presumably after the notorious mugger Orestes son of Timocrates who appears in Aristoph., *Acharnians* 1167; *Birds* 712, 1491 (with scholion).

[10]An obscure allusion, apparently reflecting the speaker's fears about his opponents' behavior during the rest of the trial.

listen to me with goodwill and, if I appear to have been wronged, to help me secure my rights.

[6] First, then, I will prove to you that my mother was Ciron's legitimate daughter. For events of long ago I will rely on reported statements and witness testimony, but for events within living memory, on witnesses who know the facts as well as proofs, which are stronger than testimony. When I've made this clear, I will then prove that it's more appropriate for us than for our opponents to inherit Ciron's property. I too will start at the point where they began their narrative of events and will try to show you what happened.

[7] My grandfather Ciron, gentlemen, married my grandmother, his first cousin, who was herself the daughter of his own mother's sister. She was not married for long but bore him my mother and died after four years. Being left with an only daughter, my grandfather married his second wife, the sister of Diocles, who bore him two sons. He brought his daughter up in the house with his wife and her children [8] and, while they were still alive, gave her in marriage, when she was of the right age, to Nausimenes of Cholargus,[11] with her clothes and jewelry and a dowry of twenty-five minas.[12] Three or four years after this, Nausimenes fell ill and died, before my mother bore him any children. My grandfather received her back into his house without recovering the dowry he'd given, because of Nausimenes' poor financial condition, and married her a second time to my father with a dowry of one thousand drachmas.[13] [9] Now then, how could one prove clearly that all these events took place in the face of the charges our opponents are now making? When I looked, I discovered how. Whether my mother was Ciron's daughter or not, whether she lived in his house or not, whether he gave two wedding breakfasts on her behalf or not, and what dowry each of her husbands received with her, all these things must be known to the male

---

[11]Probably the son of the Nausicydes of Cholargus who appears as a wealthy miller in Xenophon (*Mem.* 2.7.6) and is also known from Aristophanes (*Eccl.* 426) and Plato (*Gorg.* 487c). Since Nausimenes died poor, something had happened to his father's estate.

[12]See 2.9n. This dowry was just below an average sum; see Davies 1971: 314.

[13]I.e., ten minas this time.

and female slaves who belonged to him. [10] Therefore, I wished to obtain proof from them by torture[14] in addition to the witnesses I had, so that you would have more faith in these witnesses because they would not be tested in the future but would have already been tested in the matter of their testimony.[15] And so I asked our opponents to surrender the female and male slaves for torture on these and all the other points they might know about. [11] But our opponent, who is now going to ask you to believe his witnesses, declined the torture examination. And yet if he clearly was unwilling to do this, what else can you think of his witnesses than that they are now giving false testimony, since he has declined such an important test? I don't think there is any other conclusion. But to prove I'm telling the truth, please first take this deposition and read it.

[DEPOSITION]

[12] You consider that in both private and public matters torture examination is the most conclusive test; and whenever slaves and free men are present and some disputed point needs to be clarified, you do not use the testimony of the free men but seek to discover the truth about what happened by torturing the slaves. And reasonably so, gentlemen, since you are well aware that some witnesses before now have been thought to testify untruthfully, but nobody examined under torture has ever been convicted of not telling the truth as a result of the torture.[16] [13] Will our opponent, the most shameless of all men, ask you to believe his fabricated tales and lying witnesses, when he declines such conclusive tests? This is not our approach: we asked to resort to torture to confirm the testimony that was going to be given, but our opponent refuses, and so we think that you should believe our witnesses. Take these depositions, then, and read them to the jurors.

---

[14]The evidence of slaves was only valid if extracted under torture with the approval of both parties.

[15]I.e., if the slaves' evidence corroborated that of the witnesses, there would be a presumption that the witnesses were telling the truth before their evidence was heard.

[16]A commonplace argument that is repeated almost verbatim at Dem. 30.37, but a counter-argument could sometimes be employed (as at Ant. 5.32).

[DEPOSITIONS]

[14] Who are likely to know the events of long ago? Clearly those who were close to my grandfather. They, then, have testified as to what they heard. Who must know the facts about giving my mother in marriage? Those who betrothed her and those who were present when they betrothed her. The relatives, then, of both Nausimenes and my father have testified. Who are the ones who know that she was brought up in Ciron's house and was his legitimate daughter? The present claimants clearly testify this is true by the fact that they declined the torture examination.[17] Therefore, without a doubt you have no reason to disbelieve our witnesses but every reason to disbelieve theirs.

[15] Now we have other proofs beside these to put forward to prove that we are the children of Ciron's daughter. As was natural since we were the sons of his own daughter, he never made any sacrifice without us, but whether he was performing a small or large sacrifice, we were always there joining in it with him. And not only were we invited to these ceremonies but he always took us into the country for the Dionysia;[18] [16] we attended public spectacles with him and sat next to him, and we went to his house for all the festivals. When he sacrificed to Zeus Ctesius,[19] a sacrifice that he took especially seriously and to which he did not admit slaves or free men from outside the family, but performed all the ceremonies personally, we shared in this, laid our hands on the victims with his, placed our offerings with his, and assisted him in the other rites; and he prayed that Zeus grant us health and wealth, as was natural for him, being our grandfather. [17] Yet if he didn't consider us his daughter's children and didn't see us as the only remaining descendants left to him, he would never have done any of these things but would have invited our opponent to his side, who now claims to be his nephew. And that all this is

---

[17]For this type of argument, cf. 2.38 and n.

[18]I.e., the Rural (not City) Dionysia, which was held in Poseideon (roughly, December).

[19]Zeus in his guise as protector of the house and property. That Ciron took sacrifice to Zeus Ctesius "especially seriously" suggests that he was well off, though see below, 35n.

true is best known to my grandfather's attendants, whom our opponent refused to hand over for torture; but some of his close friends also know it very well, and I will produce them as witnesses. Please take the depositions and read them.

[DEPOSITIONS]

[18] Now it's clear not only from these proofs that our mother was Ciron's legitimate daughter but also from the actions of our father and from the attitude of the wives of his demesmen towards her. When our father married her, he gave a wedding breakfast and invited three of his friends as well as his relatives, and he gave a wedding feast to the members of his phratry in accordance with their rules. [19] The wives of his demesmen afterwards selected her, together with the wife of Diocles of Pithus,[20] to preside at the Thesmophoria[21] and perform the customary rites with her. Our father also introduced us at birth to the members of his phratry, swearing on oath in accordance with the established laws that he was introducing the children of an Athenian mother (astē) and lawfully wedded wife. None of the phratry members objected or claimed this was not true, even though a large number were present and they consider such matters carefully. [20] And you cannot think that if our mother had been the kind of woman our opponents allege, our father would have given a wedding breakfast and wedding feast, rather than hushing all this up; or that the wives of the other demesmen would have chosen her to be the joint overseer of the festival with the wife of Diocles and put her in charge of the sacred objects, rather than entrusting this office to some other woman; or that the members of the phratry would have admitted us, rather than complaining and justifying their objection, if it had not been universally agreed that our mother was Ciron's legitimate daughter. As it was, because the facts were evident and many knew them, no such dispute arose in any quarter. And to prove I'm telling the truth in this, call the witnesses to the facts.

[WITNESSES]

---

[20]This probably indicates that the speaker's father was from Pithus. See the Introduction.

[21]See 3.80n.

[21] Next, gentlemen, it's easy to recognize from the way Diocles acted when our grandfather died that we were acknowledged to be Ciron's grandchildren. I came with one of my relatives, my father's cousin, to remove his body for burial from my own house. I did not find Diocles at the house, so I entered, accompanied by bearers, and was ready to remove it. [22] But when my grandfather's widow asked me to bury him from that house, and with supplications and tears said that she herself would like to help us lay out and adorn his body, I consented, gentlemen. I went to our opponent and told him in front of witnesses that I would conduct the funeral from there, because Diocles' sister had begged me to do so. [23] When Diocles heard this, he didn't object at all but claimed he had purchased some of the things needed for the funeral and had paid a deposit himself for the rest, and asked that I pay for these. We agreed that I would reimburse him for the cost of the things he'd bought and he would produce the men who received the deposit that he claimed he'd given. And right then he casually remarked that Ciron had left nothing at all, although I'd never said a single word about his money. [24] And yet if I'd not been Ciron's grandson, he would never have made these arrangements but would have said, "Who are you? What gives you the right to bury him? I don't know you; you're not going to set foot in the house." This is what he should have said and what he has now induced others to say. As it was, he said no such thing but told me to bring the money the next morning. And to prove I'm telling the truth, please call the witnesses to this.

[WITNESSES]

[25] And Diocles was not alone, but the present claimant of the estate also said no such thing, but now he is claiming the estate after being suborned by this man. And although he refused to accept the money I brought and alleged the next day that he'd been paid by our opponent, I was not prevented from joining in the burial but assisted in all the rites; and not only were the funeral expenses not paid by him or Diocles, they came out of what Ciron left. [26] And yet if Ciron was not my grandfather, our opponent should have banned me and thrown me out and prevented me from joining in the burial. For I was not related to him: I allowed him to assist in all these rites as being my grandfather's nephew, but he should not have allowed

me to do so, if what they now have the audacity to say were true. [27] But he was so struck by the truth of the matter that at the tomb, when I spoke and accused Diocles of embezzling the money and inducing this man to claim the estate, he didn't dare mutter a sound or say any word of what he now dares to say. And to prove I'm telling the truth in this, please call the witnesses to these events.

[WITNESSES]

[28] Why should you believe what I have said? Shouldn't you because of the testimony? I certainly think so. Why should you believe the witnesses? Shouldn't you because of the torture? It's certainly reasonable. Why should you disbelieve the words of our opponents? Shouldn't you because they declined the tests? That's an absolute necessity. How then could anybody prove more clearly that my mother is Ciron's legitimate daughter than by doing so in this way? [29] I provided witnesses who testified to what they heard of the events of long ago, and where witnesses are still alive I presented those who knew all the details—who knew well that she was brought up in his house, was considered his daughter, was twice betrothed and twice married—and further I showed that on all these points our opponents have declined the torture evidence from the slaves who knew them all. By the Olympian gods, I could not produce stronger proofs than these, but I think the ones that have been given are ample.

[30] Moving on, I will now show you that I have a better right to Ciron's fortune than our opponent. And I imagine that it's a simple fact that's completely clear to you that those who are born of the same stock as Ciron are not nearer in their rights of kinship than those who are descended from him—how could they be, since the former are called collaterals and the latter, descendants of the deceased? But even though this is the case, since they still have the audacity to claim the estate, we will show this still more conclusively from the laws themselves. [31] If my mother, Ciron's daughter, were alive, and if he had died intestate, and if our opponent were his brother, not his nephew, he would be entitled to marry his daughter but not to claim his fortune, which would go to their children when they came of age:[22] this

---

[22]Literally "two years after puberty," which was commonly thought to happen at the age of fourteen, but in the legal context at sixteen.

is what the laws prescribe. If, then, not he but the children would have gained control of the daughter's property were she still alive, it's clear that since she is dead and has left us her children behind, it is not our opponents but we who are entitled to inherit the estate.

[32] Again, this is clear not only from this law but also from the one concerning neglect of parents. If my grandfather were alive and lacking life's necessities, we, not our opponent, would be liable to prosecution for neglect. The law prescribes that we look after our parents, parents meaning our mother, father, grandfather, and grandmother, and their mother and father if they are still alive, because they are the origin of the family and their property is passed down to their descendants. For this reason their descendants are bound to look after them, even if they leave them nothing. So how can it be right that, if they have nothing to leave, we are liable to prosecution for neglect if we don't look after them, but if they have left something, our opponent is the heir, not we? Surely it's not right at all.

[33] I shall now compare the first of the collaterals with the descendants and ask you about the degree of relationship of each, since in this way you would most easily understand the matter. Is Ciron's daughter or brother the nearer of kin? Clearly his daughter, as she is born of him, whereas he is merely of the same stock. Are the daughter's children nearer or his brother? The children, surely, as they are direct descendants and not merely collaterals. If, then, we have a stronger claim than a brother, surely we are very far ahead of our opponent, who is only a nephew. [34] But I'm afraid you may think me boring if I repeat things that are universally agreed. You all inherit the property of your fathers, grandfathers, and those still further back, taking up the succession by direct descent without having to go to law, and I don't know that such a case as this has ever been brought against anybody before. So I'll read the law on neglect of parents, and then try to show you why all this is happening.

[LAW]

[35] Ciron possessed a property, gentlemen, which included an estate at Phlya,[23] easily worth a talent, and two houses in the city, one

---

[23]A deme about five miles northeast of Athens.

near the shrine of Dionysus in the Marshes[24] that brought in rent and was worth a thousand drachmas, the other in which he himself lived, worth thirteen minas.[25] Besides this, he had male slaves who were hired out,[26] two female slaves and a slave girl, and the furnishings of the house he lived in, all worth, with the slaves, about thirteen minas. Altogether his visible property was worth more than ninety minas, and apart from this, he had large sums on loan on which he received interest.[27] [36] Diocles began plotting with his sister for this property a long time ago, as soon as Ciron's sons died. He did not try to find her another husband, even though she was still capable of bearing children to one, in case, if she were separated from Ciron, he should plan to dispose of his property in the proper way; but he kept urging her to stay with him by claiming she thought she was pregnant by him and then pretending she'd accidentally miscarried, so that he was continually hoping he would have children and would not adopt either of us as his son. And Diocles continually slandered my father, alleging that he was plotting against Ciron's property. [37] So he gradually persuaded Ciron to let him manage all the debts that were owed to him and the interest on them, as well as his visible property, seducing the old man by his attentions and blandishments until he took over all his property. He knew that I would seek to gain control of all this property by right when my grandfather died, but he did not try to prevent me from visiting him, taking care of him, or spending time with him, because he was afraid that I would become exasperated and angry with him. Instead, he was preparing someone to claim the property against me, promising him a very small share if he were successful but planning to take the whole property for himself; and he did not even admit to this man that my grandfather was leaving any money but pretended there was nothing. [38] As soon as Ciron died he began making preparations for the

---

[24]South of the Areopagus; cf. Thuc. 2.15.4 with Hornblower's note. See S. Hornblower, *A Commentary on Thucydides: Volume I, Books I–III* (Oxford, 1991), 266.

[25]I.e., 1,300 drachmas.

[26]The number of these slaves has probably been lost from the text.

[27]A "modest enough" estate (Davies 1971: 314), but see above, 16n. Cf. his daughter's dowries at 8.8.

funeral, demanding that I pay for it, as you have heard the witnesses testify, but pretending that he'd received the money from our opponent, and he refused any longer to receive it from me, craftily pushing me aside so it might appear that our opponent was burying my grandfather, not I. And when our opponent claimed this house and everything else Ciron left, although he said that he'd left nothing, I didn't think I ought to use force and remove my grandfather's body in such difficult circumstances, and my friends agreed with me about this, but I assisted in the rites and joined in the burial, the expenses being paid out of what my grandfather left. [39] So I acted in this way under compulsion. But to prevent them from gaining any advantage over me by alleging to you that I did not pay any of the funeral expenses, I consulted the exegete[28] and on his advice presented and paid at my own expense for the ninth-day offerings, preparing them in the finest way possible, to thwart this sacrilege of theirs and to remove the impression that they paid for everything and I nothing, but to make clear that I paid my share.

[40] This is pretty much what happened, gentlemen, and why we are involved in this business. If you knew Diocles' shamelessness and how he behaves on other occasions, you would not disbelieve a word of what I've said. The property he possesses, which now makes him so grand, is somebody else's because, when his three half-sisters by his mother were left as heiresses, he made himself the adopted son of their father, even though the deceased had made no will to this effect.[29] [41] When the husbands of two of the sisters tried to secure their fortune, he shut up the husband of the older one in his house and by plotting disfranchised him,[30] and though he was indicted for hybris,[31] he has not yet been punished for this; and he killed the husband of the younger one using a slave, whom he then smuggled out of the country, and turned the charge against his sister; [42] and

---

[28]An interpreter of sacred law and customs; here, those connected with burial.

[29]The half-sisters' father would have been Diocles' stepfather.

[30]The speaker's allegation is presumably that Diocles imprisoned the man by nailing up the door to a room and then brought or had a charge brought against him that he failed to answer and as a result lost his civic rights.

[31]By a *graphē hybreōs,* or public charge of aggravated assault.

by terrifying her with his disgusting behavior, he deprived her son, his ward, of his property—he occupies the farmland, while he has given him the stony ground. And to prove I'm telling the truth in this, although his victims are afraid of him, they may yet perhaps be willing to testify for me; if not, I'll produce as witnesses those who know what happened.[32] Please call them here first.

[WITNESSES]

[43] Such, then, is the brutality and violence of Diocles: he has deprived his sisters of their property, is not content with having that, but since he has not been punished in any way for it, he has come to deprive us too of our grandfather's fortune. He has given our opponent only two minas (so we hear) but is putting us in danger of losing not only our property but our country as well. For if you are misled into believing that our mother was not a citizen woman, then neither are we citizens, since we were born after the archonship of Eucleides.[33] So is the suit he has fabricated against us really only a trifling matter? While our grandfather and father were alive we faced no charge, but we lived the whole time free from challenge; [44] but now that they are dead, even if we win today, we will bear a stigma because our rights have been challenged, thanks to this damned Orestes,[34] who was caught in adultery and suffered the appropriate treatment for men who do such things,[35] but even so has not given up the practice, as those who know about it can testify.

You are now hearing, then, what kind of man he is, and you'll learn in even greater detail when we begin our suit against him.[36] [45] But I beg and supplicate you, do not allow me to be insulted and deprived of this estate that my grandfather left, but help me as

---

[32]The speaker's uncertainty is purely rhetorical, since he already either has the witnesses' depositions or does not.

[33]In 403/2, when Pericles' citizenship law of 451/0 (whereby citizenship depended on birth to two citizen parents) was reenacted.

[34]See 8.3n.

[35]Probably an allusion to the physical humiliation described at Aristoph., *Clouds* 1083 (cf. Suidas, s.v. *rhaphanis*).

[36]Presumably the one for hybris mentioned in 8.41, which was actually brought (cf. Lost Speech VIII). See the Introduction.

far as each of you is able. You have sufficient proof from depositions, torture evidence, and the laws themselves that we are the children of Ciron's legitimate daughter and that we have a greater right to inherit his estate than our opponents, being our grandfather's direct descendants. [46] Remember, therefore, the oaths you swore before sitting as jurors, the arguments we have put forward, and the laws, and pass your verdict for what is just.

I don't know what more I need say: I think you are fully aware of what's been said. But take the remaining deposition, that Diocles was caught in adultery, and read it to the jurors.

[DEPOSITION]

9. ON THE ESTATE OF ASTYPHILUS

Astyphilus, the son of Euthycrates, died during military service at Mytilene on Lesbos. His estate was seized by his first cousin Cleon, who produced a will that had been deposited with Hierocles, Astyphilus' maternal uncle, and in which Cleon's son, who may have been called Myronides (see below), was adopted by Astyphilus as his own son (9.5). Astyphilus' mother, however, after the death of her first husband had remarried to Theophrastus, and their son (Astyphilus' half-brother and also Cleon's first cousin) contested the estate on his own return from military service (9.3) by the present speech. He claimed that the will was a forgery and that his right to the estate was stronger both morally and legally.

The unnamed speaker's main difficulty lies in contesting the validity of the will. He can produce his own witnesses that the witnesses to the will were people who happened to be there at the time rather than close relatives and friends of Astyphilus (9.7–13); but beyond that he can adduce only circumstantial evidence: Astyphilus had never made a will before setting out on previous campaigns (9.14–15); and, more importantly, Cleon was his bitterest enemy, so why would he have adopted his son (9.16–21)? The speaker further alleges that Hierocles had been the instigator of a fraud, whereby he would produce a will in favor of anybody who would share the estate with him (9.22–26).

He then turns to moral arguments, which are based on the close affection between himself and Astyphilus, who was brought up by Theophrastus and whose affairs were conducted by him (9.27–30).[1]

---

[1] Wyse (1904: 626) comments that it is strange Astyphilus did not think of adopting the speaker (his half-brother) during his lifetime. But this would have

Stemma

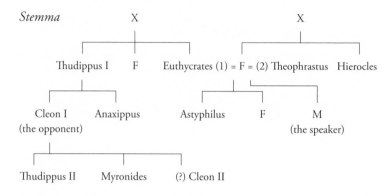

This is in stark contrast to the previously mentioned fact that Astyphilus never spoke to Cleon, because his father Thudippus had been responsible for the death of Astyphilus' father Euthycrates. The speaker, finally, comes up against the legal principle that relatives on the paternal side of a man who died intestate took precedence over his relatives on the maternal side. Against this he argues that Cleon's father had been adopted into another family, and consequently he and his son had no claim on an estate belonging to the family out of which they had been adopted (9.32–33). This is a strong point in the speaker's favor, though it is stated rather than proved,[2] and in any case the existence of the will, if genuine, overrides this issue. Overall, therefore, the speaker's legal position seems weak: he does not attack the motives of the witnesses to the will,[3] and Hierocles, as Astyphilus' uncle and a nonbeneficiary, was an obvious choice as the depositary for it. His main suit, clearly, is the apparent moral justice of his claim.[4]

---

been unusual, the more so if the speaker was the only son of Theophrastus (who would thereby lose his own heir). See Avramovic 1990: 45–47.

[2] But accepted by Avramovic 1990: 43–44.

[3] Though Avramovic (1990: 47–50) points out that the speaker instead adduces numerous witnesses to his own claims. But he perhaps exaggerates their number into "a whole army of relatives and friends."

[4] For a defense of the speaker's case, see Avramovic 1990.

Rhetorically, as Wyse observed (1904: 626), the speech builds from a businesslike opening, through increasing indignation, to end on a note of pathos. There is no formal proem, but the speaker opens directly, and perhaps in character as a straightforward soldier, with a statement of his relationship to the deceased and the fact of his death in Mytilene. He then inserts a prothesis (9.1), stating the outline of his case, before giving a narrative of Cleon's actions after Astyphilus' demise, the way in which his funeral was conducted, and the matter of the will (9.2–6). The characters of two key figures, Cleon and Hierocles, are already blackened in this forthright opening, and the speaker immediately proceeds to his attack on the validity of the will, which culminates in a further assault on the character of Hierocles (9.7–26).

The speaker relies on a series of arguments from probability (*eikos*) over Astyphilus' intentions, though these ultimately do not disprove the existence of a will: his friends and relatives were not summoned as witnesses to it (9.7–10); it was in Cleon's interest to make the contents of the will open knowledge (9.11), whereas if Astyphilus had wished it to remain secret, he would not have summoned any witnesses (9.12); but again, he should in any case have summoned those who would share the religious and civil rites with the adoptee, and moreover there was no shame in summoning as many witnesses as possible (9.13). The comparative argument follows that Astyphilus had not made a will before more perilous expeditions, and so he had no reason to do so this time (9.14–15); and then the far stronger argument over bitter enmity between Cleon and Astyphilus (9.16–21), which leads into the attack on the character, interestingly not of Cleon but of Hierocles (9.22–26).

This assault reaches a climax with the highly emotive charge that Hierocles was willing to slander the dead, and the speaker turns immediately to his moral arguments (9.27–32). These comprise standard topics: Theophrastus brought Astyphilus up and cultivated his estate, betrothed his sister, and took him to religious ceremonies. Astyphilus' relationship with his stepfather and his half-brother stands in stark contrast to his relationship with Cleon, and the point is reinforced by a second reference (cf. 9.4) to Cleon's failure to bury Astyphilus' remains. The speaker can now address the legal issue of precedence (9.32–33), which may have formed an important part of his opponents' arguments but is summarily dismissed by a second statement (cf. 9.2) that Thudippus had been adopted out of the family. In the epilogue (9.34–37) the speaker begins by summarizing the claims of the opposing sides,[5] but his main rhetorical tactic is now extended emotional appeal, beginning with "a most holy request" in 9.34 and ending with supplication of the jurors in 9.37. If Cleon's son was the member of the Council in 343/2 who was named "Myronides son of Cleon" (not "son of Astyphilus"), this should indicate that the appeal was successful.[6]

Unfortunately for the dating of the speech, the nature and date of the expedition to Mytilene are otherwise unknown. Since Astyphilus had served "all through the Theban war" (9.14), the speech must be later than 371. Commentators have therefore suggested a date in the mid 360s, linking Astyphilus with the activities of Timotheus in the eastern Aegean in 366/5; but Welsh argues that Astyphilus was on extended garrison duty on Lesbos in the 360s, and the speech may date to the end of that decade or possibly even later.[7]

9

[1] Astyphilus, whose estate this is, gentlemen, was my half-brother by the same mother. He went abroad with the army to Mytilene and

---

[5]Usher (1999: 149) notes that this breaks with convention, so too the plea in the epilogue rather than the proem for the jurors' protection against the opponent's rhetorical ability (9.35).

[6]For the date, see Develin 1989: 331. The identification is not certain, since Astyphilus' alleged adoption of Cleon's son (9.5) would normally imply that Cleon had more than one son. Nevertheless, it is possible that the Thudippus of Araphen, who was principal trierarch before 323/2, was Myronides' older brother, thus making Myronides the more likely candidate for adoption. See Davies 1971: 229, who suggests that the Cleon who was a Councilor in 336/5 may have been a third brother, but he sounds the cautionary note that Thudippus and Cleon could have been the sons of the elder Cleon's brother, Anaxippus. He is not mentioned in the speech but was one of the *epimelētai* (curators) of the dockyards in 356/5.

[7]D. Welsh, "Isaeus 9 and Astyphilus' Last Expedition," GRBS 32 (1991), 133–150.

died there.[8] I will try to prove to you what I stated in my oath, that he did not adopt a son, bequeath his property, or leave a will, and that nobody has a right to possess the property of Astyphilus except me. [2] Cleon[9] here is first cousin to Astyphilus on his father's side, and his son, whom he claims to have given him for adoption, is his first cousin once removed. Cleon's father was adopted into another family, and they are still members of that family, and so legally they are not related to Astyphilus at all. Since they had no claim on these grounds, they fabricated a will, gentlemen, a forgery (as I think I will prove), and are seeking to deprive me of my brother's property. [3] And so strong has been the belief of Cleon here both before and now that nobody other than himself will possess the estate that as soon as the news of Astyphilus' death was announced, when my father was ill and I was abroad on military service, he entered into possession of the land and said that anything else he left belonged entirely to his own son, before you voted at all. [4] But when my brother's remains were brought home, the one who pretends to have been adopted long ago as his son did not lay them out or bury them,[10] but Astyphilus' friends and fellow soldiers, seeing that my father was sick and I was abroad, themselves both laid out the remains and performed all the other customary rites, and they led my father, ill as he was, to the tomb, knowing full well that Astyphilus regarded him with affection. I'll produce the very friends of the deceased, who were among those present, as witnesses of this.

[WITNESSES]

[5] That Cleon did not bury Astyphilus, even he himself would not deny, and it has been confirmed by witnesses. When I returned

---

[8]On the date, see the Introduction. An Astyphilus moved a decree in 378/7 admitting Methymna (also on Lesbos) into the Athenian confederation, but the identification of the two men is uncertain. See Davies 1971: 230.

[9]Cleon was a *tamias* (treasurer) of Athena in 377/6. It has been suggested that his father, Thudippus, was the son-in-law of the leading fifth-century politician Cleon (see Davies 1971: 228), but it is also possible that this was the family into which the speaker claims Thudippus had been adopted.

[10]Cleon's son was clearly a minor at the time, but Cleon should have performed this duty (cf. 9.5).

home and found my opponents enjoying his property, I approached
Cleon, who said that[11] his son had been adopted by Astyphilus and
that he had left a will to this effect with Hierocles of Iphistiadae.
When I heard him say this, I went to Hierocles' house, knowing
full well that he was a very close friend of Cleon [6] but not thinking he would dare to lie about Astyphilus after his death, especially
since Hierocles was his uncle and mine too.[12] Nevertheless, gentlemen, Hierocles took no account of this and when questioned by me
replied that he had the will; he said that he had received it from Astyphilus when he was about to set sail for Mytilene. To prove he said
these things, please read this deposition.

[DEPOSITION]

[7] Since, then, gentlemen, none of his relatives was present when
my brother died and I was abroad when his remains were brought
here, it's necessary for me to prove from my opponent's own words
that the will is a forgery. Now it's likely that he not only desired to
adopt a son to leave behind but also considered how to make his will
absolutely valid and ensure that whomever he adopted, he should
possess the property, attend the family altars, and perform the customary rites for him after his death and for his ancestors; [8] and he
would be absolutely sure that all these things would not happen if he
made his will without his family being present but only if he summoned first his relatives, then the members of his phratry and deme,
and finally as many as possible of his other close friends. In that way,
anybody who might claim the estate on the ground of either kinship
or bequest would be easily proved a liar. [9] Now Astyphilus clearly
did nothing of the sort and did not summon any of these people
when he made the will my opponents claim he did, unless, that is,
anybody has been suborned by them to agree that he was present.
But I will myself produce all these people to you as witnesses.

[WITNESSES]

---

[11]There is a lacuna in the text after "his property," and the words "I approached Cleon, who said that" follow Dobree's suggested addition.

[12]Hierocles' sister was the mother of both Astyphilus and the speaker
(cf. 9.23, 27).

[10] Perhaps, then, Cleon here will say that it is not reasonable for you to use these witnesses as proof, because they testify only that they do not know Astyphilus made this will. But since the dispute is about a will and the adoption of a son by Astyphilus, I think that the testimony is far weightier for us when his friends say they were not present on the most important of issues than when people who are not related to him at all testify that they were there. [11] Besides, Cleon himself, gentlemen, who apparently is no fool, when Astyphilus was adopting his son and leaving the will, ought to have summoned any relatives he knew were in Athens and anybody else he knew Astyphilus was at all close to. Nobody could then have prevented Astyphilus from leaving his property to whomever he wished, but that the will was not made in secret would have been strong evidence in Cleon's favor. [12] Further, gentlemen, if Astyphilus did not want anybody to know that he was adopting Cleon's son or that he'd left a will, it's likely that nobody else's name would have been entered in the document as witness;[13] but if it is clear that he made a will in front of witnesses, and these were not people especially close to him but ones who happened to be there, how likely is it that the will is genuine? [13] I don't think anybody, when he was adopting a son, would have dared summon any others than those to whom he was about to leave the son in his place as a future partner in their religious and civil rites.[14] Moreover, nobody ought to be ashamed of summoning the largest possible number of witnesses to such a will, when there's a law that a man is entitled to leave his property to whomever he wishes.

[14] Consider also, gentlemen, the matter of the date my opponents assign to the will. They say that he made these dispositions when he was setting sail for Mytilene on military service: it appears from their account, then, that Astyphilus knew beforehand everything that was going to happen to him! He'd served first at Corinth,[15]

---

[13]The absence of witnesses would certainly have raised questions as to the authenticity of the will.

[14]I.e., the members of his phratry and deme (cf. 9.8).

[15]In 394; he must therefore have been born by 413/12 at the latest, and his father will have died (9.17) when he was still a child (9.20, 27), by ca. 410. See Davies 1971: 230.

then in Thessaly,[16] and all through the Theban war besides,[17] and wherever else he heard that an army was being mustered he went off there as a company commander; and in not a single one of these campaigns did he leave behind a will. The expedition to Mytilene was his last, the one on which he died. [15] Who among you could find it credible that when Astyphilus was serving on other campaigns and knew full well that he was going to be in danger on all of them, fate should befall him so precisely that he did not previously make a will about a single item of his property, but when he was about to go on service for the last time, setting sail as a volunteer and with every prospect of returning safely from this campaign—how credible is it now that he then left a will, set sail, and died?

[16] But apart from this, gentlemen of the jury, I'll produce even greater proof that there is no truth in what my opponents say. I will prove to you that Astyphilus was the bitterest of all enemies with Cleon, and hated him so much and with such good reason that he would far sooner have stipulated that none of his relatives should ever speak to Cleon than have adopted his son. [17] Thudippus, the father of Cleon here, is said to have been responsible, gentlemen, for the death of Astyphilus' father Euthycrates: he assaulted him when a dispute arose between them over the division of their land, and Euthycrates suffered so badly that he fell ill from the blows and died a few days later.[18] [18] That this is true I'm sure many of the Araphenians[19] who were working in the fields with them at the time might possibly testify for me, but I could not find any who would testify expressly to you on such a serious matter. Hierocles saw him being hit, the man who claims that the document was deposited with him, but I know he would refuse to testify against the will he is himself

---

[16]In an unknown conflict.

[17]See the Introduction.

[18]If this story is true, we would expect Thudippus to have been prosecuted for homicide, unless Euthycrates had forgiven him; there may have been other factors involved that the speaker omits. For the approximate date of Euthycrates' death, see above, 14n.

[19]I.e., fellow demesmen of the brothers from Araphen in east Attica.

producing. But nevertheless call Hierocles, either to testify before the jury or to swear an oath of disclaimer.[20]

[OATH OF DISCLAIMER]

[19] I knew exactly what he would say: it's normal for the same man to swear an oath of disclaimer about things he knows and then be ready to swear an oath that he knows all about things which did not happen; but to prove that when Astyphilus' father Euthycrates was dying he solemnly charged his relatives never to allow any of Thudippus' family to approach his tomb, I will produce as a witness of this the husband of Astyphilus' aunt.[21]

[DEPOSITION]

[20] Astyphilus, then, heard about these things while still only a child both from this man and from his other relatives, and from the moment he was old enough to understand he never spoke to Cleon, and until the day he died he considered it impious, when Thudippus bore such responsibility for his father's death, to speak with the man's son. To prove that he was at odds with Cleon the whole time, I'll produce as witnesses those who know about this.

[WITNESSES]

[21] Next, it would surely have been reasonable for Astyphilus, whenever he was in Athens, to go to the sacrifices, at which all Athenians entertain each other, with Cleon rather than anybody else, since he was a demesman and his cousin, and especially if he intended to adopt his son. To prove, then, that he never went with him, the clerk will read you the deposition of his demesmen.

---

[20]An *exōmosia,* denying knowledge of the events in question, would exempt one from testifying. Despite the speaker's pretence of uncertainty, Hierocles must have sworn the *exōmosia* before the trial, so that here the statement can just be read to the jurors.

[21]I.e., the husband of the sister of Thudippus and Euthycrates, who was also Cleon's aunt. Her evidence, given through her husband, will have been a key support for the speaker's contention that the two brothers were at loggerheads and also a balance to the testimony of Hierocles. See Avramovic 1990: 51–53.

[DEPOSITION]

[22] This, then, was Cleon's relationship with the deceased, and he thinks his son should inherit his property. But why must I speak about him? It's Hierocles, uncle both to the deceased and to me, who is so bold that he comes here with a forged will and says that Astyphilus left it in his keeping. [23] And yet, Hierocles, even though you received many kindnesses from my father Theophrastus when you were not doing as well as you are now and from Astyphilus, you do not properly return the favor to either of them: you are depriving me, Theophrastus' son and your own nephew, of what the laws granted to me, and you are inventing lies about Astyphilus now that he's dead and doing your part to make his bitterest enemies his heirs. [24] Even before the estate was claimed,[22] gentlemen, Hierocles knew full well that it would devolve to nobody else but me, and so he approached all the friends of the deceased in turn, peddling his scheme and trying to persuade people who had no right to the estate to make a claim. He said that he was Astyphilus' uncle and would declare that he had left a will, if anybody would become his partner; and now that he has made an agreement with Cleon and divided up my brother's property, he will ask to be believed as telling the truth. I reckon he would gladly even swear an oath, if somebody were to propose one to him. [25] And although he is a relative of mine, he refuses to testify even to things that have happened, while he joins in telling lies with my opponent, to whom he is not related at all, and has come up with a document of things that never happened. He thinks making money is far more important than his kinship with me. And to prove that he went round promising to produce a will if anybody would become his partner, I'll produce as witnesses the very people he approached.

[WITNESSES]

[26] What name then, gentlemen, should be given to this man, who is willing so readily to invent lies about one of the dead for his

---

[22] The speaker presumably means by Cleon rather than by himself, although the impression he tries to give is that Cleon simply took possession of the estate by *embateusis* (entry) without making a formal claim (cf. 9.3, 5, 32). See further Wyse 1904: 640.

own profit? This testimony will be no small proof to you that he isn't producing the will in Cleon's favor for nothing but has received payment. Such things, however, do they contrive together against me; for each of them thinks he has a windfall in whatever he can take from the property of Astyphilus.

[27] I have shown as best I can that the will is not genuine and that Cleon and Hierocles wish to deceive you; now I'll show you that even if I were not related to Astyphilus at all, I have a better right to his property than my opponents. When my father Theophrastus received my mother, who was also Astyphilus' mother, in marriage from Hierocles,[23] she brought Astyphilus with her, then a little child, and he lived with us the whole time and was brought up by my father.[24] [28] And when I was born and reached schooling age, I was educated with him. Please take this deposition, then that of the teachers whose classes we attended.

[DEPOSITION]

My father planted Astyphilus' father's land, gentlemen, and cultivated it and doubled its value. Will the witnesses to this come up as well, please.

[WITNESSES]

[29] Next, when my brother came of age, he received everything in correct and proper fashion, and so he never made any complaint against my father. After this my father betrothed Astyphilus' sister by the same father to a husband of his choice,[25] and he managed everything else to Astyphilus' satisfaction: he thought he'd received

---

[23]Hierocles acted as her legal representative (*kyrios*), indicating that her father was dead.

[24]He may in fact have been the boy's guardian, appointed as such in Euthycrates' will or by the Archon, and so was legally bound to take good care of Astyphilus and the estate.

[25]The performance of this duty by Theophrastus, not the now-adult Astyphilus, is a further indication of their excellent relationship. The sister and any children of hers had a stronger claim to the estate than the speaker, and so presumably they either were dead or did not claim because they believed the will was genuine. For further possibilities, see Avramovic 1990: 44–45.

sufficient proof from my father of his goodwill towards him, since he'd been brought up by him from his early childhood. The people who know the facts are also my witnesses about the betrothal.

[WITNESSES]

[30] Further, my father took Astyphilus everywhere with him when he was a boy to the religious ceremonies, just as he took me, and introduced him to the followers of Heracles, so that he might become a member of the association.[26] The members themselves will testify to you.

[WITNESSES]

Next, consider my relationship with my brother, gentlemen. First, I was brought up with him from childhood, and second, I never had a dispute with him, but he regarded me with affection, as all our relatives and friends know. I would like them to come forward as witnesses.

[WITNESSES]

[31] Can you imagine, gentlemen, that Astyphilus, who so hated Cleon and had received so many kindnesses from my father, would have adopted a son of one of his enemies or left him his property, depriving his benefactors and relatives? I think not, even if Hierocles produces forged wills ten times over; but because I am his brother and because of our other close ties, it belongs far more to me than to Cleon's son, [32] since it was totally improper of them to claim the property of Astyphilus when they were so disposed towards him and did not bury his remains but claimed the property before performing the customary rites over him. Further, they now think they should inherit Astyphilus' property not only saying there is a will but also comparing our degree of kinship, on the ground that Cleon was a first cousin on his father's side. [33] But it's not likely, gentlemen, that you will pay any attention to this man's degree of kinship: nobody has ever been adopted out of his family and then inherited from the family he was adopted out of, unless he legally returned to

---

[26]On other confraternities (*thiasoi*), hereditary groups devoted to the cult of Heracles, see Andrewes 1961: 9–12; Parker 1996: 333–334.

it. . . .[27] These men,[28] however, knowing perfectly well that Astyphilus did not adopt Cleon's son, have never given him any share of the victims' meat even though he has often come forward. Please take this deposition too.

[DEPOSITION]

[34] Consider our sworn statements, therefore, and then vote for one of us. Cleon says that his son was adopted by Astyphilus and that he made a will to this effect; but I deny this and say that all Astyphilus' property is mine, because I am his brother, as my opponents know perfectly well themselves. Do not then, gentlemen, give Astyphilus an adopted son he never adopted himself during his lifetime, but confirm for me the laws that you yourselves passed: it is according to them that I claim the estate and make a most holy request, gentlemen, that you make me heir to my brother's property. [35] I showed you that he did not leave his property to anybody, and I produced witnesses to everything I said. Help me, then, and if Cleon can speak better than I, let this do him no good without the law and justice, but make yourselves arbiters of everything. You are gathered together for this reason, that the shameless may not gain any advantage and the weaker may have the courage to pursue their just claims, knowing full well that you are paying attention to nothing else. [36] Therefore, all of you take my side, gentlemen; if you are persuaded by Cleon to vote in any other way, consider what you will be responsible for. First, you will cause the bitterest enemies of Astyphilus to go to his tomb and perform the ceremonies over him; second, you will invalidate the solemn injunctions of Astyphilus' father Euthycrates, which Astyphilus himself died before violating; and finally, you will convict Astyphilus after his death of insanity; [37] for if he adopted this man as his son, whose father was his most bitter enemy, how will those who hear about it not conclude that

---

[27]There is another lacuna in the text here, which would have told how Cleon tried to have his son recognized by the members of Astyphilus' phratry (see next note).

[28]Since Astyphilus and Cleon were both from the deme Araphen, "these men" must be members of Astyphilus' phratry. Their attitude towards Cleon's son is significant. See Avramovic 1990: 53–54.

he was out of his mind or destroyed by drugs? Further, gentlemen of the jury, you will be allowing me, after being brought up in the same house and educated with Astyphilus and being his brother, to be deprived of his property by Cleon. I entreat and supplicate you by every means I can to vote for me: in this way you would especially gratify Astyphilus and do me no injustice.

10. AGAINST XENAENETUS
ON THE ESTATE OF ARISTARCHUS

Aristarchus I, the brother of Aristomenes, had two sons, Cyronides and Demochares, and two daughters. Cyronides was adopted as the son of his maternal grandfather Xenaenetus I and so passed out of the family, leaving Demochares as heir (10.4). When Aristarchus I died, Aristomenes became the children's guardian, but Demochares died when still a minor along with one of his sisters; hence (the speaker argues), the surviving daughter of Aristarchus I became the heiress to the estate,[1] which in the normal course of events would have passed to her son when he reached maturity. Since she was unmarried, she could now be claimed by Aristomenes as next of kin or by his son Apollodorus, but Aristomenes instead gave her in marriage to an unnamed man outside the family.

Before this Aristomenes had married his own daughter to Cyronides and had handed over to him the estate of Aristarchus I (10.5), even though he had forfeited his claim to it by his adoption. Cyronides in turn had two sons, Xenaenetus II and Aristarchus II. On his death, Aristarchus II was introduced (illegally, according to the speaker) to the phratry of Aristarchus I as his son by posthumous adoption (10.6). Aristarchus II then held the estate until his death in battle and, being childless, bequeathed it to his brother Xenaenetus II. But his ownership was challenged by the unnamed son of the daughter of Aristarchus I, who claims that his mother had been

---

[1]Strictly speaking, the estate of her brother (cf. 10.8, 14) rather than her father. But it seems that, either way, she was entitled to the rights enjoyed by an heiress (*epiklēros*). See Speech 6, n. 1.

Stemma

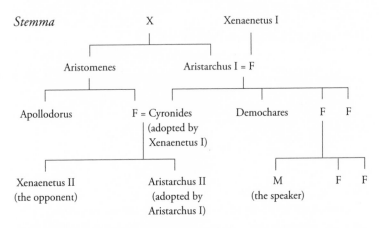

defrauded of her rightful inheritance by the machinations of Aristomenes and Cyronides.[2]

Was this, however, a fraud at all? On the face of it the speaker seems to have a good case, and it may have been the law that an adopted son (here Aristarchus II) was not permitted to bequeath the property he had thereby acquired, though interestingly the speaker does not use this argument. There were complicating factors, however, as the claimant lets slip during the course of his speech. First, the Archon had insisted that the speaker declare his mother was the sister of Aristarchus II (10.2). In doing so he was actually recognizing the posthumous adoption of Aristarchus II as the son of Aristarchus I, the very thing he argues was illegal. The Archon therefore seems to have accepted the position of Aristarchus II and to have allowed the speaker to make a claim (assuming his mother was dead) not as the grandson of Aristarchus I but as the nephew of Aristarchus II.[3] Second, why had the speaker or his mother not claimed the estate before? The alleged fraud by Aristomenes and Cyronides, both of whom were now dead, must have taken place well over thirty years earlier.[4] Against the an-

---

[2]It is unclear whether his mother was still alive and he was claiming as her legal representative (*kyrios*), or she was dead and he was claiming the estate for himself.

[3]Since *ex hypothesi* Aristarchus I now had a son, and so the estate in question was that of Aristarchus II.

[4]See below, 18n.

ticipated objection on these lines, he contends that his father had indeed tried to take action but had backed down under the threat that otherwise his wife would be claimed in marriage by her next of kin and so he would be obliged to divorce her. He and his son were afterwards prevented from acting by military service, as was the son on his return by legal disqualification because he was a state debtor (10.18–21).

These arguments are less than fully convincing, and the obvious counter to them is that Aristarchus II had long been accepted as the rightful heir to Aristarchus I. The posthumous adoption of Aristarchus II might be represented as a piece of chicanery, but it had been recognized by the Archon, and the speaker gives away the probable reason for this at 10.15: Cyronides had paid a debt on behalf of the estate (a point that the speaker does not contest), which presumably indicates that Aristarchus I had died a state debtor. Cyronides, then, paid the debt to clear his father's name and any liabilities that his heir would inherit; and the posthumous adoption of Aristarchus II, perhaps sanctioned in Cyronides' will from a sense of filial duty, was carried out to save this impoverished household (*oikos*) from extinction. It was, moreover, under these circumstances that Aristomenes generously gave the speaker's mother in marriage to a member of another *oikos* with a dowry (10.19), doing the best for her while understandably being unwilling to marry her himself (since he was already married with children) or to allow his son to marry into a poor family.

The speech is one of Isaeus' least remarkable rhetorically. The short proem (10.1–3) is full of commonplace material, including the speaker's inexperience contrasted with the clever speaking and plotting of his opponents, a hypothetical inversion,[5] and a preliminary indication of his line of argument. A brief narrative of the family background (10.4–6) is followed by the first of the speaker's proofs and what appear to be his strongest arguments: since Cyronides had been adopted out of the family, Demochares inherited his father's estate, and it should in turn have passed to his sister; and neither Aristarchus I nor Demochares had the right to make a will to any other effect, since Aristarchus I had a son and that son was still a minor when he

---

[5]For this figure, see Speech 2, n. 8.

died (10.8–10). Again, Cyronides did not have the right to introduce his son as the adopted son of Aristarchus I, nor did Aristomenes or Apollodorus have the right to do so on his behalf (10.11–14).

These points are made in a straightforward but forceful manner, preparing the ground for his arguments against two potentially damaging points in the opposition's favor. The first is a refutatory proof against his opponent's argument from probability (*eikos*) that Cyronides had paid a debt on behalf of the estate and therefore his sons had a just claim to it. The speaker meets this with the reverse probability that Cyronides would not have spent money on an insolvent estate or arranged for his son's adoption into one; therefore, it was unencumbered (10.15–17). Even more dangerous for his case was that a considerable time had elapsed since the death of Aristarchus I, and he had not challenged the possession of the estate by Aristarchus II (10.18–21). Here, in an attempt to raise sympathy, the speaker claims that when his father broached the question, he was threatened with the prospect that Aristomenes or Apollodorus would exercise their right to marry his wife (as the next of kin of an heiress), but his love for her was greater than the desire to secure the estate. Both the speaker and his father were subsequently obliged to fight in the Corinthian War, and after this the speaker was a state debtor, an honest admission but a dangerous one, since it cast doubt on his character (the debt implies that he had lost a lawsuit). Ultimately, he can only make a plea for justice, a theme that he magnifies with further considerations over the rights of a testator and his opponent's right to the estate (10.22–24). He thereby attempts to counter in advance his opponent's plea for pity after the death of his brother Aristarchus II in the war.

Pathos and prejudice are raised on the speaker's side by comparing his own position, of being deprived of his mother's estate, with that of his opponent, who stood to gain both that estate and the sizeable fortune of Xenaenetus I; he ends with the use of the emotive verb "eject" (*ekballein*, 10.24) of his mother's treatment, suggesting her physical removal from the property, even though she had in fact married into another family. The emotional level is maintained by the typical Isaean tactic of a withering assault on the character of Xenaenetus II, contrasted with the excellent behavior, generous (despite his financial difficulties) and patriotic, of the speaker (10.25).

The speech concludes with a recapitulation of the arguments and, after the mention of his military service, with a return to the character of the blunt soldier, and so without an appeal to the jurors (10.26).

The date of the speech is doubtful. Because the speaker tells us that he fought in the Corinthian War (10.20) and Aristarchus II has died during a war still in progress (10.22), most commentators take the latter to be the Theban War of 378–371. Wevers (1969: 23–25), however, argues for the Social War and a date of ca. 355.

10

[1] I wish, gentlemen, that I could tell you the truth about my claims as easily as Xenaenetus here can boldly tell lies: I think then it would immediately become clear to you whether we have come forward unjustly to claim the estate or my opponents have wrongfully possessed this property for a long time. But as it is, we are not equally matched, gentlemen. They are both clever speakers and skilled plotters, and they have often contended before you on behalf of others; but I, far from speaking on another's behalf, have never even pleaded a private suit of my own, and so I should receive much indulgence from you.

[2] Because I could not obtain justice from them, gentlemen, I was forced to add to my petition at the preliminary hearing that my mother was a sister of Aristarchus.[6] This will not, however, make your decision any easier when you consider whether, according to the laws, Aristarchus bequeathed this estate when it belonged to him or when he had no entitlement to it. This is the right question, gentlemen, since the law prescribes that a man can dispose of his own property to anybody he likes, but it has given nobody authority over the property of another. [3] This, then, is the first point I shall try to show you, if you would kindly listen to me with goodwill. You will see that this estate belonged from the start not to my opponents but to my mother as her patrimony, and second that Aristarchus took possession of it without the sanction of any law and along with his relatives is wronging my mother in violation of all the laws. I'll try to

---

[6]See the Introduction.

show you first by going back to the point from which you will most clearly understand how these matters lie.

[4] Aristarchus, gentlemen, was from Sypalettus.[7] He married the daughter of Xenaenetus of Acharnae, who bore him Cyronides, Demochares, my mother, and another daughter. Cyronides, the father of my opponent and the other one who was in unjust possession of this estate,[8] was adopted into another family, and so he no longer had any entitlement to the property. On the death of Aristarchus, the father of these two, Demochares his son became heir to his property. But he died when still a minor, as did the other sister, and my mother became heiress to the whole family estate.[9] [5] And so from the start all this estate was my mother's; but although she ought to have been married with the property to her nearest relative, she is being treated terribly, gentlemen. Aristomenes, the brother of Aristarchus the elder, who had a son and daughter of his own, refused to make her his own wife or to claim her by adjudication for his son with the estate;[10] he did neither of these things but gave his own daughter in marriage to Cyronides with my mother's property as her dowry, and from her were born Xenaenetus here and the deceased Aristarchus. [6] Here, then, is the crime; this is how she was deprived of her property, gentlemen. After this he gave my mother in marriage to my father. On the death of Cyronides they introduced Xenaenetus' brother as the adopted son of Aristarchus,[11] without the support of a single law, gentlemen, as I will show you by many proofs.

[7] I'll first produce witnesses that Cyronides was adopted into the family of Xenaenetus and died a member of it; second, that Aristarchus, whose estate this was, died before his son Demochares and

---

[7]Sypalettus and Acharnae were Athenian demes.

[8]I.e., Aristarchus II.

[9]A disputed, but probably correct use of the term *epiklēros*. See above, n. 1.

[10]They were not obliged so to act by the law, but might marry a poor heiress off with a dowry, as happened here (cf. 10.19). It is possible that Apollodorus was still a minor at the time.

[11]By the procedure of posthumous adoption, on which see Rubinstein 1993: 25–28.

that Demochares died while a minor, as did his other sister, and so the estate devolved to my mother. Please call the witnesses to this.

[WITNESSES]

[8] Therefore, the estate that is now in question, gentlemen, was my mother's from the start, since Cyronides was adopted into the family of Xenaenetus, and his father Aristarchus left his estate to his son Demochares, and he in turn to his own sister, my mother. But since they are utterly shameless, gentlemen, and think they should possess this property contrary to justice, you must understand that Aristarchus' introduction to the members of Aristarchus' phratry was not supported by a single law; if you do understand this, you will see clearly that the man who was in illegal possession of the estate was not entitled to dispose of it either. [9] I think you all know, gentlemen, that introductions of adopted children take place through a will, in which men distribute their property and adopt a son, and no other procedure is allowed. So if anybody says Aristarchus made a will himself, he will not be speaking the truth: as long as he had a legitimate son, Demochares, he would not have wanted to do so, and he was not allowed to bequeath his property to another.[12] And if they say that on the death of Aristarchus Demochares adopted Aristarchus, they will be lying about this too. [10] A minor is not allowed to have a will, for the law expressly forbids a child or woman to make a contract for the disposal of more than a *medimnos* of barley.[13] Now witnesses have testified that Aristarchus died before his son Demochares and that the latter died after his father; so even if they had made wills, Aristarchus was not entitled to inherit this property by will. Read, then, the laws according to which neither of them was allowed to make a will.

[LAWS]

---

[12] This is not in fact entirely true; see 6.28n.

[13] Roughly, 1.5 bushels or 51.7 liters. The precise scope of this law is unclear, since there are a number of examples of women engaging in financial transactions in excess of this sum. See V. J. Hunter, *Policing Athens: Social Control in the Attic Lawsuits, 420–320 B.C.* (Princeton, 1994), 19–29. Strictly speaking, the law applies to contracts, not wills.

[11] Nor again, gentlemen, could Cyronides give Aristarchus a son for adoption. It was possible for him to return to his father's family, leaving behind a son in the family of Xenaenetus, but there is no law whereby he could introduce a son of his own in his place; and if they say there is, they will be lying. So even if they say that the adoption was made by Cyronides,[14] they will not be able to point out any law by which he was allowed to do this, but from their own statements it will become even clearer to you that they are in possession of my mother's property illegally and insolently. [12] Furthermore, gentlemen, neither Aristomenes nor Apollodorus, who were entitled to claim my mother in marriage by adjudication, had any right to the estate. It would be amazing if it was not possible for Apollodorus or Aristomenes to gain control of my mother's property when married to her, according to the law that does not allow anybody to control the property of an heiress except her sons, who obtain possession of it when they come of age, but Aristomenes is going to be allowed to give her in marriage to another and then introduce a son for adoption to inherit her property. This would be truly scandalous. [13] Again, her own father, if he had no male children, would not have been allowed to dispose of the estate without her: the law prescribes that he has the power to leave his property with his daughters to whomever he wishes. But when a man who decided not to marry her and is not her father but her cousin introduces an heir against every law,[15] will this act be valid? Who among you will accept this? [14] I, gentlemen, am absolutely certain that neither Xenaenetus nor anybody else will be able to prove that this estate is not my mother's, left to her by her brother Demochares; but if they still have the audacity to say this, order them to point out the law by which the adoption of Aristarchus was carried out and who the adopter was: this is perfectly just. But I know that they will not be able to show one.

[15] So then, that the estate was my mother's from the start and she was unjustly deprived of it by my opponents, I think has been sufficiently proved by my arguments, by the testimony that has been

---

[14]By testament, since the speaker said in 10.6 that Aristarchus II was introduced to the phratry after his father's death. Further on testamentary adoptions, see the Introduction to this volume.

[15]I.e., it was Apollodorus who introduced Aristarchus II to the phratry (cf. 10.6, 8). Aristomenes may by then have been dead (cf. 10.25).

produced and by the laws themselves. Indeed, it's so clear even to my opponents that they are not rightfully in possession of this property that they do not base their case solely on the legality of Aristarchus' introduction to the members of the phratry but also allege that their father has paid a debt on behalf of this property,[16] so that if you don't think they possess it justly because of the adoption, it might appear reasonable that they have it because of the payment. [16] But I will show you by strong proofs, gentlemen, that they are not telling the truth. If, as they say, this estate was encumbered, my opponents would not have paid money on it, since it was not for them to do so, but the men who claimed my mother's hand ought to have decided what to do about it, nor would they have given a son as the adopted child of Aristarchus to this estate, if they were not going to get any advantage from it but instead incur great losses. [17] Others, when they are suffering financial hardship, give up their own children for adoption into other families, to prevent them sharing their father's loss of civic rights; did my opponents really give themselves for adoption into an encumbered property and family in order to lose their own possessions as well? This is not possible; rather, the estate was unencumbered and became my mother's, and in their greed for money and desire to rob her, my opponents made up this whole story.

[18] Some of you, gentlemen, may perhaps be surprised at the delay, wondering how it is that we allowed so much time to pass, and although we were being defrauded took no action in the matter but are only now making our claim.[17] Now I don't think it's right for anybody to have less than his due through inability or negligence, for this should not be the issue, but whether his claim is just or not; nevertheless, we can also explain this delay, gentlemen. [19] My father received

---

[16]This may imply (so Wyse 1904: 662) that Aristarchus I died a state debtor and so without civic rights (*atimos*) and that Cyronides settled the debt to prevent the confiscation of the estate and stop the loss of civic rights being passed down to the heir.

[17]Since the speaker fought in the Corinthian War (10.20), and so will have been over twenty by, say, 390; and since Aristarchus II died in the Theban (or possibly Social) War (10.22), the speaker is likely to have been well into his thirties (or fifties) at the time of the trial, and his mother's marriage must have taken place almost forty (or sixty) years earlier.

my mother with a dowry[18] and married her, but while my opponents were enjoying the estate, he had no way of getting it back, because when he raised the matter at my mother's bidding, they threatened him, saying they would themselves claim her by adjudication and marry her, if he was not willing to keep her with only a dowry. My father would have allowed them to enjoy an estate of even double the value so as not to lose my mother; [20] so this is the reason why my father did not bring a suit for the estate. After this, the Corinthian War started,[19] in which he and I were obliged to serve, so that neither of us could obtain justice. And when peace was restored,[20] I had a bit of trouble with the treasury,[21] so that it was not easy to pursue a dispute with these men. Thus we have good reasons for the way we've behaved in the matter. [21] But now it is only right, gentlemen, for my opponent to say who gave him the estate, by what laws he was introduced to the members of the phratry, and how my mother was not heiress to this property. These are the points on which you must cast your vote, not whether we are late in attempting to secure the restitution of what is ours. If they cannot explain, you would justly vote that the estate is mine.

[22] I know that they will not be able to do this, as it is a difficult task to argue against laws and justice. But they will talk about the deceased, bewailing that he was a good man who died in the war and that it is not just to make his will invalid. I myself, gentlemen, think that wills ought to be valid that somebody makes about his own property, but wills about other people's property ought not to be valid, just as those that everybody makes about his own property are valid. [23] Now this property is clearly not theirs but ours. Therefore, if he takes refuge in this argument and produces witnesses that Aristarchus made a will, order him to prove also that he did so with his own property. This is just, for it would be the most dread-

---

[18]Suggesting that Aristomenes had in fact treated her well.

[19]In 395.

[20]In 386.

[21]Another allusion to public debt and loss of civic rights (see above, n. 16), which included that of litigation. This does not necessarily conflict with the speaker's claim in the proem (10.1) that he had no experience of private litigation.

ful thing of all if Cyronides and my opponents, his children, are not only to possess the estate of Xenaenetus, worth more than four talents, but are to receive this one as well, while I, though my mother was the rightful owner and I come from the same line as Cyronides, am not to receive even my mother's estate, even when my opponents cannot bring forward the name of the person they have received it from. [24] And yet, gentlemen, just as the holder of disputed land must produce the person who has pledged or sold it to him, or prove that it was awarded to him, so is it right for my opponents to claim that the estate should be adjudicated to them only after proving their entitlement in detail, instead of ejecting my mother, the daughter of Aristarchus, from her patrimony before any hearing. [25] Doubtless, gentlemen, it is not enough for Xenaenetus to have dissipated the estate of Aristomenes in pederasty, but he thinks he should also dispose of this one in the same way. Whereas I, gentlemen of the jury, despite having slender means, gave my sisters in marriage, providing them with as large a dowry as I could afford.[22] Since I conduct myself in a law-abiding manner, perform my prescribed duties, and serve in the army, I think I should not be deprived of my mother's patrimony. [26] I have proved to you that Cyronides, the father of my opponents, was adopted out of the family and did not return to his father's house, that the father of Cyronides and of my mother left this estate to his son Demochares, who died while still a child, and that this estate then went to my mother.

---

[22] Indicating that his father was dead.

11. ON THE ESTATE OF HAGNIAS

〜〜〜〜〜〜〜〜〜〜〜〜〜〜〜〜〜〜〜〜〜〜〜〜〜〜〜〜〜〜〜〜〜〜〜〜

The suit in which this speech was delivered is one of the few examples in the Attic orators in which we have a speech from the opposing side, though in this instance Demosthenes 43, *Against Macartatus,* was delivered in a subsequent action. It is also one of the relatively rare occasions on which we know the outcome of the trial: Isaeus' client, Theopompus, won the case. The survival of the two speeches enables us to reconstruct with some confidence much of the complex stemma of the family of Buselus of Oeum, though (as with the surviving accounts of the embassy to Philip II of Macedon found in Aeschines 2 and Demosthenes 19) the accounts are not entirely reconcilable and some of the affiliations are not by any means certain.

Hagnias II died on an embassy whose date is disputed (see below). He adopted by will his niece, with the stipulation that, if she died without offspring, the estate should pass to his half-brother Glaucon (i.e., he would be posthumously adopted as Hagnias II's son). The niece, who may have been the daughter either of a sister or (some scholars now feel) of Hagnias II's second half-brother, Glaucus, did indeed die without issue, and Glaucon took over the estate (11.9). The authenticity of the will was now challenged by Eubulides II (11.9; Dem. 43.43–45), who was a second cousin to Hagnias II on his father's side and a first cousin on his mother's side. He too died, but his case was pursued on behalf of his daughter Phylomache II by her husband Sositheus, who succeeded in having the will judged a forgery.

Consequently, Phylomache II won possession of the estate, since she was Hagnias II's first cousin once removed on his father's side, giving her priority over Glaucon, who was Hagnias II's half-brother but on his mother's side (the male line taking precedence over the

Stemma

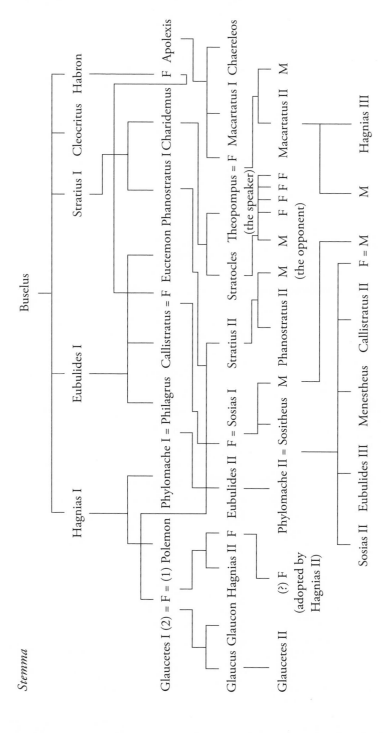

female). This happened in 361/0 (Dem. 43.31), but the overturning of the will prompted other second cousins to enter a claim: Stratius II, Stratocles, and Theopompus. Stratius II and Stratocles both died, and it was left to Theopompus to fight the claim against (he says, 11.16) Phylomache II and the mother of Hagnias II: as the daughter of Phanostratus I, the latter was at the same time her son's second cousin but, since she therefore came after Theopompus in the order of succession, she claimed the estate as Hagnias II's mother (11.17).

According to Demosthenes 43.7–8, however, there were five claimants in all: Phylomache II, Theopompus, Glaucon, Glaucus, and the mysterious Eupolemus.[1] Sositheus claims that Theopompus did a deal with the others against Phylomache II and that a written agreement was deposited with Medeius of Hagnus. Another deal (or another part of the same deal) alleged by his fellow guardian and strenuously denied was that Theopompus agreed to give Stratocles' son half of the estate if he was successful in his claim (11.24–26). It is possible, then, that Theopompus was, as one scholar has called him,[2] "a thorough-paced scoundrel," but the precise details of the inheritance claim (*diadikasia*) are obscure. What is clear is that Theopompus won the estate by demonstrating that Phylomache I was not a legitimate sister of Polemon: her granddaughter Phylomache II was therefore related to Hagnias II only as his second cousin once removed through her great-grandfather Eubulides. On this basis Theopompus was the closest relative, since Hagnias II's mother had no legal claim as mother, and he secured the estate in his turn. He was, however, subsequently prosecuted by an *eisangelia kakōseōs orphanou* for maltreatment of an orphan,[3] the son of his brother Stratocles; the case

---

[1]Davies (1971: 82–83) takes Eupolemus to be the son of Hagnias II's niece, but this would have given him the strongest claim to the estate (as Cox 1998: 6 n. 9). MacDowell (1978: 105) thinks he is the third husband of Hagnias II's mother; but Theopompus says she was represented by her legal representatives (*kyrioi;* 11.16), which implies her two sons Glaucus and Glaucon, not a husband (*contra* Thompson 1976: 26–27). Humphreys (1983: 223 n. 13) suggests the son of Callistratus.

[2]Davies 1971: 84.

[3]Cf. 11.6, 15; Harpoc. s.v. *eisangelia.* The generic term for public suits, *graphē,* is used at 11.28, 31, 32, 35.

was brought by another of the boy's guardians (possibly a brother of Stratocles' wife), on the ground that he had defrauded the boy of half of Hagnias II's estate. This speech was Theopompus' defense.

Theopompus' main argument is based on the law of succession of collateral relatives, which he has read out before the start of the speech (cf. 7.20; Dem. 43.51). In the law, which in essence distinguished between close and more distant relatives, close relatives (*ankhisteis*) were defined as relatives "as far as children of cousins." The difficulty lies in the meaning of "cousin." Since Greek uses the same word (*anepsios*) for what we would call first cousins and second cousins, it is not clear whether "children of cousins" here means "children of first cousins" (i.e., first cousins once removed) or "second cousins" (i.e., children of a parent's first cousin). Theopompus was Hagnias II's second cousin, and on the interpretation that "children of cousins" means "first cousins once removed," he was outside the required degree of kinship. But Theopompus not only won his case against Phylomache II, he also won this case against his fellow guardian, and it seems very likely that his son later won a further case on this basis (see below).

At least two juries, then, were convinced by Theopompus' interpretation of the law, and we should therefore accept that his version of it was correct, rather than that he managed to hoodwink them on both occasions. Where he may be suspected of trickery is in his argument against the right of Stratocles' son to share the estate. It is certain that the boy, as the son of a second cousin, was outside the requisite degree of kinship and so, as Theopompus argues, was not entitled himself to claim a share of Hagnias II's estate. But the opponent probably argued that Stratocles did have such a claim, even though he died before he established it, and so his son ought to inherit his father's share with the rest of his estate (as indeed Theopompus later passed on his estate, including the part that had belonged to Hagnias II, to his son Macartatus II). The jurors disagreed.

Prosecutions of Theopompus' witnesses for false testimony followed this suit (cf. 11.45). These were, however, unsuccessful, and Theopompus enjoyed the estate until his death, when it passed to his son Macartatus II. But this was not to be the end of the saga. Phylomache II became the heiress (*epiklēros*) to the estate of her father Eubulides II, and so she and Sositheus had one of their sons, Eubulides III, posthumously adopted as the son of Eubulides II (Dem. 43.14). Given the legitimacy of Phylomache I as the sister of Polemon (which Theopompus had, of course, successfully contested), Eubulides III was now in law a first cousin once removed of Hagnias II, and Sositheus claimed Hagnias II's estate on his behalf against Macartatus II by Demosthenes 43. He in effect argues that, contrary to Theopompus' earlier contention, the law in fact covered only the sons of first cousins (i.e., first cousins once removed), and Theopompus was a second cousin outside the prescribed limit. Yet it seems that once again the jurors agreed with the interpretation previously adduced by Theopompus: Macartatus II had a son, Hagnias III, who was an ephebe in 324/3 and so born around the time of this trial in ca. 344/3; since he bears the name Hagnias, this suggests that his father continued in possession of the estate of Hagnias II.

The force of Theopompus' logical reasoning is a key feature of the rhetoric of the speech. Lacking a regular proem, it is unique in the oratorical corpus in that it opens with the citation and discussion of laws (11.1–7).[4] Theopompus offers his interpretation of the laws of succession and how they apply in this case, to impress on the jurors from the start that he has the law on his side, while his nephew has no claim to Hagnias II's estate in law. He questions his opponent (11.5), criticizes his responses, and makes a preliminary attack on his character (11.6), before drawing his unconventional opening to a close with the standard proem topics of a summary of what he will prove and a promise to state the facts from the beginning (11.7).

In his narrative (11.8–10) Theopompus emphasizes that he did not contest Hagnias II's will, despite being more closely related than the niece, until Phylomache II entered her claim. He then returns to the law and the limits to the rights of collaterals, which leads into the comparative argument that if he were dead, children outside the limits would not be entitled to inherit, and so they had no claim when he was alive (11.11–12); and then to a pathetic paradox in a long period (11.13–14), with the charge that his opponent is acting like a sykophant. A second narrative follows (11.15–18) of how Theopompus successfully contested the claim of Phylomache II, then a summary of

---

[4] As Usher 1999: 154.

his position in an extended rhetorical question (11.19), before his just and legally awarded position is juxtaposed to and contrasted with his opponent's false allegations of collusion with Stratocles (11.20–26).

Theopompus' refutatory arguments here open with another attack on the mendacious and slanderous character of his opponent, followed by the persistently logical arguments that no deal could have been struck since only one voting urn was used in a double claim; hence, each party either won or lost, and there was no need for Theopompus to agree to share the estate with Stratocles' son if (as his opponent claimed) he was in any case entitled to half of it. Theopompus uses an argument from dilemma in 11.24 followed by *hypophora,* and as before, he summarizes his position with an extended rhetorical question. Further refutatory arguments, explaining his opponent's failure to go to law earlier through another examination of the relative status of his rival claimants, are again made all the more rhetorically effective by the appended charges of sykophancy and slander (11.27–31).

Theopompus now summarizes his legal arguments and what he sees as "the essential rights of the case," reiterating the legitimacy of his position and the lies of his opponent (11.32–36). As before, he puts forward a series of logical conditions and states the conclusions that must follow from them, with the underlying contention here that the wrong process was being used.[5] With his legal position securely established, Theopompus can move on to a potentially very damaging topic in the context of a maltreatment case, that of his opponent's emotional appeal concerning his wealth and meanness, and his ward's poverty (11.37–40). He refutes this by means of a third narrative (11.40–46), in which he sets out the wealth of his own and Stratocles' estates (which will have started off equal).[6] Refutatory arguments follow, again directed against the mendacious and slanderous claims of his opponent over the size of his own estate, which was not (he claims) enhanced by the addition of the estates of his wife's brothers (11.47–49). He emphasizes, in commonplace fashion, that he performed liturgies and paid his taxes, and our text ends with the proposal that his estate be pooled with his ward's and then

---

[5] The rhetorical tactic of *metalēpsis.* See Thompson 1976: 42–43.

[6] See in more detail on this Thompson 1976: 47–54.

equally divided. Theopompus perhaps went on to substantiate his own charge (11.31) that his opponent was trying to get his hands on his ward's wealth, in contrast to Theopompus' services on behalf of the boy, but unfortunately our manuscript breaks off at this point.

The dating of Isaeus 11 and the other events is, perhaps unsurprisingly, problematic. There appear to be two fixed points, the first of which is accepted by most scholars and derives from the identification of Hagnias II with the ambassador who was captured by the Spartan Pharax on an embassy to Persia in 397/6, handed over to the Spartans, and executed (cf. *Hell. Oxy.* 7.1; Harpoc., s.v. *Hagnias*).[7] This date has been strongly disputed by Humphreys, who notes that Harpocration equates his Hagnias with a man mentioned by Isaeus in his Lost Speech XIV, *Against Eucleides,* and does not refer to Speech 11. Further, the embassy of 397/6 appears to have been unsuccessful, although Isaeus here talks of the "business that turned out advantageously for the city" (11.8). Humphreys therefore prefers a later embassy, perhaps the one to Amyntas, king of Macedon, in 375 or 373.

The commonly accepted date of 396 for Hagnias II's death would mean that there was a period of roughly thirty-five years during most of which (it seems) the niece would have been in control of the estate, yet we hear of no marriage or children. The later date eradicates this problem[8] and also allows for later birth dates for Hagnias II's mother and her close family (Stratius II, Phanostratus I, and Stratius I). The second and firmer date (if we accept that the documents in Dem. 43 are genuine) is the awarding of the estate to Phylomache II in 361/0. Theopompus then contested the award to Phylomache II, and the present speech will have been delivered in the early 350s, while Demosthenes 43 will date to the late 340s.

11

[LAWS]

---

[7] For a full discussion, see Humphreys 1983.

[8] The niece could now have died as a minor, *pace* Davies 1971: 82.

[1] I've read you the laws for this reason, because according to the first of these, my opponent maintains that the boy[9] is entitled to half the estate, a claim that is not true. Hagnias was not our brother, but the law concerning a brother's property[10] has given the right of inheritance first to brothers and nephews, if they are on the father's side: this is the nearest degree of relationship[11] to the deceased. [2] In the absence of these, it second names the sisters by the same father and their children. In their absence, it gives the right of succession to the third degree, cousins on the father's side as far as children of cousins. If this degree is also lacking, it goes back again and gives control of the estate to those on the mother's side of the deceased, on the same principles as it originally gave the right of inheritance to those on the father's side. [3] These are the only rights of succession the lawgiver recognizes, in more concise wording than my paraphrase, but he indicates his desired intention in this way. This boy is not related by kinship to Hagnias in a single one of these titles but is outside the prescribed degrees of kinship. But in order that you understand precisely the points you are going to vote on, let my opponent state concisely in which of the above-mentioned degrees the boy is related to the man who left the estate. If he is shown to be related in any way, I willingly concede that half the estate is the boy's. [4] But if he cannot state any of these, surely he will be clearly proved to be acting as a sykophant against me[12] and trying to deceive you in contravention of the laws. I shall therefore bring him up before you and question him,[13] reading the law clause by clause, and in this way you will learn whether the boy is entitled to the property of Hagnias or not. [To the clerk] Please take the laws; and you, come up here, since you are so clever at slandering and twisting the laws. [To the clerk again] You read.

---

[9]The son of Theopompus' brother Stratocles; see the Introduction.

[10]This law is quoted at Dem. 43.51.

[11]"Degree of relationship" renders *genos,* a difficult term to translate. Thompson (1976: 3–4) suggests the awkward phrase "inheritance class."

[12]See 1.42n.

[13]Questioning of an opponent (*erōtēsis*) was not uncommon. A well-known example is to be found in Plato's *Apology* (24c–25a).

[LAWS]

[5] Stop. I shall question you. Is the boy a brother of Hagnias, or a nephew, the son of a brother or sister, or a cousin, or the son of a cousin on his mother's or father's side? Which of these titles, to which the law gives the right of succession? And mind you don't say that he is my nephew. It is not a question now of my estate, since I'm alive. If I had died childless and he were claiming my property, this would be a fitting reply to the question. But today you are saying that half of Hagnias' property belongs to the boy. You must therefore state the prescribed degree of kinship by which the boy is related to Hagnias. So tell these jurors here what it is.

[6] You observe that he cannot state the relationship but gives every answer except the one you need to know. And yet a man who is doing the right thing should not be embarrassed but should be able to answer at once, and not only this, but take an oath and produce witnesses about the degree of relationship, so that you gave him more credence. As it is, in matters on which he has not given a reply, or produced witnesses, or sworn an oath, or read a law, he thinks that you, who have sworn to vote according to the laws, should believe him and condemn me in this impeachment contrary to the laws; that's how wicked and shameless a man he is. [7] But I will not act like this at all; no, I will state my relationship and the grounds on which I am entitled to the estate, and I will prove—and you will agree with me—that the boy and all those who previously claimed the estate against me are outside the prescribed degree of kinship. I must state what has happened from the start; and from this you will recognize both my right of succession and that my opponents are not entitled to the estate.

[8] Hagnias, Eubulides,[14] Stratocles, Stratius (the brother of Hagnias' mother), and I, gentlemen, are all the children of cousins: our fathers were cousins, the children of brothers by the same father. When Hagnias, then, was preparing to sail off as ambassador on

---

[14]Eubulides also had a half-brother, Menestheus, the son of Philagrus by his second wife Telesippe (Dem. 43.44–45). He was equally a second cousin of Hagnias II but will have been dead by the time of Phylomache II's claim. See Davies 1971: 81; Thompson 1976: 10–11.

that business that turned out advantageously for the city,[15] he did not leave his property with us, his nearest relatives, in case anything should happen, but adopted a niece as his daughter;[16] if anything happened to her, he left his property to Glaucon, his half-brother by the same mother, and he wrote these dispositions in a will. [9] Some time after this Eubulides died,[17] the daughter Hagnias adopted also died, and Glaucon received the estate in accordance with the will. Not once did we think we should contest his will, but we thought that his intentions regarding his own property should prevail, and we abided by them. But Eubulides' daughter, together with her accomplices,[18] claimed the estate and obtained it, winning a lawsuit against those who claimed on the basis of the will; she was outside the prescribed degree of kinship[19] but hoped, it seems, that we would not bring an action against her, because we had not contested the will either.[20] [10] Since the estate had now become adjudicable to the next of kin,[21] we, Stratius, Stratocles, and myself, all prepared to bring a suit. But before our claims were heard, Stratius died[22] and so did Stratocles; thus I am left as the sole surviving relative on the

---

[15]The reference is obscure; see the Introduction.

[16]One of only three known examples in Athens of the adoption of a female, two of which appear in this speech (cf. 11.41). See 7.9 and n.

[17]In 361/0.

[18]Cf. 11.16. We are only informed that her husband Sositheus acted on her behalf (Dem. 43.9). His name, in turn, is only known from the Argument to Dem. 43 and so is not absolutely certain.

[19]Because of her grandmother's disputed status. See below, 16n.

[20]According to Dem. 43.4, Theopompus appeared as a witness for Glaucon against Eubulides' daughter. For possible implications of this, see Thompson 1976: 18–19.

[21]Since the court's decision had set aside the will, the estate was now intestate, and so the next of kin could claim it.

[22]If Hagnias II died in 396 as most scholars accept, his mother must have been very old by the late 360s (see below, 16n) and Stratius II will also have been a very elderly man; but Hagnias II probably died some twenty years later than this, thus bringing down the ages of his mother and uncle (see the Introduction). Stratius II left sons who were adults (11.15, 19) but did not pursue the claim (being outside the requisite degree of kinship). One of them, Phanostratus II, was a member of the Council in 371/0.

father's side, being the son of a cousin, and the only person who had the right of inheritance according to the laws, now that all the others who possessed the same degree of kinship as myself are dead.

[11] But how will you know that I possessed the rights as next of kin, while the children of the others, including this boy, did not? The law itself will show you. Everybody agrees that the rights as next of kin belong to cousins on the father's side as far as the children of cousins. But the point we must now consider is whether the law gives these rights after us to our children. So take the law and read it to the jurors.

[LAW. *If there is no relative on the father's side as far as the degree of the children of cousins, those on the mother's side are to inherit in the same order.*]²³

[12] Note, gentlemen, that the lawgiver did not say that if there is no relative on the father's side as far as the degree of the children of cousins, the children of first cousins' children are to inherit, but he assigned the right of inheritance now, in our absence,²⁴ to the relatives of the deceased on the mother's side, to brothers and sisters, their children, and so on, in the same order as was set down at the start. But he placed our children outside the prescribed degree of kinship. How, then, can those to whom the law does not award Hagnias' estate even if I were dead think that, when I am alive and in possession in accordance with the laws, they have the right of succession themselves? They cannot possibly think this. [13] Furthermore, if they do not share the right of succession when their fathers were related in the same degree as myself, neither does this boy have it, since his father was a relative in the same degree as they were. Isn't it appalling, therefore, that when the laws have expressly given me the right of inheritance in this way and have placed my opponents outside the prescribed degree of kinship, my opponent here should

---

²³The text of the law quoted here (the only example of this in the manuscripts of Isaeus) almost certainly is a later addition, deriving from what is said in 11.12.

²⁴I.e., when there are no children of cousins on the male side, such as the speaker.

have the audacity to act like a sykophant?[25] They did not think they should dispute it or pay a deposit when I laid claim to the estate, when the matter ought to have been settled if he had anything just to say, but now they make trouble for me in the boy's name and put me into the greatest of dangers. [14] And now he doesn't accuse me over money that we agree belongs to the boy, nor does he argue that I took any of this money (if I had managed the property as badly as he has done, I would deserve to be prosecuted for it), but he is concocting this kind of suit against me to secure property that you voted was mine, after giving anybody who wished the opportunity to claim it. Has he sunk to this depth of shamelessness?

[15] I think, then, you realize from what I've already said that I am not doing the boy any wrong nor am I in the least bit liable to these charges; but I believe you will understand this still more precisely from the rest of the story, especially when you hear how the adjudication of the estate to me took place. When I brought the action for the estate, gentlemen, my opponent, who is now impeaching me, did not think fit to pay a deposit on the boy's behalf, nor did Stratius' sons, who are related in the same degree as the boy, either for this[26] or any other reason think that they had any right to this property; [16] for my opponent would not even be making trouble for me now, if I had allowed him to plunder the boy's property and had not opposed him. These men, then, as I said, knew that they were outside the prescribed degree of kinship and did not claim the estate, but kept quiet; but those who were acting on behalf of Eubulides' daughter, who is related in the same degree as the boy and Stratius' sons, and the legal representatives (*kyrioi*)[27] of Hagnias' mother[28] decided to bring an action against me. [17] But they had

---

[25]See 1.42n.

[26]There is a lacuna in the text here.

[27]See above, n. 1. Sositheus alleges that Glaucon and Glaucus, and indeed Eupolemus (if he is meant here), were in cahoots with Theopompus (Dem. 43.7).

[28]If Hagnias II was over thirty in 396, his mother will have been born by ca. 445 and so by this time was about eight-five; by bringing his death down some twenty years, her age and that of her brother Stratius II can be reduced commensurately, and their father Phanostratus I was then born ca. 455. Their first

such difficulty deciding what to enter in their counter-claim about the degree of kinship that when the woman who was in possession of the estate and those who were explaining her kinship lied about it, I easily proved that they had dared to enter what was not true;[29] but those who represented Hagnias' mother, who is related in the same degree as I am (she was Stratius' sister) but is excluded by the law that gives preference to males, omitted this argument, and thinking they would gain an advantage over me wrote that she was the mother of the deceased—this was the nearest relationship of all by blood, but as everyone would agree is not within the prescribed degrees of kinship. [18] I then wrote that I am the son of a cousin, and since I had proved that those women were not within the prescribed degrees of kinship, I had the estate adjudicated to me by you; and none of their pleas prevailed, neither when the woman in possession of the estate said that she had previously won a decision over those who claimed on the basis of the will, nor when the other one said that she was the mother of the man who left the estate, but the jurors on that occasion attached such importance to justice and their oaths that they cast their vote for me, whose claim was based on the laws. [19] And yet if I defeated the women this way, by showing that they were not at all related to Hagnias according to the prescribed degree of kinship; and if my opponent did not dare to bring an action against me claiming half the estate for the boy; and if Stratius' sons, who are related in the same degree as this boy, do not even now think they

---

cousins Stratocles and Theopompus had children who were minors at the time of this speech in the early 350s and were themselves perhaps born ca. 410. Therefore, their father Charidemus may have been about fifteen years younger than his brother Phanostratus I but need not have been the considerably younger age that an earlier death for Hagnias II would imply (for which see Davies 1971: 81–82; a considerable age gap is not, of course, impossible: cf. the alleged sons of Euctemon in Speech 6).

[29]Theopompus' claim was based on his assertion that Phylomache I was not the legitimate, full sister of Polemon (Dem. 43.29, 39–40), a claim contested by Sositheus (id. 22, 24, 26, 29, 32, 35–36, 49, 63) but accepted by the jurors. As Davies notes (1971: 79), her marriage to her cousin Philagrus "creates a strong presumption of legitimacy," but this does not, of course, disprove Theopompus' contention. Philagrus later married Telesippe (Dem. 43.44–45) and had a son Menestheus, on whom see above, 8n.

should bring an action against me for the estate; and if I am in possession of the estate by your adjudication and can prove that even today my opponent cannot state the prescribed degree of kinship by which the boy is related to Hagnias—what more must you learn, what more can you want to hear about this matter? I think what I've said is sufficient for you as men of good sense.

[20] Again, my opponent, who is ready to lie at any opportunity and thinks his own depravity does him no harm, has the audacity to slander me on many other matters, which I will deal with presently; but in particular he now says that Stratocles and I made a deal as we were about to bring suit concerning the estate. But of all those who were prepared to claim the estate, we were the only ones for whom making a mutual agreement like this was impossible. [21] Since Eubulides' daughter and Hagnias' mother were not basing their claim on the same grounds in their suits against me, they might have made an agreement that if one of them were to win, she would give a share to the loser, as a separate voting urn would be used for each of them.[30] But our situation was not like this, since we were making two claims based on the same degree of relationship for half the estate each; only one voting urn is used for those who are claiming on the same grounds, and so it would be impossible for one to lose and the other to win, but the risk was the same for both of us together, so we could not possibly have joined together or made an agreement about the estate. [22] But when Stratocles died before our claims for half of the estate each were heard, and there was no further participation in the estate by Stratocles or by this boy, because of the law, but the entire inheritance came to me by right of succession if I could defeat those in possession, it was only then that my opponent invented and fabricated these fictions, expecting he would easily deceive you by these stories. None of them could have happened, but every detail in them has been provided for, as can easily be seen from the law. Take it and read it to the jurors.

[LAW]

---

[30]The voting procedure was different in an inheritance case in which, since there might be more than two parties, there was a separate voting urn for each claimant, with the exception described in the next sentence (cf. Dem. 43.10). For the regular procedure, see 5.17n.

[23] Does the law seem to you to give the opportunity for an agreement? Or doesn't it provide for the exact opposite, even if an agreement previously existed, by expressly prescribing that each party bring a suit for his share, by providing one voting urn for those who claim on the same ground, and by making this the procedure in claims for adjudication? But despite these legal provisions and the impossibility of there being an agreement, he has had the audacity to invent a lie as great and illogical as this. [24] And not only has he done this, but he's told the most inconsistent story possible, to which you must pay close attention, gentlemen. He says that I agreed to share half the estate with the boy, if I won my case against those in possession of it. Yet if he too had some share by degree of relationship, as my opponent states, what need was there for this agreement between us? Half the estate was equally adjudicable to them, if what they are saying is indeed true. [25] But if they had no entitlement by degree of kinship, why would I have agreed to give them a share, when the laws have given me the right of inheritance to the whole estate? Was it that it was impossible for me to claim without their consent? But the law gives the right to anybody who wishes, so they could not say this. Or did they have some testimony for me about the case, and if they did not testify, I would not have the estate adjudicated to me? But I was claiming on the ground of kinship, not on the ground of bequest, so I didn't need any witnesses. [26] And indeed, if it was impossible for me to have come to an arrangement with Stratocles during his lifetime and if his father did not leave the estate to the boy, since he did not have any of it adjudicated to him, and if it was unlikely that I agreed to share half the estate with him, but you awarded this estate to me by adjudication and my opponents neither claimed it then nor ever thought they should make a claim, how can you consider their arguments credible? I think you simply cannot.

[27] My opponent, then, pretends (since you might reasonably be amazed that they didn't bring a suit for half the estate at the time) that it was my fault that they did not claim against the others, because I had agreed to share the estate, so for this reason they did not pay the deposit, and also that the laws prevented a suit against me, because orphans are not allowed to sue their guardians; but neither of these statements is true. [28] My opponent could not point to a law that forbids him to bring suit against me on behalf of the boy,

because there is no law against this, but just as the law has provided for a public suit (*graphē*) against me, so it has granted either me or the boy the right to bring a private one (*dikē*). Moreover, they did not fail to claim the estate from those who were in possession of it because I agreed to give them a share, but because they had no right to this property whatsoever. [29] I know full well that, even if I had agreed the boy would receive half the estate from me by adjudication, they would never have carried out this agreement or even attempted to do so, knowing that since they were not within the prescribed degree of kinship, if they had anything that did not belong to them, they would easily have been deprived of it by the next of kin. As I said before, the law does not grant any right of succession at all to our children after us but to the relatives of the deceased on the mother's side. [30] So first Glaucon, the brother of Hagnias, would have come forward, and they could not say they had a closer relationship than he had but would clearly have been outside the prescribed degree of kinship; and then, if he'd been unwilling, the mother of Hagnias and Glaucon would have come forward, since she had an entitlement by kinship to her own son,[31] and so if she had contended against those who had no entitlement by degree of kinship, she clearly would have received half the estate from you, since justice and the laws have given her a right to it. [31] For these reasons, then, my opponent did not claim the estate, not because he was prevented from doing so by me or by the laws, but these are excuses that he has made in order to enter into these sykophantic proceedings. Drawing on them he has lodged a public suit (*graphē*) and by slandering me hopes to get money and remove me from the guardianship. And he thinks he's being clever in employing these devices, because if he doesn't succeed, he will not lose anything of his own,[32] but if he does achieve his objective, he will then be able to squander the boy's property as well with impunity.

[32] You must not, therefore, listen to my opponent's arguments, or permit or accustom people to bringing public suits (*graphai*) about

---

[31]I.e., as his cousin, not as his mother.

[32]Prosecutors of guardians for maltreatment did not risk the usual penalties in a public suit for securing less than twenty percent of the votes; see 3.46n.

matters for which the laws have prescribed private suits (*idiai dikai*).³³
The rights of this case are perfectly simple and easy to understand:
I'll deal with them briefly and entrust them to your memory, before
turning to the rest of my defense against their charges. [33] What
are these rights, then, and how do I define them? If my opponent
says the boy has a share in Hagnias' property by degree of kinship,
let him bring suit for half the estate before the Archon, and if you
vote for him, let him take it; this is what the laws prescribe. But if
he does not base his claim on this ground and says that I agreed to
share it with the boy, though I declare that there is no truth in this,
let him bring an action (*dikē*), and if he proves that I made such an
agreement, then let him enforce its execution; this is what's just.³⁴
[34] But if he says that the boy can pursue neither a property suit
nor a personal suit, let him name the law that prevents this, and if
he can show it, let the boy receive his share of the property in this
way too. If, on the other hand, he says that there is no need either for
the half share to be adjudicated or to sue me for it, because it already
belongs to the boy, let him register it with the Archon among the
terms for leasing the boy's property, and the lessee will secure it from
me as the boy's property. [35] These are the essential rights of the
case. These are also what the laws prescribe, not, thank heaven, that
I be prosecuted by public suits (*graphai*) in matters about which they
have instituted private suits (*idiai dikai*) or that I run personal risks
because I am not sharing this estate with the boy, which I received
by your vote when I defeated those who were in possession of it. If I
were in possession of anything that admittedly belonged to the boy
and had administered it badly to his detriment, then it would be
right to prosecute me by this public suit, but not, by heaven, when
it's my own property.

[36] I think, by heavens, that you are well aware and all equally
understand that he has acted completely unjustly in this matter and

---

³³There are some similarities between the public/private distinction here and
the distinction between criminal and civil cases in common law, though there
are also differences. The main point is that a *graphē* would have more serious
consequences for the defendant if he lost the case.

³⁴The speaker probably envisions a suit for damages (*dikē blabēs*) arising out
of a broken agreement.

has never spoken a word of truth about anything else, but has cleverly plotted everything out of greed, slandering us, twisting the laws, and seeking unjustly to get the better of you and me. So I don't know what more I need to say about this.

[37] I see, gentlemen, that most of his speech concerns my fortune and that of the boy and that he represents the boy's circumstances as thoroughly impoverished but for me he creates with his speech a picture of wealth; further, he accuses me of behaving dishonorably in that I do not offer to contribute towards the dowry of any of Stratocles' four daughters, even though (so he says) I have the child's property. [38] I certainly wish to discuss this too, since he hopes with his words to arouse in you a prejudice against me over the money I've acquired and pity for the children if you conclude that they are destitute. You must not, therefore, remain ignorant on any of these points, but you must understand them precisely, so that you will know he is lying, just as with everything else. I, gentlemen, would admit to being the worst of all men if it were shown that Stratocles left an impoverished estate and I was prospering but paid no attention to his children. [39] But if the property he left them was greater and more secure than my own, and large enough to provide handsomely for his daughters without diminishing his son's wealth from the remainder, and if I am managing it so well that their fortune has been considerably increased, I could not reasonably be blamed for not giving them my own money as well, but I would rightly be praised for preserving and increasing their wealth. And I can easily show that this is the case. [40] First, therefore, I'll describe the details of the property in full and, after this, how I think I should manage the boy's property.[35]

The patrimony Stratocles and I had was large enough to be sufficient but not large enough to perform public services.[36] A proof of this is that each of us received a dowry of twenty minas with his wife, but so small a dowry would not be given to somebody with a

---

[35]The manuscript ends before he reaches this part of the speech.

[36]I.e., it was less than 3 talents (the figure suggested by Davies 1971: xxiv). But he does claim to have been performing liturgies later (11.50), when he had acquired the estates of Hagnias II and Macartatus I. See further Thompson 1976: 58–59.

large fortune. [41] In addition to this estate, however, Stratocles happened to receive property worth more than two and a half talents, since Theophon, his wife's brother,[37] on his death adopted one of his daughters[38] and left her his property: land at Eleusis worth two talents, sixty sheep, one hundred goats, furniture, a fine horse from when he was a cavalry commander, and all the rest of his possessions; [42] Stratocles controlled these for nine whole years and left a fortune of 5 talents 3,000 drachmas,[39] including his own patrimony but excluding the fortune Theophon left his daughter; his property comprised land at Thria worth two and a half talents, a house at Melite bought for 3,000 drachmas, and another at Eleusis bought for 500. This was his real estate, from which the revenue from the land was 12 minas and the houses 3, a total of 15 minas; he also had about 4,000 drachmas lent at interest, the yearly income from which totals 720 drachmas at a monthly rate of 9 obols.[40] [43] His total income was therefore 22 minas and more; besides this, he left furniture, sheep, barley, wine, and fruits, and the sale of these brought in 4,900 drachmas; also there were 900 drachmas in the house. In

---

[37] Omitted from the stemma here. Since his estate was administered by Stratocles for nine years (11.42), Theophon will have died ca. 369. Therefore, the daughter he adopted must have been born before 369, and since the dowries of Stratocles' four daughters were being settled a decade later (11.37, 39), all Stratocles' children were probably born in the 370s. Theophon was presumably a cavalry commander (phylarch) in the 370s.

[38] For adopting a daughter, see above, 8n.

[39] The sums listed below total 4 talents 5,300 drachmas, a shortfall of 3,700 drachmas. This could be the property undisclosed by the opponent (11.43) or perhaps more likely indicates exaggeration by Theopompus. There is also the question of the 2.5 talents mentioned in 11.41 as the value of Theophon's estate, which Stratocles controlled for nine years, thereby (it seems) increasing his own fortune from one below the liturgical class (cf. 11.40) to 5.5 talents. The income might be claimed by the girl's future husband, thus diminishing further the size of Stratocles' estate (as Davies 1971: 88), though he could claim some of it as expenses for the girl; and if his investments prospered, the girl's estate may also have increased considerably.

[40] I.e., 1.5 drachmas per 100 drachmas per month, an interest rate of 18 percent. By contrast, the annual rental income of three minas (5 300 drachmas) from properties worth 3,500 drachmas was about 8.6 percent.

addition, his (the boy's) mother included in the inventory in front of witnesses fines recovered on interest-free loans, amounting to almost 1,000 drachmas. And I'm not yet talking about the other property that was left but that my opponents are not disclosing, only the real property and what was admitted by them. Please call the witnesses to what I've said.

[WITNESSES]

[44] Stratocles' fortune is even more than this, but later I'll give an account of the moneys pilfered by my opponents. But how much is my fortune? I have a property at Oenoë worth 5,000 drachmas and one at Prospalta worth 3,000, plus a house in the city worth 2,000; in addition to this is the estate Hagnias left, worth about two talents—I know it would not fetch more than that. This gives a total of only 3 talents 4,000 drachmas, 110 minas less than the boy's fortune.[41] [45] And I'm also including in my reckoning the fortune of my son, who was adopted out of the family, but I did not include in the boy's fortune Theophon's estate, two and a half talents, for which he adopted the boy's sister. Their family property could easily be worth 8 talents, but Theophon's money has been counted separately. As for me, the estate Hagnias left is not yet securely mine; actions for false witness are pending, [46] and the law prescribes that if anybody is convicted of false witness, the claims for an estate are to be heard again from the beginning;[42] but the boy's property left to him by Stratocles is admitted and uncontested. To prove this is the amount of my property, including that of my son who has been adopted out, and actions for false witness over Hagnias' property are pending, take the depositions and read them.

---

[41]As Davies points out (1971: 88), Theopompus does not include a number of certain or possible extra items, including his wife's dowry of 2,000 drachmas (11.40), sundry elements of the kind he lists for Stratocles, any loan income, and (on Davies' contention against 11.49) the estate of Macartatus I.

[42]It has been thought unlikely that the conviction of a single witness for false testimony automatically led to the reopening of the inheritance case (see, e.g., Harrison 1968: 161 n. 2). But Theopompus' words are taken at face value by Thompson 1976: 55.

[DEPOSITIONS]

[47] Is the difference between each of our fortunes small, then, or rather is it not so great that mine is nothing in comparison with that of Stratocles' children? So it's not right to believe my opponent's statements: although they have been left this large fortune, he dared to slander me by lying about the size of mine. He includes in his reckoning that I have received three estates and, being in affluent circumstances, am hiding my wealth so that you may gain the least possible advantage from it.[43] People who cannot say anything fair about the issues must produce arguments like these so that by slandering their opponents they can gain an advantage over them. [48] But you are all my witnesses that my wife's brothers, Chaereleos and Macartatus, were not among those who performed public services but those who possess little property. You know that Macartatus sold his land, bought and manned a trireme, and then sailed off to Crete. The affair was no secret but even prompted a debate in the Assembly; some feared he might cause war between us and the Spartans instead of peace.[44] [49] Chaereleos left the property at Prospalta,[45] which would not fetch more than thirty minas. The brother who left this estate happened to die before Macartatus, Macartatus died with the property he took when he sailed off: he lost everything in the war, including the trireme and his own life. The estate at Prospalta

---

[43]I.e., in the performance of liturgies.

[44]It is tempting to equate this episode with the affair of Demaenetus in 396 (*Hell. Oxy.* 6.1–3, 8.1–2) and to link Macartatus I's death with the suit for which Lysias' speech *On the Estate of Macartatus* was written. But there are significant differences of detail that were correctly noted by Davies 1971: 85; and if both brothers were dead by 395, their sister, Theopompus' wife, was either considerably younger or Theopompus was much older than it would otherwise appear. Davies therefore dates the episode to a time after the Peace of Antalcidas (386) but before 380 to fit in with the limits of Lysias' logographic activity. Thompson (1976: 56) prefers a date after the Common Peace of 371 (which breaks the link between this Macartatus and the Lysias speech), suggesting that Macartatus I was probably involved in collecting booty. But it is more likely that he was acting as a naval mercenary commander; see L. Casson, "A Trireme for Hire (Is. 11.48)," *CQ* 45 (1995), 241–245.

[45]That mentioned in 11.44.

was left and passed to their sister, my wife, and I was persuaded by her to let one of our sons be adopted into the family of Macartatus.[46] I was not trying to avoid performing public services if this property accrued to me, [50] since my situation remained unaltered after I had given him up: I did not perform fewer public services than before because of this but was one of those who paid the war taxes and performed all the duties you prescribed. But my opponent is making these statements to discredit me as being wealthy but useless to you.

I shall make one proposal as my strongest argument of all, which I know will appear just to you. I am willing to join my estate with that of the boy and let each of us take half the total, whether it is large or small, so that neither party has any more than is appropriate; but he will not agree to this.

[THE REST OF THE SPEECH IS MISSING.]

---

[46]This son is the Macartatus who is prosecuted in Dem. 43. Theopompus' explanation is reasonable, though some have suspected that there was more to this than his wife's persuasion or the alleged avoidance of liturgies (cf. 11.47). See Davies 1971: 86; Thompson 1976: 58. Macartatus II subsequently returned to his natural family by leaving one of his own sons as the adopted son of Macartatus I.

12. ON BEHALF OF EUPHILETUS

〰〰〰

This speech is, strictly speaking, a fragment, since it is preserved by Dionysius of Halicarnassus in his essay on Isaeus (*Isaeus* 17). It further differs from the preceding speeches in that its subject matter is civic rights; together with some other fragments, this indicates that Isaeus did not restrict himself solely to matters of inheritance.

Euphiletus, son of Hegesippus, was struck off the register of the deme Erchia during one of the periodic revisions of the register. He brought suit against the demesmen and two arbitrators found in his favor (12.11),[1] but the demesmen refused to back down, and Euphiletus exercised his right of appeal to the court of the Thesmothetae.[2] The penalty if he lost was enslavement and the confiscation of his property. The speech was delivered by an advocate (*synēgoros*), Euphiletus' elder half-brother (the son of Hegesippus by a previous marriage), and the preserved fragment, admired by Dionysius for its argumentative skill, is from the proofs section.

The speaker begins with possible motives why Hegesippus might have adopted Euphiletus. He argues from probability (*eikos*) that adoption was unlikely because Hegesippus already had two sons, and bringing up Euphiletus caused him considerable expense (12.1– 3). Nor was it likely that he, the speaker, would testify falsely on

---

[1] On the legal problems raised by the involvement of arbitrators, see Wyse 1904: 716–717.

[2] The precise procedure involved here is unclear. It may have been a private action (see Rubinstein 2000: 61 n. 99). For the view that it was the members of the deme who were appealing, see M. Just, "Le rôle des διαιτηταί dans Isée 12, 11," *RIDA* 15 (1968), 107 –116.

Euphiletus' behalf when he would have to share his patrimony (12.4). Similarly, the other relatives had more reason to testify against Euphiletus than for him (12.5–6), and the opponents could not have produced better witnesses than these if they had been on trial (12.7– 8). The speaker then turns to a nontechnical proof (*atechnos pistis*), the oaths that his mother, father, and he himself were ready to swear to Euphiletus' legitimacy (12.9–10): the offer by the mother to take an oath may have been particularly effective.[3] He goes on to contrast the reliability of his witnesses, as kinsmen, with the opposition's lack of evidence to the contrary, which strongly influenced the arbitrators (12.11), and backs this up with the hypothetical inversion that just as the opponents would have used the arbitrators' decision as a strong proof if it had been in their favor, so it should now count for Euphiletus (12.12).

The law ordering the revision of the deme register was proposed by Demophilus in the archonship of Archias (346/5). It clearly caused a good deal of litigation, as is evidenced also by Lost Speech VI (*Against Boeotus;*[4] cf. Dem. 39) and Demosthenes 57, *Against Eubulides*. The present speech will have been delivered, after two years with the arbitrators (12.11), in 344/3, which in turn is evidence for the longevity of Isaeus' forensic career.

12

Introduction[5]

The deme of Erchia is summoned to the court by a member who has been rejected by its vote, on the ground that he was unjustly excluded from the citizenship. The Athenians had passed a law ordering a scrutiny of the citizen roll by demes and prescribing that anybody who was rejected by the votes of his demesmen was not to share in the citizenship; but those who were unjustly rejected were to have the right of appeal (ephesis) to the court by summoning the demesmen, and if they were

---

[3]See Usher 1999: 168–169.

[4]Nothing survives of this speech.

[5]Dionysius (*Isaeus* 16) introduces the excerpt he quotes with these remarks.

excluded a second time, they were to be sold as slaves and their property confiscated. It was under this law that Euphiletus summoned the demesmen of Erchia, on the ground that they had unjustly expelled him and instituted this lawsuit. The facts have already been precisely stated and confirmed by witnesses; the following passage, in which he seeks to strengthen the testimony, is in my opinion composed with great precision, but you must decide for yourself whether my judgment of it is appropriate.

[1] So then, gentlemen of the jury, you have heard not only us but also all our relatives testify that Euphiletus here is our brother. Now consider first what motive our father could have for lying and adopting this man as his son, if he were not. [2] You will find that all men who do such things either have no natural children of their own or are forced by poverty to adopt foreigners, in order to receive some assistance from them because through them they have become Athenian citizens. Our father has neither of these motives, since we are his two natural sons, so he would not have adopted this man because he had no heir. [3] Nor again does he need any material support or comforts from him since he has sufficient resources, and apart from this, you have heard testimony that he brought Euphiletus up from childhood, educated him, and introduced him to the members of his phratry—and this involves no small expenditure. So it is unlikely, gentlemen of the jury, that our father attempted such an unjust thing for no advantage. [4] Moreover, no one could suppose that I am so totally insane as to give false testimony for him in order to share my patrimony with more people,[6] since afterwards I would not be able to claim that he is not my brother. None of you would put up with listening to me if I now make myself liable to prosecution by testifying that he is our brother, but afterwards openly contradict this. [5] So it's not just I, gentlemen of the jury, who is likely to have testified truthfully, but also the other relatives. Consider first that our sisters' husbands would never have given false testimony about him. His mother had become stepmother to our

---

[6] The speaker, being a *synēgoros*, could also testify on Euphiletus' behalf.

sisters, and usually stepmothers and stepdaughters have great differences with each other. So if Euphiletus were their stepmother's child by any other man and not by our father, our sisters would never, gentlemen of the jury, have allowed their husbands to testify. [6] Again, our uncle, being a relative on our mother's side and not related to him at all, surely would never have agreed, gentlemen of the jury, to give false testimony for Euphiletus' mother that is manifestly to our detriment, if we are introducing him as our own brother when he is a foreigner. And besides, gentlemen of the jury, how could any of you convict of false testimony Demaratus here and Hegemon and Nicostratus, who in the first place clearly have never practiced anything shameful and who second are our relatives, know all of us, and have each testified to their own kinship with Euphiletus here? [7] So I'd be pleased to learn from the most esteemed of our opponents[7] whether he can produce some other kind of evidence to prove himself an Athenian apart from those we are using to prove who Euphiletus is. I do not think he could say anything other than that his mother is an Athenian (*astē*) and married, and his father is a citizen, and he would produce his relatives as witnesses that he was telling the truth in this.

[8] Next, gentlemen of the jury, if our opponents were on trial, they would ask you to believe the evidence of their own relatives rather than their accusers; but as it is, when we produce all these proofs, will they ask you to believe what they say rather than Euphiletus' father and me and my brother and the members of the phratry and all our relations? Furthermore, our opponents are acting out of personal hostility while not running any risk, whereas by testifying we are all rendering ourselves liable to prosecution. [9] And in addition to the depositions, gentlemen of the jury, in the first place Euphiletus' mother, who our opponents admit is an Athenian (*astē*), was ready to swear an oath before the arbitrator in the Delphinium[8] that Euphiletus here really was the child of herself and our father. And who should have known this better than she herself? Second, gentlemen of the jury, our father, who probably can recognize his

---

[7]Perhaps a reference to the current demarch; the original one was now dead (12.11).

[8]As did Plangon at Dem. 40.11.

own son best after his mother, was ready then and is ready now to swear that Euphiletus here really is his own son by a mother who is an Athenian (*astē*) and a wedded wife. [10] In addition to this, gentlemen of the jury, I was thirteen, as I've already said, when he was born, and I am ready to swear that Euphiletus here really is my brother by the same father. So, gentlemen of the jury, you would be justified in considering our oaths more trustworthy than their arguments; we know the facts precisely and are willing to swear oaths about him, whereas they are saying things they have heard from his enemies or are making up themselves. [11] In addition, gentlemen of the jury, we are producing our relatives as witnesses before you as we did before the arbitrators, and you should not disbelieve them; but when Euphiletus brought his earlier suit against the whole deme[9] and the demarch at the time, who has since died, even though the case was before the arbitrator for two years,[10] our opponents were unable to find a single piece of evidence that Euphiletus here is the son of any other father than ours. The arbitrators took this as the strongest proof that our opponents were lying, and both decided against them. Please take the deposition about the previous arbitration.

[DEPOSITION]

[12] You've now heard that they lost the arbitration on that occasion. So, gentlemen of the jury, just as our opponents would have declared it to be strong proof that he is not the son of Hegesippus if the arbitrators had decided for them, I now ask that the opposite be taken as evidence for us that we are telling the truth, since the arbitrators decided they were wronging Euphiletus by later deleting his name, even though he was an Athenian and had been legally registered in the first place. I think you have heard enough, gentlemen of the jury, to prove that Euphiletus here is our brother and your fellow citizen and was unjustly insulted by those who conspired against him in the deme.

---

[9]On the prosecution of associations, see Rubinstein 2000: 43–44, 81.

[10]The reasons for this long delay are unclear. Since an arbitrator was in office for only one year, the speaker may be referring to the period in which the opponents failed to give evidence (perhaps because the demarch had died), which led to a second hearing.

LOST SPEECHES AND FRAGMENTS

〰〰

We have evidence for over forty lost speeches of Isaeus. Fragments of some survive in quotations by Dionysius of Halicarnassus, and other shorter sentences, single words, and simple titles are preserved in later lexicographers. I give here translations of the fragments and sentences, following the numbering of Thalheim's Teubner edition[1] and with roman numerals for speeches, arabic for fragments. Full references may be found in the Teubner and in Forster's Loeb edition. Where the fragment comes from and is introduced by Dionysius, I give a translation of Dionysius' own words in italics. Speeches of which only the title survives are omitted.

III. AGAINST ARISTOGEITON AND ARCHIPPUS, ON THE ESTATE OF ARCHEPOLIS

Dionysius (*Isaeus* 15) reports on this speech as follows:

In the action against Aristogeiton and Archippus a person claiming an estate, who is the brother of the deceased, serves a summons on the man in possession of the invisible property for discovery of objects,[2] *but the person in control of the estate enters a counter-indictment against the summons, saying that the property has been left to him in a will. Two points are in dispute: first, whether a will was made or not, and second, if the will is now controverted, who should control the estate. After first dealing with the legal question and having shown from this perspective that an estate that is adjudicable should not be in anybody's possession*

---

[1]T. Thalheim, *Isaeus. Orationes* (Leipzig, 1903).
[2]For the *dikē eis emphanōn katastasin*, cf. 6.31 and n.

before a judgment has been made, the speaker then proceeds to his nar-
rative, by which he shows that the deceased never made the will. Isaeus
does not set out even this narrative in a simple, concise, and straightfor-
ward way, but because of its length divides it into sections and for each
point calls witnesses, has challenges read out, produces contracts, and
uses evidence, proofs, and all kinds of arguments from probability.

Fr. 1

After this reply they produced another will, which they said
Archepolis made in Lemnos.[3]

Fr. 2

Four wills having been forged by them.

V.   AGAINST ARISTOMACHUS[4]

Fr. 3

On the plot of land he left old men and cripples.

VII. AGAINST THE DEMESMEN, CONCERNING A PLOT OF LAND

Dionysius (*Isaeus* 10) cites the beginning of this speech.
Isaeus, in a dispute about a plot of land held by the members of his
client's deme, to whom the plot had been mortgaged, introduces the sub-
ject with the following opening words.

Fr. 4

I very much wish, gentlemen of the jury, that I had not been
wronged by any citizen, or otherwise that I had met opponents of

---

[3] The reference to Lemnos makes it likely that the Aristogeiton involved here
was a descendant of the famous tyrant slayer, whose daughter settled there in
the early fifth century; see Davies 1971: 474.

[4] Or "Aresaechmus."

the kind I could be in dispute with and not feel anxious. But as it is, the most distressing thing possible has happened to me. I am being wronged by my fellow demesmen, whose robbing me I cannot easily overlook, but with whom it is unpleasant to be at odds, since I must sacrifice with them and attend their common gatherings. It is difficult to bring an action against a large number of opponents, since their large number contributes in no small measure to the appearance that they are telling the truth. Nevertheless, since I have confidence in my case, even though I am beset by many difficulties, I do not think that I should shrink from trying to obtain justice from you. I beg you, therefore, to excuse me if, young as I still am, I have ventured to speak before a court; but although it goes against my character, I am compelled to do this because of those who are wronging me. I shall try to tell you about the matter from the start as briefly as I can.

It is clear from a citation by Harpocration (s.v. *Sphēttos*) that the land in question was in the deme Sphettus, of the tribe Acamantis. The suit may have been an inheritance claim (*diadikasia;* Rubinstein 2000: 82 n. 20).

VIII. AGAINST DIOCLES, FOR VIOLENCE (HYBRIS)[5]

Fr. 5

My brother and Cteson, a relative of ours, met Hermon as he was leaving for Bothynus.

The Diocles of this and the next speech is the same man who is attacked at 8.41–42 (see the Introduction to Speech 8).

IX. AGAINST DIOCLES, CONCERNING A PLOT OF LAND

Fr. 6

I will prove to you that this land does not belong and never has belonged to the heiress but was part of the patrimony of Lysimenes,

---

[5] This fragment seems more suited to XIII: one of the references to the latter in Harpocration comes under the entry "Bothynus." Bothynus was a village on the Sacred Way from Athens to Eleusis.

the father of Menecrates; Lysimenes was in possession of the whole of his patrimony.[6]

X. AGAINST DIOPHANES, DEFENSE IN AN ACTION CONCERNING A GUARDIANSHIP

Fr. 7

Part of the money he paid in person, and he instructed them to receive the rest from others.

Fr. 8

Having paid off part myself, namely, two talents and thirty minas, and with the farmer instructed to pay the rest.

XI. AGAINST DOROTHEUS, IN AN ACTION FOR EJECTMENT (EXOULĒS)

Fr. 9

He has sunk to such a depth of depravity and audacity at the same time.

XII. AGAINST ELPAGORAS AND DEMOPHANES

Fr. 10

After the return from Piraeus,[7] as I hear, they were revenue commissioners,[8] to whom matters of confiscated goods were referred.

A papyrus fragment (*P. Oxy.* 3.415) may belong to this speech.

---

[6]Further on "patrimony" (*patrōia*), see Harrison 1968: 125.

[7]I.e., after the restoration of the democracy in 403.

[8]Cf. Lys. 16.7. Further on these *syndikoi,* see Rubinstein 2000: 45.

XIIA. AGAINST EPICRATES

Fr. 10a

I'll produce, then, gentlemen of the jury, not only this deposition but also another absentee deposition[9] made by Myronides, who was the oldest of the demesmen.

XIII. AGAINST HERMON, CONCERNING A SURETY

Fr. 11

He threw Hermocrates into prison, alleging that he was a freedman, and did not release him until he had exacted payment of thirty drachmas.

XIV. AGAINST EUCLEIDES, CONCERNING THE RELEASE OF A PLOT OF LAND[10]

Fr. 12

A little above the Three-headed statue[11] by the road to Hestiaea.

Fr. 13

My private property would not be my own.

A man named Hagnias was mentioned in this speech; see the Introduction to Speech 11.

XV. AGAINST EUCLEIDES THE SOCRATIC[12]

Fr. 14

That reward money for certain people was placed on the altars.

---

[9]For the *ekmartyria,* cf. 3.18 and n.

[10]I.e., from mortgage.

[11]Of the god Hermes, according to Harpocration (s.v. *trikephalos*).

[12]Harpocration (s.v. *hoti*) questions the authenticity of the speech.

This speech may have been identical with the preceding one, though it is unclear why Eucleides, a Megarian, was involved in a suit concerning land in Attica. Eucleides appears in Plato's *Phaedo* (59c) and *Theaetetus* (142a–143c).

XVI. ON BEHALF OF EUMATHES, IN VINDICATION OF HIS FREEDOM

Dionysius (*Isaeus* 5) introduces this fragment as follows:

There is a speech of Isaeus for Eumathes, a metic who was engaged in banking at Athens. The heir of the man who has freed him is trying to reenslave him, and one of the citizens asserts his freedom and pleads in his defense. The proem of the speech is as follows.

Fr. 15

Gentlemen of the jury, I was of service to Eumathes here on a previous occasion, as was only right, and today I shall try, as far as I can, to save him with your assistance. Hear a few words from me, so none of you will think that I have rashly or in some other way unjustly interfered in Eumathes' affairs. When I was trierarch in the archonship of Cephisodotus,[13] word was brought to my relatives that I had died in the sea battle.[14] Since I had deposited some money with Eumathes here, he sent for my relatives and friends and told them of the money he was holding for me, and he handed over the whole sum with scrupulous honesty. As a result of this, when I returned home safely, I became even closer to him and, when he was setting up his bank, I procured additional capital for him. Afterwards, when Dionysius was trying to enslave him, I asserted his freedom, knowing that he had been freed by Epigenes before a court. But I will say no more about this.

---

[13] 358/7. Cawkwell argued that the Archon's name should be emended to Cephisodorus (Archon 366/5); see G. L. Cawkwell, "Notes on the Social War," *C&M* 23 (1962), 34–49 (at 34–35).

[14] If the Archon date is correct, this will be the battle fought off Chios in 358 at the start of the Social War.

Fr. 16

Xenocles wronged me by asserting the freedom of Eumathes when I was trying to enslave him as part of my inheritance.[15]

Fr. 17

But look at the recent past, gentlemen of the jury; this is right in front of you.

XIX. AGAINST ISCHOMACHUS

Fr. 18

There is no Lysides among the Twelve Hundred.[16]

XX. AGAINST CALLICRATES

Fr. 19

Nevertheless, since he gave all these orders at the same time.

XXII. AGAINST CALLIPHON

Fr. 20

Six hundred drachmas at one-third interest.[17]

XXIV. AGAINST CALYDON,[18] CONCERNING A GUARDIANSHIP

Fr. 21

And the bathhouse near the statue of Anthemocritus.

---

[15]The speaker is apparently quoting his opponent's speech.

[16]The Twelve Hundred are the wealthiest, liturgical class of citizens. On the possible identity of this Ischomachus, see Davies 1971: 265–268.

[17]A high rate of interest, but not unheard of.

[18]Davies (1971: 283) identifies Calydon with the eponym of a naval symmory (i.e., the organizer of a group of taxpayers) between 356 and 340.

XXIII. AGAINST HAGNOTHEUS

This speech is mentioned by Dionysius (*Isaeus* 14), who introduces fragment 22 as follows (*Isaeus* 8): *Isaeus in the defense which he composed for a guardian being prosecuted by his own nephew, begins in the following way.* Dionysius also cites fragment 23 (*Isaeus* 12), which may be from the same speech, despite the apparently contradictory positions of the speakers. Harpocration (s.v. *epismainesthai*) gives the title as "On Behalf of Calydon against Hagnotheus," but it is possible that he confuses two speeches, and the cases of Calydon and Hagnotheus were unconnected.[19] Davies notes (1971: 4) that Dionysius does not mention the name Calydon in his discussion.

Fr. 22

I wish, gentlemen of the jury, that Hagnotheus did not have so shameful a desire for money that he plots against the property of others and brings suits like this one. But since he is my nephew and in control of his father's estate, which we handed over to him and which is not small but in fact is enough for the performance of public services, I wish he would take care of it and not covet my property. Then he would enjoy a better reputation with everybody if he had preserved his wealth, and if he had increased it, he would have shown himself a more useful citizen. But since he has wasted, sold, and shamefully and wickedly squandered it, as I wish he had not, and since he has now attacked mine, trusting the members of his political club (*hetaireia*)[20] and relying on fabrications, I am compelled, it seems, to regard it as a misfortune that I have such a man as a relative and to defend myself before you as vigorously as I can against the claim he has made and his irrelevant slanders.

---

[19]Harpocration further talks of a suit for ejectment, whereas the passages quoted by Dionysius concern guardianship; see Forster 1927: 446; *contra* Harrison 1968: 97 n. 1.

[20]These clubs were formed partly to support their members in litigation. In the fifth century, Antiphon and Andocides had both been associated with oligarchic *hetaireiai*.

Fr. 23

Why, by heavens, should you believe what I have said? Isn't it because of the witnesses? I certainly think so. Well, why should you believe the witnesses? Isn't it because of the torture? It's certainly reasonable. And why should you disbelieve the words of my opponents? Isn't it because they declined the tests? You certainly must.[21] It's clear, then, that I am investigating these things and subjecting matters to torture, but my opponent is clearly making it a matter of slanders and words, as somebody would do who simply wants to get what he can. If he had any thought for justice and were not seeking to mislead you in your views, he should not be doing this, by Zeus, but should be moving towards an accounting in the presence of witnesses and examining every item in the accounts, asking me questions like: "How much do you reckon for war taxes?" "So much." "On what basis were they paid?"[22] "On such and such a basis." "In accordance with what decrees?" "These ones here." "Who have received them?" "These people." And he should consider the testimony of my witnesses on these issues, the decrees, the amount of war taxes, the sums paid, who received them, and if everything were in good and proper order, he should trust my accounts, but if not, he should now produce witnesses regarding any false entries in the accounts I presented to them.

XXVI. AGAINST LYSIBIUS, CONCERNING AN HEIRESS

Fr. 24

My opponents, however, fabricating such things in the name of the deceased.

---

[21]"Decline the tests" refers to their rejection of the speaker's challenge that they allow certain slaves to be interrogated under torture. For this commonplace, cf. 8.28.

[22]The special war taxes (*eisphorai*) were levied as needed. The tax would be a percentage of the citizen's property, with the amount varying according to the need.

Fr. 25

We think that the next of kin should marry the heiress and the property should belong to her for the time being, but when sons come of age, they should have possession of it.[23]

XXX. AGAINST MENECRATES

Fr. 25a

Both the ground around the house and the house itself.

XXXV. AGAINST THE MEMBERS OF A RELIGIOUS ASSOCIATION[24]

Fr. 26

And that the plot of land should not become thickly shaded.

Fr. 27

Since they indicated by the removals of these boundary stones that the plot of land was somebody else's.

XLI. AGAINST STRATOCLES

Fr. 27a

Important matters.

Fr. 27b

He offered a smaller sacrificial victim than was prescribed.

---

[23]For the law prescribing this, cf. 8.31.
[24]For the *orgeōnes*, cf. 2.14 and n.

XLIV. AGAINST TLEPOLEMUS, A SWORN AFFIDAVIT [25]

Fr. 27c

Since he did not think he should borrow more.

XLV. UNIDENTIFIED FRAGMENTS [26]

Fr. 28

And my opponent, the most wicked of all men, claims that you should believe their statement that they have paid us rather than our statement that we have not been paid, even though they do not produce any witnesses in whose presence they say they paid us. And yet it is obvious to everybody that men who defrauded this man's father when he was in possession of his civic rights would not have paid us voluntarily, and that in our situation we would not have been able to recover the money.

Fr. 29

Everything I possessed apart from mortgaged property had been spent on public services, and nobody would have lent me any more if I tried to borrow against it, since I had already committed the revenue from it. Even though I have an undisputed right to it, my opponents, by bringing so serious a suit and alleging that the property is theirs, prevented me from using the money to have repairs done.

Fr. 30

I think that the greatest of public services is to conduct one's daily life in a manner that is law abiding and modest.

---

[25] For the sworn affidavit (*antōmosia*), cf. 3.6 and n.

[26] The first two of these are from Dionysius of Halicarnassus, *Isaeus* 13.

Fr. 31

They who punish wrongdoers prevent the rest from being wronged.

Fr. 32

Laws that are passed should be rigorous, but the punishment should be milder than they prescribe.

Fr. 33

What need is there for witness testimony in such circumstances, when those who are judging know some of the facts themselves, namely, that the boy was well, and acquire some from eyewitnesses and learn others from hearsay?

Fr. 34

Whenever he came, he usually stayed at my house. Whenever I came, I used to stay at his house.

Fr. 35

Being from the family of Anaxion[27] and Polyaratus.

Fr. 36

I denounced him before the Areopagus.

---

[27]The name occurs elsewhere in Athens only as that of a treasurer of Athena in the mid sixth century; see Davies 1971: 26.

APPENDIX

In the manuscripts of Isaeus the eleven speeches are each preceded by an Argument (*Hypothesis*) written at some time later in antiquity. These Arguments summarize the speeches and classify them according to the categories of Greek *stasis* ("issue") theory, by which a speaker might identify the central question at issue in any given dispute.[1]

ARGUMENT TO SPEECH I (*On the Estate of Cleonymus*)

The nephews of the deceased Cleonymus claim his estate as direct heirs. They admit that the will that Pherenicus, Simon[2] and Poseidippus produced in their own favor was genuinely written by Cleonymus and deposited with the magistrates when he was angry with their guardian Deinias; but they allege that he afterwards tried to annul the will and summoned the City Magistrate but died suddenly. They also allege that Polyarchus, their grandfather and Cleonymus' father, prescribed that if anything happened to Cleonymus, he was to leave the property to them. The issue is a double definition in dispute: one side relies on the original will; the other says that Cleonymus summoned the magistrate to annul it and relies on the last acts of Cleonymus.

---

[1]On "questions at issue" (*staseis*) in rhetorical theory, see D. A. Russell, *Greek Declamation* (Cambridge, 1983), 40–73; and in detail, M. Heath, *Hermogenes. On Issues* (Oxford, 1995).

[2]Simon clearly was a friend, not a relative of Cleonymus (cf. 1.31–2).

ARGUMENT TO SPEECH 2 (*On the Estate of Menecles*)

Menecles adopted a son and lived for twenty-three years after the adoption. When his brothers[3] claimed the estate, a certain Philonides testified that it was not actionable, since Menecles had left a son. The brothers denounced him for false witness, and the son undertakes the defense against them on his behalf. This speech is the opposite of the one *On the Estate of Cleonymus* (Speech 1): the speaker in that case defended kinship; here, he defends a will. The issue is a counter-plea with a controversy on a conjecture;[4] for he says that the deceased had the right to adopt a son, then the point of conjecture was that "he did not adopt me under the influence of a woman."

ARGUMENT TO SPEECH 3 (*On the Estate of Pyrrhus*)

Pyrrhus adopted one of his sister's sons, Endius, who held the estate for more than twenty years. Then on his death Xenocles brought a suit for the property on behalf of Phile, his wife, and made a formal declaration that she was a legitimate daughter of Pyrrhus; the estate was also being claimed by Endius' mother. He was found guilty of false witness; but Nicodemus also testified that he had betrothed his sister according to the laws and Phile was her daughter. Endius' brother declares that Phile is a bastard, the daughter of Pyrrhus by a prostitute, and was so given in marriage by Endius to Xenocles. The issue is one of fact; the action, one of false witness against Nicodemus.

ARGUMENT TO SPEECH 4 (*On the Estate of Nicostratus*)

Nicostratus having died abroad, Hagnon and Hagnotheus, being first cousins born of his father's brother, claim his estate against Chariades, who declares that he is his heir by bequest, that is by will.

---

[3]Menecles in fact had only one brother, who also had a son (2.10, 21).

[4]The case was not in fact an *antilēpsis* ("counter-plea"), for there was no question that Menecles had the right to adopt a son.

Isaeus the orator, being a relative of Hagnon and his family, speaks as their advocate.[5] The issue is one of fact.

ARGUMENT TO SPEECH 5 (*On the Estate of Dicaeogenes*)

Dicaeogenes died childless but with four sisters, and Proxenus came forward with a will in which the deceased Dicaeogenes adopted his (Proxenus') son, Dicaeogenes, with a one-third share of his property. They parceled out the whole property on this basis, but eventually Dicaeogenes, the son of Proxenus, came forward saying that he had been adopted as heir to the whole property; he won and took possession also of the two-thirds held by the deceased's sisters. Later, the sons of the sisters won a suit against Dicaeogenes, who agreed to hand the two-thirds back again to them clear of charges and free of claims, with Leochares acting as a surety for this. In this suit, with Dicaeogenes and Leochares denying the agreement, the sons of the sisters are making a claim concerning the two-thirds from the one as having agreed to hand them back and from the other as surety.[6] The issue is one of fact, for they deny the agreement.

ARGUMENT TO SPEECH 6 (*On the Estate of Philoctemon*)

Euctemon's son Philoctemon adopted Chaerestratus, the son of one of his two sisters and Phanostratus, by a will deposited with Chaereas, the husband of the other sister, and died while his father was still alive. Later, when he too died, Chaerestratus claimed the estate in accordance with the law. When Androcles made a declaration that it was not adjudicable because Euctemon had a legitimate son, Antidorus,[7] Chaerestratus and his supporters formally contested the declaration, claiming that both Antidorus and his sister were bastards, and the law explicitly states that no rights of kinship exist for a bastard son or daughter. The issue is one of fact, for it is unclear

---

[5]Most probably an error. See the Introduction to Speech 4.

[6]The case was in fact brought against Leochares as surety.

[7]This was in fact the name of one of the guardians (6.39, 47); the names of Euctemon's two alleged children (both boys, not "Antidorus and his sister") are nowhere mentioned.

whether Philoctemon adopted Chaerestratus as his son and again whether Antidorus and his sister are legitimate.

ARGUMENT TO SPEECH 7 (*On the Estate of Apollodorus*)

Eupolis, Thrasyllus, and Mneson were brothers. Of these, Mneson died childless and Thrasyllus left a son, Apollodorus; the sole survivor Eupolis wronged Apollodorus in many ways. Therefore, Archedamus, the grandfather of the man making the speech, being married to Apollodorus' mother after the death of her husband Thrasyllus and pitying Apollodorus as an orphan, demanded a large sum of money from Eupolis on account of the wrongs he had done to Apollodorus. Mindful of this, Apollodorus introduced Thrasyllus, the son of his half-sister and grandson of Archedamus, to the members of his phratry as his adopted son. Thrasyllus had already been entered among the members of the *genos* and of the phratry but not yet on the deme register when Apollodorus died. After his death Thrasyllus was entered on the deme register; nonetheless, the daughter of Eupolis, the uncle of Apollodorus, claimed against Thrasyllus, alleging that Thrasyllus had not at all been entered among the members of the phratry and *genos* according to the wishes of Apollodorus, but the adoption was fictitious. This is the argument; the issue is one of fact; and so handling the speech with utmost thoroughness and skill, the speaker describes in full the hostility of Apollodorus towards Eupolis, which provides a sure indication that he did not want his property to be inherited by Eupolis' daughter.

ARGUMENT TO SPEECH 8 (*On the Estate of Ciron*)

When Ciron died without legitimate children, his nephew (his brother's son) claimed the estate and took over the property from his widow. After this the man giving the speech indicts the nephew, alleging that he is a son of Ciron's daughter and that the wife of the deceased handed the estate over to the nephew on her own to give him a part and profit from the rest. This is the argument; the issue is one of fact, the question being whether the claimant is a legitimate son of Ciron's daughter or not. Combined with this also is the question of qualification: the nephew contested the claim, arguing that even if we grant that she was the legitimate daughter of Ciron, since she is dead and her son is now the claimant, the nephew, the brother's son, ought to have precedence over the offspring of a daughter, in accordance with the law that prescribes that the descendants of males take precedence over the descendants of females. The speaker very skillfully ignores this law completely and contends on the basis of the difference between the parents, showing that just as a daughter is closer in kinship to the deceased than a brother, so her son prevails over a brother's son. The case, then, is strong in justice but weak in law; and Isaeus effects his treatment of the topics with his accustomed skill.

ARGUMENT TO SPEECH 9 (*On the Estate of Astyphilus*)

Astyphilus and the man delivering the speech were half-brothers by the same mother. When Astyphilus died, a certain Cleon, his first cousin, produced a will, claiming it had been made in favor of his own son. The brother of Astyphilus attacks the will as a forgery. The issue is one of fact.

ARGUMENT TO SPEECH 10 (*Against Xenaenetus on the Estate of Aristarchus*)

A certain Aristarchus was the father of four children, Cyronides, Demochares, the mother of the man delivering the speech, and another daughter; of these, during his lifetime he gave Cyronides for adoption as heir to the estate of Xenaenetus, his maternal grandfather, and left the rest of his children as his own heirs. Afterwards, Demochares died childless and so did one of the daughters, and the whole estate passed by law to the mother of the man delivering the speech. And this was how things stood; but after the death of Aristarchus, Aristomenes, his brother, who now by law became guardian of his brother's children, gave his own daughter in marriage to Cyronides, the son of Aristarchus who had been adopted out of the family, after promising to secure Aristarchus' estate for him. He indeed succeeded in doing this; for when a son was born to Cyronides, first they gave the child the name of his grandfather, calling him Aristarchus, and then had him adopted into his grandfather's family on the ground that the latter had given instructions for this, and Aristomenes handed over to him the whole of his grandfather's estate. But he died still childless and constituted his own brother Xenaenetus as his heir in a will. This being the case and Xenaenetus being in possession of the estate of Aristarchus the elder, the son of Aristarchus the elder's daughter claims the estate from him, saying that he himself is the sole heir by law of Aristarchus the elder's property. For Cyronides (he argues) was adopted out of the family, and his father, since he had a legitimate son Demochares, could not adopt a child; and neither could Demochares, who was a minor, himself adopt a son into his father's family, nor the other daughter who predeceased him. Therefore (he argues) since the adoption of Aristarchus the younger was by law invalid, his (Aristarchus the younger's) will no longer stood: how could he transmit to another what he had not rightfully acquired? With the will annulled, the estate naturally passed to the man delivering the speech, as son of the legitimate daughter of Aristarchus the elder. This is the argument; the issue is practical, concerned with the validity of a written document; for the questions are whether such a will ought to stand and which side has the juster claim.

ARGUMENT TO SPEECH 11 (*On the Estate of Hagnias*)

A certain Hagnias had several cousins: Theopompus, his brother Stratocles, Stratius, and Eubulides. Just before his death he adopted a daughter, stipulating in his will that if anything should happen to the daughter, the estate was to pass to Glaucon, his half-brother by the same mother. After arranging this he died, and his daughter received the estate and died. When Eubulides also died, his daughter brought an action against Glaucon and secured the estate. After this, with Stratocles and Stratius dead too, Theopompus brought an action against her on his own and received the estate. It is against him that the son of his brother Stratocles brings an action through a guardian, claiming that the inheritance belongs equally to Theopompus and his brother's son. The issue is practical.

INDEX